P9-DSY-167

STARPOWER

AN ASTROLOGICAL GUIDE TO SUPER SUCCESS

by

Jacqueline Stallone

PUBISHED IN U.S.A. BY
STARPOWER PUBLISHING, INC.

I wish to dedicate this edition of *Starpower* to my dear husband S. Marcus Levine, M.D. who had the courage to melt my ice cubes. As my son Sylvester said, when he gave me away for the fourth time, "You have just witnessed a minor miracle!"

1st edition of revised *Starpower*.
© 1999 STARPOWER Publishing, Inc.
P.O. Box 491550, Los Angeles, CA 90049
All rights reserved.

LIBRARY OF CONGRESS CATALOGING IN-PUBLICATION DATA
Stallone, Jacqueline.
    Starpower : an astrological guide to supersuccess / Jacqueline Stallone.
        p.   cm.
    ISBN 0-9676854-0-0
    1. Astrology. 2. Success-Miscellanea. 3. Celebrities-United States-Miscellanea.
I. Stallone, Jacqueline. II. Title. III. Title:
Star power.
BF1729.S88S73   1989   89-12382
133.5—dc2O   CIP

Book Design by Shahryar Amiri, XERXES Studio
Cover Design: Shahryar Amiri & Pierre-Marc Atlan
Art Direction & Production: Pierre-Marc Atlan
Editor: Karen Geller-Shinn
Research & Assistant Editor: Rhonda Chee Atlan
Printing by PALC, (800) 219-1999
PRINTED IN THE UNITED STATES OF AMERICA

The Excitement...The Power...The Man...

ROCKY III

a ROBERT CHARTOFF–IRWIN WINKLER production · SYLVESTER STALLONE
BURT YOUNG · CARL WEATHERS and BURGESS MERE
BUTLER, A.S.C. · music by BILL CONTI · produced
directed by SYLVESTER STALLONE

COMING THIS SUMMER

With love
Jacqueline Stallone

JACQUELINE STALLONE reveals in full detail the secrets to success that have brought fortune to Hollywood stars, and she shows readers how to apply those principles in their own lives. Packed with celebrity gossip and call-it-like-it-is advice, STARPOWER explores not just the traditional 12 divisions of the zodiac, but the 36 sub-categories that make all the difference in discovering hidden personality strengths and dangers. It offers specific directions for finding a person's best career choices, for choosing the most compatible lover, and for making smart decisions that reap happiness, success, wealth, and power. You'll also be privy to delicious revelations about the rich and celebrated, such as:

why Gemini Jack Kennedy had the perfect wife in Leo Jacqueline Bouvier.

why Libra John Lennon was a fated soul mate for Aquarius Yoko Ono.

why Leos Madonna and Sean Penn should have never even gone on a second date, let alone said, "I do"!

why Aries Warren Beatty is able to exert such irresistible charm over women.

Amazingly accurate and eye-opening, STARPOWER is at once a brassy, bawdy look at all the stars, and an authoritative and detailed guide written by a professional astrologer. Jacqueline Stallone shows you how her book has worked for her and her famous son ... how it has worked for Hollywood's brightest stars ... and now she shows you how it can work for you — bringing a future filled with passion, money, career changes, and wonderful new adventures.

JACQUELINE STALLONE has practiced astrology since the 1950s, and can be contacted through her web site at: www.jacquelinestallone.com

CONTENTS

CHAPTER 1

DECANS

YOUR TICKET TO SUCCESS

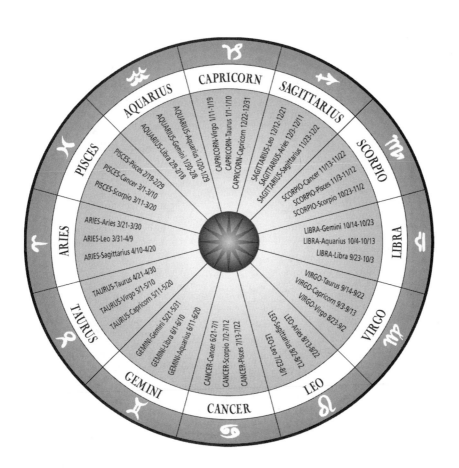

FIND YOUR DECAN!

I hope you've got your pencils sharpened because we're going to have an astrology review before we get down to talking turkey about YOU. Pay attention to the guidelines I'm setting out! Most of you probably already know your *Sun sign*. Some of you may have an awareness of your *Moon* and *Rising signs* as well, and a few of you astrology fans might even be in possession of your own natal charts. To get a specific, in-depth horoscope I would recommend that you visit an expert astrologer. For our purposes, however, knowing your *Sun sign* is the only prerequisite to the course.

Astrologers through the ages have paid the most attention to the placement of the Sun in your chart, because it is the most powerful planet in the solar system—it rules the show. Where the Sun is in relationship to the Earth when you were born has a profound influence on you. The sign that the Sun is in when you are born indicates what qualities of character you have, your potential powers and abilities, your active and outward behaviors.

Now, if you're an astute star watcher, you're going to ask the question that yours truly and others before me have asked. Why aren't all individuals born within a given Sun sign alike? For example, I'm a SAGITTARIUS and my sister is a SAGITTARIUS and we are as different as night and day. So, how do we account for these differences? What force of the planets changes to affect me in one way and my sister in another? The answer lies in the Decan of each *Sun sign*.

WHAT IS A DECAN?

It takes 30 days for the Sun to move through each sign of the zodiac. As it travels along, we are able to check the degree of its presence most accurately every ten days. Imagine watching a train on a track chugging along and then pausing to refuel or change passengers at those various ten-day checkpoints. We use the word Decan (pronounced "deck-han") or more formally, *decanate*, to describe which ten-day period of the sign the Sun is in. So, when you say, "I'm an AQUARIUS," we'll ask, "To what degree?" We'll look for ten-day or decan changes to understand the different energies of the Sun that are affecting you. If you were born in the 1st Decan of AQUARIUS (1/20 to 1/29), you'll have AQUARIAN traits in full force and thus earn the title AQUARIUS-Aquarius. If you were born during the 2nd Decan of AQUARIUS (1/30 to 2/8), your AQUARIAN aspects should be diluted and balanced by your nearest Air sign neighbor, Gemini, so we call you the AQUARIUS-Gemini decan. If your birthday falls into the last ten days, or 3rd Decan of AQUARIUS (2/9 to 2/18), your degree of AQUARIAN attributes will be the mildest of the lot as you pick up some noticeable traits from Libra, the third Air sign. That's why you're AQUARIUS-Libra. As you can see from the chart, 3rd Decans are in close to the Cusps - the dividing lines between the Sun signs. To make matters a bit more technical, a 3rd Decan of any sign can grab subtle aspects from the Sun sign directly ahead. So, AQUARIUS-Libra decans might display Piscean nuances in some areas. Usually, a lst Decan of a sign won't receive vibrations from the sign preceding theirs. That's because the Sun train travels counterclockwise around the zodiac clock, starting with ARIES and moving all the way around to PISCES. So far so good. Let's review:

- 1st Decans of any given *Sun sign* are going to be the most intense of that sign, they're the extremists;
- 2nd Decans are less extreme, more toned down—in general they're more balanced individuals; and
- 3rd Decans are unusual hodge-podges of ingredients, unique and unpredictable.

You may also want to think of your decan as shading or coloring. Of course, we may know that you're a PISCES, but what kind of a fish are you? Do you swim in a school with others, or do you float aimlessly alone? So you see, within each Sun sign some general principles will apply to each person born under that sign and some very surprising decan differences may hold the key to your unique personality. Knowing the hallmarks of your Sun sign and your decan is the best way to take advantage of how truly distinct you are.

COMPOSITION OF THE ZODIAC

Unless you've lived in a shoebox all your life, you've got to know that there are 12 Sun signs, the same number of months in the year. Each Sun sign is said to be ruled by a planet. In my terms, the planet that is associated with your Sun sign will place more interest in a specific area of your life than in others. For example, if you are a VIRGO, the planet Mercury, your ruler, will highlight intellectual concerns.

I've chosen to stick to the nine planets that have been studied for centuries, without discussing the influence of some of astronomy's more recent discoveries. The newer planets are important to watch when charting specific plans of action, but I rarely use them when looking at birth charts. You can trust that the planet listed below that corresponds with your Sun sign will designate the field in which you learn your greatest lessons.

Sun Sign	Planet	Indications
Aries	Mars	Drive and Motivation
Taurus	Venus	Putting Talent and Love to Use
Gemini	Mercury	Communication and Association
Cancer	Moon	Emotions and Mood
Leo	Sun	Vitality and Ego
Virgo	Mercury	Analytical Thinking
Libra	Venus	Creativity and Morality
Scorpio	Mars	Channeling Desires
Sagittarius	Jupiter	Challenges and Opportunities
Capricorn	Saturn	Discipline and Achievement
Aquarius	Uranus	Transformations
Pisces	Neptune	Dreams, Illusions and Karma

Is everybody with me so far? Good. Once we've established your ruling planet, the second question we'll answer is into which category your Sun sign falls—CARDINAL, FIXED, or MUTABLE. These three groups describe motion. The CARDINAL signs are the fast travelers - the sharks of the zodiac. If CARDINAL describes your Sun sign, you probably insist on flying first class. Or, perhaps you'll rent a helium balloon just to create a stir when you arrive at your destination. You love shortcuts and leading the traffic from the fast lane of a five-lane freeway. When you move toward an objective, you prefer top speed, not pausing to take a break or check out the sights. Unless, of course, you can afford the luxury of being chauffeured in a limo—one method of travel that most CARDINAL movers adore.

Not that a FIXED sign wouldn't hop aboard that same limo. It's just that if you're a person whose Sun sign falls into a FIXED pattern, you won't want to go anywhere without being thoroughly prepared. You'll plan out the whole trip ahead, carefully mapping out milestones that you must reach before you get to your final goal. And, you would just as soon drive your dependable old Ford that you know won't break down in the middle of the journey. FIXED movers pace themselves, and rarely fail to reach their destination. When it all boils down to endurance, a FIXED sign will pass right by a CARDINAL sign, who has probably been pulled over for speeding.

Finally we have the signs who'll take the alternate route—the MUTABLE signs. If your Sun sign belongs to the unpredictable, versatile groups of MUTABLE travelers, you'll try any form of transportation possible. You'll sneak off on a bicycle, take the bus, hitchhike, or blow your savings on a souped-up sports car. You may spend part of your life heading off on detours and then suddenly emerge as someone "with a remarkable sense of direction." Sometimes you'll pay strict attention to traffic signals and other times you'll be so distracted that you may find yourself gridlocked. Even though you swing between different modes of motion, you are always moving, inside and out. Of the three categories, those whose Sun signs are MUTABLE will absorb more sights along the way than either the CARDINAL or FIXED movers, regardless of whether they actually reach their original destination.

Cardinal	Fixed	Mutable
Aries	Taurus	Gemini
Cancer	Leo	Virgo
Libra	Scorpio	Sagittarius
Capricorn	Aquarius	Pisces

All right. Now that we know what planet motivates you, and what mode of movement you most often employ, the third question we ask is what is your substance, your element. The four elements are Earth, Air, Water, and Fire. One of the most eloquent voices of astrology, Carl Jung, related the elements to the following four parts of the human psyche:

FIRE represents Emotion
EARTH represents Sensation
AIR represents Intellect
WATER represents Intuition

Fire Signs	Earth Signs	Air Signs	Water Signs
"Doers"	"Attainers"	"Thinkers"	"Feelers"
Aries	Taurus	Gemini	Cancer
Leo	Virgo	Libra	Scorpio
Sagittarius	Capricorn	Aquarius	Pisces

Your element is your human makeup, your CONTENT. Your mode of transportation (Cardinal, Fixed, or Mutable) can also be described as your STYLE. When we look at and examine each Sun sign we'll take into account how your ruling planet and your STYLE combine with your CONTENT, your element. As a FIRE sign do you burn quickly or do you live on a low, steady simmer? If you're made of EARTH, do you stand your ground like a concrete block or are you always getting ready for an earthquake? As an AIR sign, you could be light and breezy, or constantly blowing in forceful gusts. In the event that you belong to one of the WATER signs, you could be a whirlpool of emotions, or as serene and flowing as the rivers to the sea.

Still with me? I hope so! This is just the easy stuff. It starts to get very intricate when we return to your decan, which will be a specific mix of your ruling planets and your respective STYLES of motion, as they work together with your element. (Decans never combine elements. Even if you are a 3rd Decan of LEO, a LEO-Aries, ruled by SUN-Mars, styled as FIXED-Cardinal, you are still all FIRE.)

WHAT TO LOOK FOR IN YOUR DECAN

Some say that each planet has a light and a dark side. Whether that is physically true or not, it is true in my experience that each person has a light and a dark side. I've yet to meet one living soul who is all "light" with no room for improvement. Nothing thrills me more than meeting someone who is working to overcome their "darker" shortcomings and, believe me, I have had occasion to run into some of the real dregs of society. We're talking "fringe element," if you know what I mean. Even with the sorriest of the lot, there is always a flicker of positive potential, a light place within them, offering him or her a chance for self-improvement. The bottom line is that we have a choice. Astrology sets no limits on your ability to embrace the very best within yourself; it lets you choose to do so. Astrology is simply a guide, you have to take the trip yourself. It can serve as your conscience, making you aware of the ways in which you short-circuit your "light" power, pointing out the pitfalls you create for yourself.

I'll give you examples of some famous individuals who have had an impact on our lives. Some of them have become legendary. They have achieved true *Starpower* and will live long after they have left our midst. Others are only the *shooting stars*, those who burn brightly at first and then disappear from public view. A few of my examples will be those who have not fulfilled their light-side potential, who may have chosen their darker nature and its limitations. And, finally, I'm going to be listing a couple of celebrities that I just happen to want to gossip about to you. Don't forget, I'm a SAGITTARIUS, 1st Decan, SAGIT-TARIUS-Sagittarius, otherwise known as BLAB and GAB. We are infamous for not keeping secrets. So, don't blame me, blame it on JUPITER, the planetary ruler of the 1st Decan of Sagittarius.

I'll tell you now that one of the quickest ways to uncover the dirt in anyone's chart is to size up what's going on in their twelfth house, karma. This is where we astrologers discover your past life secrets, what lessons you've already learned, and what you're here to work out in this lifetime. This house is also referred to as the house of Self-Undoing, or the house of Entrapment. In some cases we'll be getting the buzz on where certain celebrities are sabotaging their true greatness.

Be ready for me to gossip a bit about you, too. We may hit on some of your twelfth-house secrets. But most particularly, we'll be talking about what you're really like in affairs of the heart. Rumor has it, for instance, that all SCORPIOS are sexual. Is it true? And, if so, what does that mean? Are all VIRGOS really prudes? Well, stay on the line, and listen up. We've got 36 decans to hash!

LOVE AMONG THE DECANS

Whether you are married, single, searching for love, or running desperately from attachment, you probably place a lot of importance in this part of your life. I know that I do! And I know that my particular needs and wants could be totally different from yours. Astrology gives us very useful insights in our search for our perfect "other." Based upon your birth Sun sign, and more specifically understood on decans and how they interrelate, astrologers can make some fairly accurate assumptions about the outcome of certain relationships.

It has been my vast experience that when it comes to giving first-time advice to the lovelorn, we astrologers can talk endlessly, and you're still going to do what you want to do, aren't you? Oh, if you come looking for answers to career decisions or money matters or how to handle your bossy ARIES-Aries mother-in-law, you'll listen to every word. But, if you are an impulsive GEMINI dashing after a stubborn TAURUS, you probably don't want to hear me say that the relationship is going to be a constant chase.

Nevertheless, remember the adage, Forewarned is forearmed. At least you won't walk into the bullring with your eyes closed. When you recall the wise advice that you ignored, you can say to yourself, "this is exactly what Jacqueline said would happen," at which point you'll have to decide if you're willing to work on your relationship or if it is time to grab your red cape and skedaddle.

We'll look at the Love Combos of each decan with every other decan a little later. I've made it very simple by scoring the Combo on a zero to ten basis. If your current relationship earns a low score from me, don't run off to the nearest bar and drink yourself under the table. But remember that you may hit bumps in the road together, so prepare yourselves for getting through the rough time. If you are currently single and committed to finding a love that has lasting power, look for the Combos that win top scores.

No genius who has ever lived has ever summed up the essence of love. Nor has any Einstein formulated the pure chemical components of the perfect match between two people. It can't be done. That is what makes love so unmanageable, often so very painful, and why it gives us the most powerful highs of our life. It is mysterious and intense, a quest that is as expansive as the universe.

When we deal with that bizarre creature, the love bug, we can borrow some basic tools from astrology. Pay attention to these handy rules of thumb; they might save you from wasting precious time with the wrong person or from having your wallet emptied without any return on your dollar. They might even save you from having a broken heart, and that's no laughing matter. Statistics show that more people die of sheer heartbreak than actual cardiac arrest. These same figures tell us also that 90 percent of all crimes are crimes of passion.

Astrology highlights emotional compatibility, ego conflicts, life-style similarities and differences, sexual attractions and preferences, inclinations to share home and family together. The optimum, of course, is the whole package: romance, friendship, passion, financial security, emotional and intellectual support. With the whole package there is a spiritual oneness and then something very fundamental: It is a relationship that works. For some people, finding their match is as difficult as stumbling over the next Hope diamond. Some never do and are constantly facing disappointments in their chosen mates. Some are meant to go solo. They're the ones that I'll be pointing out as the "Bachelor decans" whose inner motto is "give me freedom or give me death." Others want love, but are just plain lazy, and will marry young for convenience, status, or material comfort. Still others are just too picky, waiting for Mr. or Mrs. Right to fall from the skies right into their laps.

In any case, I strongly advise you to look for the best, for you. If your relationship is lacking in some important area, work to improve it. Ask yourself, "do I want to change?" Waiting for your partner to do the changing alone can be like "waiting for Godot"—an eternal anticlimax! If he or she is unwilling to do the work with you, get a lawyer.

Seriously, I believe that every couple has the potential to make it, if they are committed to making changes within themselves. At the same time, I believe that the reason the divorce courts have become as populated as honeymoon hotels is that the newlyweds ignored telltale warnings in each other's personalities before they traipsed down the aisle. Think of the heartache that could have been spared had they consulted one another's horoscopes.

And that, my patient and dutiful students, is what three marriages and more love affairs than I can count have taught me. My experience and the power of astrology have produced the trusty guidelines for combining Sun signs, which I promised you. I've already done the hard work for you in calculating how each decan combines with all the other decans, based on the time-tested rules that follow.

OPPOSITIONS

Many astrologers agree, from years of observation, that OPPOSITIONS in love or marriage are difficult. An OPPOSITION is the sign directly opposite from you on the zodiac wheel. We always hear "opposites attract," but this cliché wears out as fast as I can tell a secret. The two of you attract because one has an ingredient that the other lacks and needs. There is a magnetic pull that seems magically to draw you together. But once you are in his or her space you can become lost, homesick, overwhelmed. We find a lot of sensual passion between OPPOSITIONS—and twice as much conflict! You simply are too different from one another. Go visiting, but don't go to stay unless you are willing to give up your old habits. An OPPOSITION can teach you your greatest lessons, fill that void in your makeup, confront you with your faults, and improve you. You will find rare and unusual friendship with an OPPOSITION, an opportunity not to miss. Unless your decan qualities balance you out, however, I rarely advocate rushing out to buy your trousseau when involved with an OPPOSITION.

One of the most tempestuous love affairs between OPPOSITIONS occurred between Marilyn Monroe, a GEMINI, and Joe DiMaggio, a SAGITTARIUS. It was a passionate mismatch—they adored one another and drove each other nuts.

The "relationship" between writer/actor SCORPIO Sam Shephard and actress TAURUS Jessica Lange, can point up the deep attraction between OPPOSITIONS that doesn't necessarily get the couple to the church on time. Even when baby makes three!

Incidentally, in researching examples of famous marriages between OPPOSITIONS, I found that there are truly very few out there. It's not an easy dynamic, so do take note of which Sun sign could take you on a rough ride.

Aries	OPPOSES	Libra
Taurus	OPPOSES	Scorpio
Gemini	OPPOSES	Sagittarius
Cancer	OPPOSES	Capricorn
Leo	OPPOSES	Aquarius
Virgo	OPPOSES	Pisces

CUSP NEIGHBORS AND YOUR OWN SUN SIGN

The second general rule suggests that it is not so wise to date your neighbors, the Sun signs that border yours, and in most cases very risky to marry someone whose birthday falls within thirty degrees, or thirty days from yours. The logic here is that if you are together with your own sign, there is no contrast, you're too much alike. Can you imagine two GEMINIS together? Two sets of twins trying to find spiritual oneness with each other? Stereophonic schizophrenia!

I married my own decan, another SAGITTARIUS-Sagittarius, and was I in for a hellish experience. Here I thought I had it made: I had this adorable jockey, cute as a button, who came right up to my armpit. I was thrilled that I'd finally found a man who'd let me hold the reins. Boy, was I dumb. We were both fighting so hard for independence and control; pretty soon he seemed to be about seven feet tall and I'd become a regular dwarf next to him.

If my experience with my own sign isn't convincing enough, what about Sylvester's travesty of a marriage to Brigitte? That's right, they're both Moon Child CANCERS, which was one too many Crabs under one roof in that household. Unfortunately, the unhappiness that Sly felt so deeply when it was over prevented me from having any satisfaction in saying, "I told you so." You'd think he would have learned after it didn't work with his first wife, Sasha, another CANCER!

Cusp neighbors are great to have for borrowing a cup of sugar now and then, but usually there seems to be no major chemistry. Of the many men who I have dated and enjoyed, I have never spent five minutes with a CAPRICORN, of any decan, that was anything better than miserable. Interestingly, the sign that follows yours is known as your "pesty" neighbor, whereas the sign that precedes yours is your "support system," your backup when you need advice or consolation. Take a look at some of your friendships and see if they fall into these two patterns. In neither case should the love sparks be evident. If they are, just be sure you know who's the pest and who's the support.

Astrology is trying to teach us that we need BALANCE. We need enough differences and enough similarities to complement one another. So, we look for this balance with the following combinations: TRINES, SEXTILES, and sometimes SQUARES. A TRINE is the sign behind or in front of you four stops down the street. It is also a member of your family of elements.

ARIES	trine	LEO	trine	SAGITTARIUS	(Fire)
TAURUS	trine	VIRGO	trine	CAPRICORN	(Earth)
GEMINI	trine	LIBRA	trine	AQUARIUS	(Air)
CANCER	trine	SCORPIO	trine	PISCES	(Water)

TRINES are usually happy combinations. You like each other. You have similar backgrounds and values. Yours will outlast other relationships. There are exceptions to this rule that I've taken into account in scoring the decan combos, which you'll soon see.

The immortal love affair between Richard Burton, a SCORPIO, and PISCES Elizabeth Taylor was a TRINE bonding if ever there was one. Two Water signs make for deep, emotional attachments and their marriage was the ultimate in romance. Astrologically, they were a match made in heaven! We'll be taking a closer look later at why this positive TRINE hookup ran into trouble.

Another one of Liz's hubbies, Eddie Fisher, a LEO, found his TRINE connection with ARIES Debbie Reynolds. Their mutual FIRE components made them an excellent balance for one another. Don't worry that your love affair may suffer the same fates as either of these two couples if you are currently involved in a TRINE. And don't sit around and figure that you've got it made, either. The combination of your common elements is a great starting place. You still have to work at it. Making love last is now up to you!

SEXTILES occur with every other Sign, and a SEXTILE connection can be as much fun as the word suggests. You are in for a marvelously romantic experience, especially if your birthdays fall between thirty and sixty days from one another.

In most SEXTILE unions there is, in addition to basic chemistry, an ability to complement one another in professional and financial matters. When all hell broke loose for Richard Nixon, an ambitious CAPRICORN, his wife, Pat, a compassionate PISCES, kept him from going off the deep end for good.

If you have an opportunity to meet either one of your SEXTILE matches, take advantage of the astrological magic that can happen.

ARIES	sextile	GEMINI	and	AQUARIUS
TAURUS	sextile	CANCER	and	PISCES
GEMINI	sextile	LEO	and	ARIES
CANCER	sextile	VIRGO	and	TAURUS
LEO	sextile	LIBRA	and	GEMINI
VIRGO	sextile	SCORPIO	and	CANCER
LIBRA	sextile	SAGITTARIUS	and	LEO
SCORPIO	sextile	CAPRICORN	and	VIRGO
SAGITTARIUS	sextile	AQUARIUS	and	LIBRA
CAPRICORN	sextile	PISCES	and	SCORPIO
AQUARIUS	sextile	ARIES	and	SAGITTARIUS
PISCES	sextile	TAURUS	and	CAPRICORN

Once you get beyond the sixty-day period and within the bounds of the ninety-day period, or ninety degrees either way around the zodiac wheel, you are encountering a Sun sign in your SQUARE. SQUARES are controversial combinations and have to be judged on a decan-by-decan basis. As a 1st Decan SAGITTARIUS, I happen to love challenge and challenge is what I'll find in my SQUARE. Not everyone wants the challenge, so please ask yourself, if you happen to be a jealous SCORPIO, whether you can handle the challenge of an airy, aloof

AQUARIAN, or the attention-hungry LEO. He or she may be the great love of your life, but you'll have to put your old possessive nature to sleep.

The SQUARE between GEMINI Mel Brooks and VIRGO Anne Bancroft has been working beautifully for decades. When all the other movie marriages have bit the dust, theirs just seems to keep on punching.

On the other hand, TAURUS Debra Winger and LEO Timothy Hutton SQUARED off to a standoff when they found they couldn't take or just didn't want the challenge in their relationship.

Before signing marriage certificates with anyone whose Sun sign SQUARES yours, really ask yourself if you are the type of person who thrives on challenge, or one who requires more stability. If you don't know the answer now, you certainly will after I've finished with your decan!

Aries	SQUARE	Cancer and Capricorn
Taurus	SQUARE	Leo and Aquarius
Gemini	SQUARE	Virgo and Pisces
Cancer	SQUARE	Libra and Aries
Leo	SQUARE	Scorpio and Taurus
Virgo	SQUARE	Sagittarius and Gemini
Libra	SQUARE	Capricorn and Cancer
Scorpio	SQUARE	Aquarius and Leo
Sagittarius	SQUARE	Pisces and Virgo
Capricorn	SQUARE	Aries and Libra
Aquarius	SQUARE	Taurus and Scorpio
Pisces	SQUARE	Gemini and Sagittarius

Sometimes no aspects are indicated between Sun signs. In those cases you're on your own. Follow your heart and your instincts and learn to be "weatherwise." Through the centuries, astrologers have noted that FIRE and AIR signs get along, while EARTH and WATER mix well together. WATER and FIRE are natural enemies, aren't they? What can put out the FIRE of a brazen ARIES better than a bucketful of WATER from SCORPIO? The same applies to EARTH and FIRE. Dump a pile of mud from CAPRICORN on the burning ego of LEO and all you've got is ash!

AIR and WATER are similarly composed, but it takes too long for the emotional torrents of CANCER to evaporate to reach the airy heights of LIBRA. AIR and EARTH don't interact at all - one's upstairs and the other's down below. A practical TAURUS takes one look at flighty GEMINI and thinks the other is from outer space.

The intricacies of these combinations get even more involved as we now are ready to meet each decan. Score yourselves an A+ for this minicourse in Astrology 101. We'll turn our focus away from these more general premises of astrology as we zoom in on what I certainly hope will be some candid close-ups on YOU.

KARMA CLOCK

FIND YOUR BIRTH TIME!

The preceding clock probably doesn't look like any clock you've seen recently, and well it shouldn't. This is the astrologer's handy-dandy Karma Clock on which we can tell the time of your destiny. To clock your own all you'll need is the time of your birth. If you don't know what time you were born, look at your wristwatch this very instant, and that is the time you'll use to check the Karma Clock. This is the basic rule of the more complex practice known as Horary, or the Birth of the Question. I use Horary for my own and Sylvester's project planning with astounding results. If you have an important question you'd like charted, visit your friendly local astrologer. If he or she doesn't know Horary, think twice before spending your money on an amateur. In the meantime, you can still dabble with this approach even if you don't know your actual time of birth. Mark your birth time, if known, or the time you've asked the question, the Horary, on the Clock and read the section that applies to you.

BORN BETWEEN 6 A.M. & 12 P.M.

Born above the astrological horizon, you are more of a late bloomer. You may spend time pursuing different interests until you find your true calling. Similarly, you may spend time exploring different love interests until you find your true love! There is both a shrewd and individualist spirit that fuels all your actions. You may also find that you thrive in the morning hours.

As you are clocked in the East, you are the master or mistress of your destiny. The success that you achieve will be a result of your own endeavors spread over time. Ultimately, you will find that you are resourceful and confident, because you do not depend on anyone or anything to create your happiness.

Birth hours in this sector include Abraham Lincoln at 6:15 a.m., Liza Minnelli at 7:58 a.m., Tony Curtis at 9 a.m., and George Washington at 10:05 a.m. My daughter, Toniann, born at 8 a.m., is famous in our family for controlling her destiny!

BORN BETWEEN 12 P.M. & 6 P.M.

Your time also is clocked above the astrological horizon. Your success may come to you later in life, following years of hard work. Don't give up; it pays off. Education figures prominently in all that you do.

This path shows you as being extremely monogamous in nature. In your younger years you may hide behind the scenes, only to emerge with a huge splash later on. Few people know your true powers.

Being stationed in the West, you will have a need for others, whose companionship and support can make or break your ultimate success. Many people in this sector feel they have been born with a mission to serve and have no choice but to let destiny control their path. Learning when to act, when to lay low, and whom to trust are of key importance. Fate smiles on you when you are in touch with your instincts. Martin Luther King, Jr., was born in the West and above the horizon, at 12:30 p.m. Others born in this time period include poet Ralph Waldo Emerson at 1:16 p.m., Jacqueline Onassis at 2:30 p.m., Carole Lombard at 2:41 p.m., and one of my favorite composers, Frederic Chopin, at 5:50 p.m.

BORN BETWEEN 6 P.M. & 12 A.M.

You are born below the astrological horizon. This means early starts, early love affairs, early success! You probably love jumping up at the crack of dawn and greeting the new day. Things should come easily to you. You have a personal magnetism that gets you into the center of the action right off the bat.

You are born in the West. Astrologically, this means that your destiny is in the hands of other people. Selecting the right individuals to guide and assist you is of prime importance. Be careful who you trust but once someone has earned that trust, don't take it for granted. Great leaders, thinkers, and writers emerge from this birth-hour period, such as Sigmund Freud at 6:30 p.m., the great actress Sarah Bernhardt at 8 p.m., Mozart at 8 p.m. as well, the impressionistic artists Matisse and Degas both around 8:30 p.m., and Prince Charles of England at 9:14 p.m.

This sector is also full of birth times for movie stars, everyone from Ava Gardner at 7: 10 p.m., to Hedy Lamarr at 7:30 p.m., to Sidney Poitier at 9 p.m., to the legendary Marlon Brando at 11 p.m., and the immortal Bette Davis at 11:50 p.m. I suppose I'll also mention my sons Sylvester and Frank Stallone, both born in different years at 7 p.m. Because of their choices in careers, their destinies are in the hands of the public. What's a mother to do?

BORN BETWEEN 12 A.M. & 6 A.M.

When your birth hour strikes below the horizon, we find early genius and talents, special gifts you have been given that will gain you. Recognition at a young age. Growing older may not be easy for you. Though you may have a wide social circle, you can be quite the loner when you are impassioned with your work. You can also experience an intense early love affair that forces all later loves to play second fiddle.

The East side of the clock where you are born tells us that you don't wait for things to happen for you, you make them happen. All good fortune that arises will spring out of your actions. You're not afraid to stir the waters and you'll accept all consequences in so doing. When you control destiny to this degree, others may envy you. This time frame gave birth to some of my greatest heroes—Winston Churchill at 1:30 a.m., artist, sculptor, and inventor Michelangelo at 1:45 a.m., inventor and artist Leonardo Da Vinci at 3 a.m., and the composer Claude Debussy 3:30 a.m. Naturally, I've got to love this sector the most because it's the one that set me on my path. I clocked in at 2 a.m.!

Your Karma O'Clock time tells the big picture of a life span. But what about the little picture, the daily events, which when added up together can alter your existence for better or for worse? Well, if you are truly sincere about using your decan Starpower potentials to the hilt, don't skip over the next part of what I've got in my astrological goodie bag.

The second most important planet, after the Sun, is the Moon. Where the Moon falls in your horoscope will show your emotional depths, how your inner feelings will affect your outward behavior. Check any table of Moon charts, or call your local planetarium to find out where your Moon was at the hour and date of your birth. If it falls into a complementary decan, you know you are a balanced individual; if not, you're going to have to work harder to overcome conflicts within yourself. In either case, you can rely on the Moon's activity to help you on a day-to-day basis by following guidelines that have been set for centuries.

Back in the good old days, long before anyone had a Rolex to check the time, nothing was done without first checking the positions of the Sun and the Moon. Harvests and marriages and battles were all arranged by the study of those two biggies. As the Moon takes 30 days to complete the zodiac orbit, we have assessed that it spends every $2^{1/2}$ days in each sign. Some days during a given month, you'll experience various highs and lows, depending on the Moon's effect on your decan. Without having to check a daily astrological chart for the Moon's positioning, simply keep on eye on the Moon up in the sky. Or, check almost any calendar for dates when the full moon or the new moon are due. At the same time you can draw big X's on the days of both solar and lunar eclipses.

Generally, the full moon makes us all emotional, more so than at any other time of the month. More violent crimes occur during a full moon, as well as the reporting of more false fire alarms, than at other times. Mental patients are known to be negatively affected during the full moon; the rest of us can also get to feeling "loony" as well. Obviously, hasty decisions made during the three-day full moon period can be disastrous for everybody.

Therefore, make it your business to use this period for emotional R&R. Spend time with loved ones in familiar surroundings, to minimize any uneasy feelings that might arise. People who are known to you who may be going through a trying time should be treated with love and affection. Full moons are great for Good Samaritan work, and rotten for anyone to undergo surgery. Hippocrates made sure all his students were aware that the full moon can cause water retention in the tissues, which increases the likelihood of hemorrhaging. If more doctors paid attention to astrology, they wouldn't have to spend so much money on malpractice insurance.

The new moon tends to give everybody sudden hefty bursts of energy. Generally, this is an excellent time to start projects, sign contracts, and go on blind dates. Don't, however, let the vibrant new moon make you so rash or overconfident that you act without proper consideration first. With caution and planning, you can use the new moon to help you do wonders. You are being given an extra cosmic boost!

If you have Cancer, Capricorn, Aries, or Libra in your decan, please prepare carefully for all full or new moons. The Cardinal crew gets double whammied by Moonpower.

Every decan can make use of the eclipses, depending on what month they occur. If the following flow chart shows that your sign is negatively affected during that particular month, do not travel, change jobs, make investments, or get married. If you see a positive aspect indicated in the chart, take all the wildest risks you've ever dreamed, embark on new ventures, the sky's the limit! I swear by these Moon movements and have seen them work like a charm.

When the Sun is in ARIES, lunar and solar eclipses, new and full moons will have positive, negative, or questionable effects on:

+	-	?
ARIES	LIBRA	VIRGO
GEMINI	CANCER	TAURUS
AQUARIUS	CAPRICORN	PISCES
LEO		SCORPIO
SAGITTARIUS		

When the Sun is in TAURUS, lunar and solar eclipses, new and full moons will have positive, negative, or questionable effects on:

+	-	?
TAURUS	SCORPIO	ARIES
CANCER	LEO	GEMINI
PISCES	AQUARIUS	LIBRA
CAPRICORN		SAGITTARIUS
VIRGO		

When the Sun is in GEMINI, lunar and solar eclipses, new and full moons will have positive, negative, or questionable effects on:

+	-	?
GEMINI	SAGITTARIUS	TAURUS
LEO	VIRGO	SCORPIO
ARIES	PISCES	CAPRICORN
LIBRA		CANCER
AQUARIUS		

When the Sun is in CANCER, lunar and solar eclipses, new and full moons will have positive, negative, or questionable effects on:

+	-	?
CANCER	CAPRICORN	LEO
VIRGO	LIBRA	SAGITTARIUS
TAURUS	ARIES	GEMINI
SCORPIO		AQUARIUS
PISCES		

When the Sun is in LEO, lunar and solar eclipses, new and full moons will have positive, negative, or questionable effects on:

+	-	?
LEO	AQUARIUS	VIRGO
LIBRA	SCORPIO	CAPRICORN
GEMINI	TAURUS	AQUARIUS
SAGITTARIUS		PISCES
ARIES		

When the Sun is in VIRGO, lunar and solar eclipses, new and full moons will have positive, negative, or questionable effects on:

+	-	?
VIRGO	PISCES	LIBRA
SCORPIO	SAGITTARIUS	AQUARIUS
CANCER	GEMINI	ARIES
TAURUS		LEO
CAPRICORN		

When the Sun is in LIBRA, lunar and solar eclipses, new and full moons will have positive, negative, or questionable effects on:

+	-	?
LIBRA	ARIES	SCORPIO
SAGITTARIUS	CAPRICORN	PISCES
LEO	CANCER	VIRGO
GEMINI		TAURUS
AQUARIUS		

When the Sun is in SCORPIO, lunar and solar eclipses, new and full moons will have positive, negative, or questionable effects on:

+	-	?
SCORPIO	TAURUS	SAGITTARIUS
VIRGO	AQUARIUS	ARIES
CAPRICORN	LEO	LIBRA
PISCES		GEMINI
CANCER		

When the Sun is in SAGITTARIUS, lunar and solar eclipses, new and full moons will have positive, negative, or questionable effects on:

+	-	?
SAGITTARIUS	GEMINI	CAPRICORN
AQUARIUS	PISCES	TAURUS
LIBRA	VIRGO	SCORPIO
ARIES		CANCER
LEO		

When the Sun is in CAPRICORN, lunar and solar eclipses, new and full moons will have positive, negative, or questionable effects on:

+	-	?
CAPRICORN	CANCER	AQUARIUS
SCORPIO	ARIES	GEMINI
PISCES	LIBRA	SAGITTARIUS
TAURUS		LEO
VIRGO		

When the Sun is in AQUARIUS, lunar and solar eclipses, new and full moons will have positive, negative, or questionable effects on:

+	-	?
AQUARIUS	LEO	PISCES
SAGITTARIUS	SCORPIO	CANCER
ARIES	TAURUS	VIRGO
GEMINI		CAPRICORN
LIBRA		

When the Sun is in PISCES, lunar and solar eclipses, new and full moons will have positive, negative, or questionable effects on:

+	−	?
PISCES	VIRGO	ARIES
TAURUS	SAGITTARIUS	LIBRA
CANCER	GEMINI	LEO
CAPRICORN		AQUARIUS
SCORPIO		

Now that you know how potentially powerful you are, by having studied your decan traits, with an understanding of your karmic birth timing, and by using wise planning and judgment with the preceding charts, we're going to check what all the other planets are going to be doing to your decan for the next ten years, and then I'm going to turn you loose. So let's go and see what the Astral Itch has in store for you during the first decade of the 21st Century.

CHAPTER 3

ARIES

MARCH 21 - APRIL 20

First Decan	Second Decan	Third Decan
ARIES-Aries	ARIES-Leo	ARIES-Sagittarius
3/21 - 3/30	3/31 - 4/9	4/10 - 4/20

Once upon a time, an ARIES was overheard
to say in passing, "Why can't everyone be like me?"

Sign:	Fire · Doers
Symbol:	The Ram
Planet:	Mars
Body Talk:	Head & Face
Style:	Cardinal

MEET THE BOSS...

ARIES men and women are the notorious commanders of the zodiac. No matter what decan you fall into, you undoubtedly love to push everything and everyone around. If you can't find a great crusade to push, you'll grab a broom and start pushing it. Unless, of course, you can find someone else to do the sweeping for you. That is your preference, is it not?

Domineering, authoritative, slave-driving. Energetic, positively ambitious, and usually optimistic. With any Ram we have to take the bad with the good. The best aspect of all of you ardent sheep put together is that no matter what your means you do achieve your ends. You get the job done, there's no two ways about it.

In love, let's just say: ARIES men and women, you like being *on top*. Literally!

As a FIRE sign, ruled by Mars, you have a constitution that burns fast, hard, and hot. You'll take over like leaping flames, engulfing your competition with choking smoke. When you're in action there is almost no stopping you.

In general, ARIES individuals have a fresh, sometimes naive quality. Sure, you like to think of yourself as a pragmatist, scoping out possibilities ahead of you. Still, most of you haven't yet learned the realities of a complicated world. You keep it very simple. You believe you are the master or mistress of your destiny, so why can't you control the destiny of the events around you? When circumstances not to your liking occur, you become outraged. You fume and gnash your teeth, punch holes in walls, or try to ram down the obstacle that has fallen in your path. Then, when all of your efforts fail, you get a bad case of the bean-bag blues, like poor little disappointed lambs. Well, never fear, your Cardinal style never allows you to stay down for long. "Up and at 'em" is the creed of each and every one of you supercharged go-getters.

FIRST DECAN OF ARIES

"I'M AGGRESSIVE, I'M VERY AGGRESSIVE!"

ARIES-Aries	CARDINAL-Cardinal	MARS-Mars

You are the 1st Decan of the first Sun sign of the zodiac. No wonder you're always calling yourself "Number One." With double Cardinal style, you demand to fly with a first-class ticket. Being put on the waiting list makes you stark raving mad. You'll recruit an entire army to get your way, if need be. Mars, in double influence, shapes almost all ARIES-Aries into highly energized pistols of raw drive. I'll bet you don't sleep very much. You probably get up at night and move around, ordering the mice back into their holes. Or, you'll inspect the execution of chores done by others, making extended lists of improvements.

A 1st Decan ARIES without a cause to fight for, or a flag to carry, is like a man without a country. You RAM-Rams belong in positions of authority, with projects that are actually more like missions in your terminology. When asked to do something that you consider too menial, or worse, when someone tries to give you an order, you can become ill. Flexibility is a word I don't think is included in your vocabulary.

YOUR DARK SIDE

All right, we've already established that you are an extremist. We can add "brash" and "overbearing" to the list that's already been covered. The trait at the bottom of this stack of bothersome traits is truly your one flaw: intolerance. Perhaps because you expect so much from yourself, because you work so hard at achieving your aims and goals, you can't imagine why others don't do the same. You have no patience for weakness or failings in others.

Come on, admit that you carry around a catalog of prejudices. I hope you are working on getting rid of your know-it-all attitude, but my guess is that your mates, friends, children, or co-workers have already complained about it.

Now the only reason that I'm hitting you so hard with these derogatories is that I know you're man or woman enough to take it. To actually get you to face up to your faults we second-stringers have to do a little ramming ourselves, if you know what I mean.

YOUR LIGHT SIDE

As difficult as it is for you to acknowledge your shortcomings, you've got so much self-confidence you could have a sale on the surplus. That's why your arrogance is usually forgiven, and why your behavior is never seen as insecure or tentative.

You are clear on what is important and you pursue priorities. The positive aspect of your bossiness is that you aren't afraid to delegate responsibilities. An ARIES-Aries can often inspire others to get off their lazy butts and go for the gold. There's something about your openly aggressive personality that makes you endearing. Maybe it's those cute, curly horns you Rams wear. If I hadn't gotten such great mileage out of my famous headbands, I'd invest in a pair just like yours!

BOTTOM LINE FOR YOUR POWER

Simply remember that you've got what it takes to accomplish anything and everything. As long as you take a spoonful of humility once a day, you'll quickly learn to be much more tolerant of others. Every now and then take a walk in someone else's shoes just so you can hop back into yours that much better equipped for what you're really meant to do. For strength, commitment to a cause, undying and powerful energy, you're making all the right moves as: a *Leader*.

BODY TALK

The 1st Decan of ARIES rules the head and face regions of the body. See, that's the reason you get labeled "headstrong", "hardheaded" or "brow-beating." It's probably a physical reality that you have a very tough noggin that can withstand heavy blows and knocks. Just as a word of caution though—your thick-skinned helmet is not impenetrable. ARIES-Aries folks have a multitude of stress-causing events going on at all times. The first place that you can get attacked is right smack dab in the middle of the forehead. Please, follow your doctor's orders if you are having chronic headaches; 1st Decan Rams rarely take sick, but when you do, it can be serious. Do take extra vitamins in any case. The rapid-burning firepower of your sign is always depleting needed nutrients.

Well, there's nothing very sexy about a skull, but there is something especially seductive about your eyes. All that MARS-Mars energy is funneled into beams of intense light that pour out of you. Haven't you ever just looked across a dinner table and rendered a member of the opposite sex helpless with an interested, focused glance? You may even have forgotten that you gave someone the eye and then wonder why he or she turned up on your doorstep one night all packed and ready to move in.

If you are afflicted with any optical problems, please invest in a pair of contact lenses, not glasses. Covering up your greatest asset would be a crying shame. In the event that you have a secret fetish for hats, by all means indulge yourself. Your decan wears them well, and for the most part, in good health. Cheers!

YOUR BEST-BET CAREERS

Short of a stint in the military, which, whether you're a man or a woman is just perfect for you, your employment options must include the chance to give orders. For example, the corporate look suits you, as long as you're standing on the higher rungs of the ladder. When you go raiding other stock-held companies, their "Bored" of Directors won't even know when you pull the rug out from under them.

You'll charge right ahead in any field where you can lead a brigade into action. Sports coaching is an ARIES-Aries hog heaven. We could use a few of your type in our national search for more natural resources. Go have a talk with OPEC and give them a copy of your rules and regulations. Or start an oil-drilling outfit of your own. If there's gold in them-thar hills, a 1st Decan ARIES will find it.

Interestingly, a lot of you feminine Ramettes have found yourselves in professional situations often occupied by men, doing twice as good a job as your male predecessor. If you happen to have chosen to stay at home and mind the store, you're sure to run the household with the strong arm of a military officer. By the way, had your kids even gotten out of diapers before you asked them to clean up their rooms?

YOUR BEST-BET LOVE COMBOS

ARIES-Aries Man: You love the challenge. You love the chase. You'd love a woman for whom you could duel a rival. Once you get her, which you usually do, you are fiercely territorial. Like a male dog pursuing a bitch in heat, a double Ram feels that once he's tagged her as his, she's his no matter what. You may even become inconsiderate toward the same sweet little thing that you wooed so passionately. Come to think of it, you can be a real dog!

In lovemaking you go by the book. Which book is that you ask? Um, I think it's the one written by a caveman many centuries ago. You know the one. It's got all those pictures of big fellas clobbering dizzy blondes over the head and dragging them home to their bachelor caves. Well, even though your moves are a tad brutish, you do have lasting power, that's for sure.

Since taking advice isn't something you're accustomed to doing, you probably won't listen to my suggestions for a suitable match. But, in case any gals out there are wondering who on earth would put up with you, I'll say for the record that Ms. LEO-Leo, your trine, isn't a bad choice. Her vanity will convince you that you've just dragged home the prize of a lifetime. Every time you slip and say something blunt in a social situation, she'll cover for you with her gregarious charm. As long as you're out conquering the nation, she'll be content to stay at home and rule the cave.

ARIES-Aries Woman: Because you tend to focus so much of your energy toward achievement, Ram-paging around on this project or that, you probably don't spend a lot of time musing about romance. Not that having a wonderful man is such a dreadful thought to you.

On the contrary, when you come home and take off your work fatigues, you'd give your left hoof to have someone playful handing you something more comfortable to slip on.

The problem you may encounter all too often is that you haven't been able to control your emotional, sensual leanings the same way you control everything else. Deep down inside you'd really like to be treated tenderly, as if you were a docile, subservient, womanly lamb. Then, when the lights go low, the aggressive side of you goes high. Your lovemaking partner will be startled when you start calling out football terms in bed. Oh, the many faces of an ARIES-Aries woman can confuse even the most sensitive male.

Given these swift changes of temperature, have I got a guy for you ... he's funny, lightning-fast, talented, and can talk his way straight to your heart. Plus, he'll constantly alternate between his different personalities.

Of course, he's a GEMINI-Gemini. Please stick to the 1st Decan of this Air sign. His MUTABLE-Mutable style is the only one to mix with a Cardinal girl like you. Whatever problems do arise, his vivid imagination will keep your interest at a bubbling perk. Sounds kinky, doesn't he?

DECAN PAIRS WITH ARIES-ARIES

LOVE SCALE SCORES

0 = Forget it! • 1 = Don't be a masochist... • 2 = Why bother? • 3 = Fun for one date. • 4 = It won't last! • 5 = You could do better! • 6 = Romance will fade... 7 = Great buddies! • 8 = Pure passion • 9 = True love. • 10 = Eternal bliss!

STARS OF ARIES-ARIES

March 21:	Rosie O'Donnell
	Matthew Broderick
March 22:	Matthew Modine
March 23:	Joan Crawford
	Richard Greico
March 24:	Bob Mackie
	Harry Houdini
March 25:	Elton John
	Sarah Jessica Parker
March 26:	Diana Ross
	Martin Short
March 27:	Quentin Tarantino
	Mariah Carey
	Gloria Swanson
March 30:	Celine Dion
	Warren Beatty
	Tracy Chapman
	Vincent Van Gogh

SECOND DECAN OF ARIES

"I'M AGGRESSIVE AND I'M VERY PROUD!"

ARIES-Leo	CARDINAL-Fixed	MARS-Sun

You are no less of a Ram than your neighbor decan ARIES-Aries. But, as an ARIES-Leo, you are mellowed by the golden glow of the sun, the planet that influences Leo. The Sun in your decan gives you a mark of nobility, a sense of pride that you stand apart from the rest. We won't find you ramming down gates to get attention, because you have been endowed with a special finesse. You often achieve your goals with a seeming lack of effort, which makes you an unmatchable foe for those who fall for your outward ease.

Your Cardinal style of rushing off on a crusade at the drop of a hat has been held in check by your Fixed temperament, which likes to weigh the odds before you attempt the risk. Once you have gone ahead with an undertaking you not only need to be in charge, as any ARIES does, you also want major recognition in the form of applause, compliments, even out-and-out worship, which is unique to your decan. Come on, admit you like to hear that you're the greatest several times a day. So what if you've already decided that you are a top-notch individual, you just want to make sure everybody else knows it.

Having a personality that likes to give orders and have people tell you how wonderful you are while you're telling them what to do, doesn't sound like the best way to get to be Ms. or Mr. Popular. Surprisingly, you are usually adored by the select few that you do allow into your inner circle. You are militantly protective of family and friends. An insult to them is an insult to you. You'll go after the culprit in full battle attire, and, knowing how the spot of Leo in you makes you a great dresser, you'll probably look fabulous as you head out to the warpath.

YOUR DARK SIDE

I'm not even going to try beating around the bush. You're an awful snob, pure and simple. You'll only eat at certain restaurants. You'll pour out a whole bottle of decent wine just because the vintage doesn't match up to your royal tastes. God forbid that you should ever have to buy clothes off the rack. Even hearing the name "K-Mart" is enough to send chills down your spine.

When caught up in one of your frequent important endeavors, you'll hit some snaggy boring detail and conclude that the whole thing is beneath you. You'll throw your hands up and expect one of the little guys to come and do the cleanup. You're actively short-circuiting your own power because you don't want to get your hands dirty. What a waste of precious Mars energy, I should say.

Oh, wait, speaking of clean. You are a clean freak. You demand immaculate surroundings, and if the stable of household help you've hired hasn't kept them so, you'll dash into your private quarters and have a roaring temper tantrum. Thank God that your pride won't allow you to display your anger to the extent that other ARIES do.

YOUR LIGHT SIDE

Most Rams aren't known for their diplomacy, but those of you born in this ten-day period are the exceptions. Where the rest of your Sun sign has a tendency to be blunt or inarticulate, you have an eloquent, gracious manner of speech. Like the very Sun that influences your decan, you can dazzle and charm when you so choose.

Aside from that little chip you wear on your shoulder, your qualities usually command true respect from your peers. Plus, you never, ever take loyalty for granted, going to great lengths to show your appreciation. For that matter you rarely take anything for granted, fueled as you are by Mars and the Sun, the two greatest sources of vital energy. You probably greet each day with a fresh outlook, ready to carry on where you left off the day before.

BOTTOM LINE FOR YOUR POWER

Your bright magnetism and discerning taste will always be your best friends — if you'll let them. At first you'll have to climb off your high horse and pay your dues. It surely won't take you long until you've earned acclaim and stature to keep you in the saddle for a lifetime.

As long as you sincerely believe in what you are doing, that your cause is worthy of your noble intentions, you can move mountains. At heart you are distinguished, exceptional, a cut above. When you are willing to do the work, you can actually be: a *Crusader*.

BODY TALK

Recall, if you will, that ARIES-Leo folk enjoy being told how swell they are. That's why your ears are your prized features. When someone says something nice about them, they perk up as if to respond, "the better to hear you with, my dear." Seriously, now, the hearing ability of Ram/Lion breeds is uniquely sharp and sensitive. If a clever member of the opposite sex leans over to whisper, or even—gasp—blow in your ear, you turn into putty in their hands.

If you do find yourself under the weather it may very well be with inner ear infections or fleeting bouts of vertigo. Basically, with ARIES rulership of the head and Leo influence over the heart, You are in excellent condition. Lucky you—your metabolism is so balanced that you may never have to work hard to lose weight or stay in shape. Aren't you glad you won't have to give away any of your designer clothes?

To accentuate the positive, I do hope you've indulged in all the latest glamorous accessories for your ears. Even you gents - a subtle diamond stud in your manly lobes can be very exciting.

YOUR BEST-BET CAREERS

As you undoubtedly already know about yourself, a behind-the-scenes or low-profile position is no place for you. You must have high visibility. Being a figurehead for a major company is an excellent use of your public appeal and your authoritative manner. Try becoming a spokesperson for a top-brand product on TV. After all, you do have a dramatic flair, don't you?

You are perfectly suited for a career in international diplomacy. All the time that you're charming the pants off your competition, you'll be winning your side of the debate. See, running your point of view into the ground with finesse can be an artful practice.

You can also employ your snobbish tastes by establishing your own local country club. That way you can earn bucks while you hold court. No kidding, take a look at ARIES-Leo Betty Ford, born on April 8. Her crusade to fight alcoholism and drug abuse led her to create an extraordinary clinic in a spa-like setting, which has saved the lives of thousands. Or, for you Ram/Lions who don't have drinking problems, go right ahead and develop that perfect bottle of wine you are always demanding. Wouldn't you love to see your face on rows and rows of bottles? Not to mention the fact that smashing grapes is excellent therapy.

Many of you may have inclinations to enter the arts. However, you may not have the patience to stick it out while your career is building. The question I asked my children back in the early years, when all three had decided to go into the entertainment industry, I'll now ask you: Can you handle it? You've got what it takes to get the attention, but it doesn't happen overnight, no matter what anyone tells you. You Ram/Lion mixes may have commitment to a cause, but the lean years are ones you'd probably prefer to skip. Think about it before you charge off on that course.

YOUR BEST-BET LOVE COMBOS

ARIES-Leo Man: As good fortune would have it, the men of this decan tend to be my personal favorites. Maybe it's that regal bearing, or that swashbuckling debonair habit you have of kissing a damsel's delicate hand and saying, "May?" How nice of you to ask before pinning her to the bed! As you can imagine, you don't have to worry about making any woman's heart go pit-a-pat! We all secretly pine for a brute in knight's armor anyway.

Still, your cavalier attitude can get you into big trouble. Your snob syndrome is actually again the root of the evil. Especially your opinion that most women aren't eligible to permanently join your league. Oh, but that doesn't mean you'll stop your conquest until the right one comes along. No wonder your ears are so sensitive. You've gotten so used to hearing the word cad cried out that you almost take it as another compliment.

Because of your need to marry within your own tribe, you should look to your other Fire signs for that appropriate mate. Go for a 1st Decan, a "pure-blooded" SAGITTARIUS-Sagittarius. She'll match you in the bedroom with a playful sense of humor while you display your tender yet forceful masculine "bent." She won't even get upset about your adventurous past.

ARIES-Leo Woman: You girl Sheep with hearts of Lionesses have an extremely romantic inner nature. In fact, you fall in love once every hour on the hour. Well, at least you're regular.

As you are in other areas, when it comes to good sense in your love life, you still get caught up with appearances. If a striking young man struts by, you could almost drop the hand of your latest amour and go chasing down the street after the new prospect. What's even worse, you don't act natural around guys. You'll purr and primp and priss the minute a male enters the room. When he exits, you're back to being just one of the rest of the girls. In the meantime, the rest of the girls are ready to pull your hair out for being such a show-off. I guess you feel that if you don't make the overtures, they aren't going to get made. Some men may appreciate your forward moves, but others will be taking giant steps backward while you're coming on to them.

Basically, what we're talking about is that you secretly enjoy doing a little chasing yourself. You'd like for your love affair to have a touch of drama, to be one more of those many crusades you like to lead. If you'll hop to it, I'll send you off on a mission that could land you a lifetime of pleasure. Catch a GEMINI-Libra by the toe and he'll keep you on yours. He's one of those more balanced 2nd Decans, like you. Also, he's got such a gift of gab that he'll tell you how beautiful you are as you persuasively command him into your chambers.

DECAN PAIRS WITH ARIES-LEO

LEO-Aries (8/13-8/22) 6
VIRGO-Virgo (8/23-9/3) 3
VIRGO-Capricorn (9/4-9/13) 2
VIRGO-Taurus (9/14-9/22) 1
LIBRA-Libra (9/23-10/3) 5
LIBRA-Aquarius (10/4-10/13) 5
LIBRA-Gemini (10/14-10/22) 4
SCORPIO-Scorpio (10/23-11/2) 7
SCORPIO-Pisces (11/3-11/12) 5
SCORPIO-Cancer (11/13-11/22) 6
SAGITTARIUS-Sagittarius (11/23-12/2) 9
SAGITTARIUS-Aries (12/3-12/11) 8
SAGITTARIUS-Leo (12/12-12/21) 8
CAPRICORN-Capricorn (12/22-12/31) 7
CAPRICORN-Taurus (1/1-1/10) 4
CAPRICORN-Virgo (1/11-1/19) 3
AQUARIUS-Aquarius (1/20-1/29) 2
AQUARIUS-Gemini (1/30-2/8) 5
AQUARIUS-Libra (2/9-2/18) 5
PISCES-Pisces (2/19-2/29) 4
PISCES-Cancer (3/1-3/10) 4
PISCES-Scorpio (3/11-3/20) 6

LOVE SCALE SCORES

0 = Forget it! • 1 = Don't be a masochist... • 2 = Why bother? • 3 = Fun for one date. • 4 = It won't last! • 5 = You could do better! • 6 = Romance will fade... 7 = Great buddies! • 8 = Pure passion • 9 = True love. • 10 = Eternal bliss!

STARS OF ARIES-LEO

March 31:	Liz Claiborne	April 5:	Bette Davis
	Cesar Chavez		Spencer Tracy
	Christopher Walken	April 6:	Billy Dee Williams
April 2:	Emmylou Harris	April 7:	Francis Ford Coppola
April 3:	Marlon Brando	April 8:	Patricia Arquette
	Alec Baldwin	April 9:	Hugh Hefner
	David Hyde Pierce		
	Eddie Murphy		
	Picabo Street		
April 4:	Robert Downey, Jr.		
	Christine Lahti		

THIRD DECAN OF ARIES

4/10 - 4/20

"I'M AGGRESSIVE AND I'M INDEPENDENT!"

ARIES-Sagittarius	CARDINAL-Mutable	MARS-Jupiter

I always say that if I had to come back as an ARIES, I'd hope that the good Lord would see to it that I was born in the last ten days of the sign. You are my favorite Rams—a little kooky, but as strong as they come. You're a man or woman on the go, no question, aggressive as any ARIES must be, but flexible to an extent that no other Ram can be. Jupiter, the planetary ruler of Sagittarius, is usually seen as the planet of expansion. Your life is simply a treasure trove of possibilities, forever to be explored. And, as it so happens, almost all ARIES-Sags have a damn good time while they're out on an expedition.

The Cardinal style of ARIES gives you the focus to get to the top, while your Mutable influence allows you to try approaches to getting there that others never imagined.

Imagination may, in fact, be one of your well-honed attributes. The Sag in you makes you quite the philosopher, as you ask yourself and others about the broader issues of life. Thank the dear Lord that your ARIES drive keeps you from wandering off into left field.

Being a 3rd Decaner, you'll sometimes confront your own feelings that you don't fit in everywhere, or that your personality is too unusual for just everyone to understand. Guess what? You're right. That's what makes you so lovable. As talented and able as you are, you don't fall into that unbecoming trap of self-conceit. So what if we don't always know what you're talking about? We still like you!

YOUR DARK SIDE

The expansionist push of Jupiter has left its mark on you, there's no mistaking it. There is a restless, uncomfortable air about an ARIES-Sagittarius that clearly conveys "I'm not satisfied yet." You want to do too much. Oh, sure, you'll maintain your witty banter most of the time, but you never really take the opportunity to congratulate yourself for a job well done. You derive little or no pride from your accomplishments and failure doesn't exactly make you dance a jig.

In work situations, you'll start out authoritative as most ARIES are prone to do. Suddenly, you'll lose your zeal and run off to pursue another goal. The rest of the crew will be left standing, scratching their heads in confusion.

In play, most ARIES-Sags tend to wild excess. Do you drink too much? Do you stay out all night long? Do people call you the life of the party, even when you secretly wish you had stayed home reading a book? When you do stay home, don't you wish there was something exciting to go out to do? I'll bet you do. You are a complicated creature—half Ram, one-quarter Horse, one-quarter Archer. No wonder you never feel totally put together!

YOUR LIGHT SIDE

Your restless energy, when channeled, has a transforming power. Your risk-taking facility gives you the freedom to swing on a star, if that's what you choose to do. Further more, you are highly observant, and don't miss out on opportunities that pass others by. The ARIES-Sagittarius decan is the tops at turning lemons into lemonade.

You are scrupulously honest when it comes to the almighty dollar. You'll always get your share and make sure that others get theirs. It's your sportsman or sportswoman mentality—you like to play, and you'll play fair. If anyone hands you a "fixed" deck, you'll stand up and protest the dirty dealing.

When your restlessness is calmed, you have what it takes to put unusual ideas into action. You'll usually get a throng of followers to believe in your project, because no matter what you're feeling on the inside, you always exhibit a sense of humor. It is your number one asset.

The most inspiring illustration of your potentials can be seen in the Personality of Thomas Jefferson, born on April 13, an ARIES-Sagittarius Hall of Famer. Had he been a pushier Ram, he might have intimidated the masses, but his philosophical idealism won out. You see, he never sat around on his aristocratic rear, worrying that he was too strange for Politics. He merely used his restless energy and helped to create the grand nation that we call home. That is Starpower.

BOTTOM LINE FOR YOUR POWER

There is no question that you are a doer and no question that you know how to navigate an unconventional course. Put the two together and you'll win over millions, while they enjoy the products of your labor. As long as you're able to take pleasure and pride in what you do there is absolutely nothing that can hamper your success.

Accept the fact that you're a bit of an oddball and capitalize on your strengths. At full tilt you have tremendous force as: an *Innovator*.

BODY TALK

Don't ask me why, but I'm not the first to observe that your special feature is your nose. It's true. An ARIES-Sag's nose is the best device for sniffing out action and adventure. Whether it's long, short, pert, wide, freckled, or sunburned, your nose is attractive and unique. I'll bet all of your love affairs started when someone was unexpectedly drawn to your darling schnoz. It was probably the way you flared your nostrils from across the room. You can communicate so much with it—from scorn to desire to vulnerability. You Ram/Horse/Archer breeds do flare with flair!

Do you ever get nosebleeds, blocked nasal passages, or chronic allergies? If so don't be alarmed—that should be as bad as your health gets. Even all that excessive partying you do never seems to make a dent in your vitality. If pressed to deprivation, you can also go without food or rest for days on end. Basically you've got all the right ingredients for long-distance running. In addition to your nasal prowess, which allows you to take in deep inhalations of air, your thighs, as indicated by Sag's rulership, should be in excellent shape.

Do wear Noskote® if you're going to be out in the sun all day. No sense letting your grand beacon of friendliness get all red or peely, is there? If it isn't kept up, how are you going to give any of those playful Eskimo-nose kisses you love to give?

YOUR BEST-BET CAREERS

As a 3rd Decan at the edge of ARIES, you'll also pick up some Taurian values, especially in any creative pursuit. If your current employment lacks challenge or is a fairly conventional profession, hightail it out of there as fast as you can gallop. Mobility is the operative word for you. Traveling sales rep may not be your idea of a glamorous job, but once you've hit the road with your wares, you'll be pleasantly surprised at how well you'll score.

Or enter the world of independent contracting and consulting. Your clients will be thrilled when you come on to their turf and instruct them on how to solve their problems. That way you can play at being the boss without getting stuck in the same old rut.

ARIES-Sags aren't necessarily the blabber mouths of the zodiac, but you probably love to play with language, coming up with slogans, rhymes, and riddles. That's because you're so "punny." You'll find that the competition and pace of the ad biz suits you to a tee. Talk about the need for innovation and movement!

Physical fitness, as I mentioned before, seems to come naturally to your decan. Your natural love has become a national rage and you could profit from it. Mind you, your best shot will be in private gyms or clubs. Being tied down to a set schedule established by a public school system could upset your system.

One last word of advice: Explore as many hobbies as you can fit into the hours of the day. If you don't feed your fancies, you'll turn into a gloomy Sheep/Mule.

YOUR BEST-BET LOVE COMBOS

ARIES-Sagittarius Man: You'd probably like to try a woman of each decan, wouldn't you? Ever sing the song "I'm A Wanderer"? When you get fired up about business or even some dumb old football game, you use 100 percent of your focus. In your love life it's a very different story. That horrifying word is what troubles you, isn't it? The one that is spelled C-O-M-M-I-T-M-E-N-T.

It's those overly active olfactories of yours, sniffing out adventure in the next gal that might come along. Lord have pity on the one who doesn't notice your restless tendencies. The irony of your fickle heart is that your hormones are usually pretty content for you to be a one-woman man. Where other ARIES will be out enticing women into their rooms, you don't really care that much. Sex isn't your goal. You just enjoy the sport of skirt chasing.

As I said previously, some decans are best suited for the bachelor life. You male ARIES-Sags may just want to let your noses pull you from flower to flower without ever choosing to pluck one up for keeps. If that is not the case, if you are willing to reform, then listen to a very unusual proposition. Being a little off-center, as you are, you might go for a Water sign and find that your elements, although not fully complementary, will balance each other out. You need to have your jets cooled, after all. Give a go with Ms. CANCER-Pisces. She's emotional, dreamy, and nurturing. Every time you dash off on another whirl, she'll pack you a delicious lunch. How can you not fall in love with someone that thoughtful?

ARIES-Sagittarius Woman: Thank goodness, you 3rd Decan ARIES girls aren't as afraid of settling down as the males of the decan. You've probably got vivid, imaginative thoughts running through your mind about the wonderful, international jet-setter you're going to meet and marry. I'll bet you've met a few. I'll bet you've dated several. What went wrong? I'll tell you exactly what's wrong with the men you choose over and over: They are too much like you. You've got similar tastes, similar family backgrounds. You probably even work together.

You need a man who is so full of areas to explore within himself that you don't stand a chance of getting bored. I would recommend an Air sign, for starters. Scratch GEMINIS and LIBRAS though; you've got enough Cardinal/Mutable style for two. That leaves you with Monsieur AQUARIUS-Aquarius, Fixed in style yet so different from your own. The millions of causes he champions will fascinate your philosophical interests. If things work out as well as I think they will, I've heard you do know how to let loose and ride. *Happy hunting!*

DECAN PAIRS WITH ARIES-SAGITTARIUS

ARIES-Sagittarius   &   ARIES-Aries (3/21-3/30) 7

                                                    ARIES-Leo (3/31-4/9) 7

                                                    ARIES-Sagittarius (4/10-4/20) 5

                                                    TAURUS-Taurus (4/21-4/30) 2

                                                    TAURUS-Virgo (5/1-5/10) 1

                                                    TAURUS-Capricorn (5/11-5/20) 2

                                                    GEMINI-Gemini (5/21-5/31) 4

                                                    GEMINI-Libra (6/1-6/10) 3

                                                    GEMINI-Aquarius (6/11-6/20) 6

                                                    CANCER-Cancer (6/21-7/1) 7

                                                    CANCER-Scorpio (7/2-7/12) 5

                                                    CANCER-Pisces (7/13-7/22) 8

                                                    LEO-Leo (7/23-8/1) 9

LEO-Sagittarius (8/2-8/12) 8
LEO-Aries (8/13-8/22) 6
VIRGO-Virgo (8/23-9/3) 5
VIRGO-Capricorn (9/4-9/13) 3
VIRGO-Taurus (9/14-9/22) 1
LIBRA-Libra (9/23-10/3) 3
LIBRA-Aquarius (10/4-10/13) 5
LIBRA-Gemini (10/14-10/22) 2
SCORPIO-Scorpio (10/23-11/2) 2
SCORPIO-Pisces (11/3-11/12) 3
SCORPIO-Cancer (11/13-11/22) 4
SAGITTARIUS-Sagittarius (11/23-12/2) 7
SAGITTARIUS-Aries (12/3-12/11) 5
SAGITTARIUS-Leo (12/12-12/21) 7
CAPRICORN-Capricorn (12/22-12/31) 3
CAPRICORN-Taurus (1/1-1/10) 2
CAPRICORN-Virgo (1/11-1/19) 4
AQUARIUS-Aquarius (1/20-1/29) 9
AQUARIUS-Gemini (1/30-2/8) 6
AQUARIUS-Libra (2/9-2/18) 4
PISCES-Pisces (2/19-2/29) 5
PISCES-Cancer (3/1-3/10) 6
PISCES-Scorpio (3/11-3/20) 3

LOVE SCALE SCORES

0 = Forget it! • 1 = Don't be a masochist... • 2 = Why bother? • 3 = Fun for one date. • 4 = It won't last! • 5 = You could do better! • 6 = Romance will fade... 7 = Great buddies! • 8 = Pure passion • 9 = True love. • 10 = Eternal bliss!

STARS OF ARIES-SAGITTARIUS

April 10:	Omar Sharif
April 12:	David Letterman
	Andy Garcia
	Shannen Doherty
April 14:	Julie Christie
	Emma Thompson
April 15:	Samantha Fox
	Leonardo Da Vinci
April 16:	Charlie Chaplin
	Ellen Barkin
April 18:	Conan O'Brien
	James Woods
April 19:	Jayne Mansfield
April 20:	Joey Lawrence

CHAPTER 4

TAURUS

APRIL 21 - MAY 20

First Decan	Second Decan	Third Decan
TAURUS-Taurus	TAURUS-Virgo	TAURUS-Capricorn
4/21 - 4/30	5/1 - 5/10	5/11 - 5/20

Unaware that anyone was listening, a TAURUS once said,
"I'd like to have my security reinforced."

Sign:	Earth - Attainers
Symbol:	The Bull
Planet:	Venus
Body Talk:	Neck & Shoulders
Style:	Fixed

MEET THE TROOPER...

"I'M MATERIALISTIC"

The planet Venus, an orb of emotions and feelings, affects you, my earthy TAURIANS, with the most positive of all results. You robustly appreciate life, the beauty of the earth, the uniqueness of the moment. You take the time to stop and smell the roses.

Slow and steady though you may be, you are nobody's doormat. In your quiet, pleasant way you could rival any ARIES at getting the job done. Many astrologers refer to your temper, calling up the fighting title, "Raging Bull." Still, your power is at its peak when you simply are holding your ground, firmly and tenaciously as only you can. You win at a stare down; you have the necessary endurance to overcome blows that would topple a whole battalion of fighters; you never start what you can't finish. You understand the word commitment.

Yes, you are infamously stubborn in relationships, but when it's time to call the whole thing off, you'll still be in the ring, waiting for the frustrated lover to come running back to your strong embrace.

FIRST DECAN OF TAURUS

"I'M MATERIALISTIC, I'M OPENLY MATERIALISTIC!"

TAURUS-Taurus	FIXED-Fixed	VENUS-Venus

The question I always ask everyone who comes to me for advice, when they're facing obstacles ahead, is: Can you handle it? This is a question I never have to ask anyone born in the TAURUS-Taurus decan. I know you can handle anything and everything. If I don't keep my SAG-Sag trap shut, old earthy BULL-Bull will try to handle me.

You're someone to be admired, you have your feet on the ground. You'll always get where you're going, even if it takes you longer than you'd originally planned. Along the way you'll end up accomplishing a myriad of tasks that no other decan could ever handle.

You may not relate that well to most human beings, having shy Venus beaming down on you double strength. At the same time, you are unusually intimate with various and sundry creatures of Nature. Again, we find that Venus gives you a sense of oneness with animals, plants, and trees. Do you ever feel that the wind rustling in the leaves is speaking to you? Do you ever talk back?

Let me ask you something else, just between you and me. Do you ever talk to your appliances? Because, if you do, you aren't lapsing into momentary madness, you are behaving in a reasonable manner for your decan. You're materialistic, you relate to things. Who cares whether it's a little weird? After all, your appliances probably run like charms because you said such sweet things to them!

YOUR DARK SIDE

TAURUS-Taurus can also be translated as: HOLDING ON-Holding on. You do not want to let go of anything or anyone. Do you still have your old teddy bear, that raggedy thing you got when you were five? Did you ever really get over your first broken heart?

Okay, so your closets are tidy and organized, but why oh why don't you have a yard sale and get rid of some of the extra baggage? Look at Shirley MacLaine (4/24), beautifully talented and versatile though she may be, she's still holding on to all of her past lives!

At your darkest, you 1st Decan TAURIANS hold on to old and useless bull-ish rage, hurt feelings from the past that you have never put aside. "Slow to anger, but never to forgive" might be your silent oath.

These negative tendencies will only wear you down in the end. In the end, no one else will be your undoing, because no one is a match for you except YOU.

YOUR LIGHT SIDE

You are a pure-breed, all Venus, all TAURUS, all Earth. There is nothing wimpy or half-baked about you, man or woman. You are breathtakingly present.

You learn your lessons. With an abundant reserve of common sense, you'll rarely make the same mistake twice. Life to you is essentially good, always a sure-footed steady path forward.

The good news of your "holding-on" pattern is that you have an excellent memory. You have a realistic self-confidence, not inflamed or exaggerated like your ARIES neighbor next door.

You are practically a genius when it comes to handling money. Boy, do I envy you there! You are neither miserly nor free-spending. Instead of letting your capital just build up so you can run around hollering, "I'm rich," you'll invest in items of value. With your innate sense of material worth, you get every one of those little dollars and cents working for you.

Though you may feel shy or reserved in the company of strangers, even friends, or family, everyone wants you for their best pal. You are warm, usually even-tempered, frequently funny. You're downright lovable, even at your most stubborn points.

BOTTOM LINE FOR YOUR POWER

If you can learn to forgive and let go of yesterday's long-lost disappointments, you'll find yourself that much stronger to carry only the responsibilities that will propel you along the road to your success. With your ability to make use of everything, you can even use the rage of the moment to learn wisely for the future. You can then find the good in every lousy break you've had in your life and build an existence that is a fortress of well-being. Therein is your essence, you are: a *Builder*.

BODY TALK

Bulls are associated with the neck and shoulder regions, and with the TAURUS-Taurus decan, we find the outstanding feature of yours to be the prize jewels of that area: the throat and voice.

You lady TAURIAN 1st Decans are renowned for your delicate and long throats, as well as for your rich, warm voice. With male BULL-Bulls we find proud and defiant thrusts of the throat. Though you may speak in measured beats, at low volume, the impact of your voice is immeasurable. Think of the two actors, Al Pacino (4/25) and Jack Nicholson (4/22). Some of their most brilliant speeches were uttered in a whispered hush. Talk about vocal power!

When wooing the opposite sex, you've got a whole bag of vocal tricks helping you out. Do you coo? Do you hum? In the throes of passion, do you excite your lover with the deepest earthy sighs and moans? I truly suspect that you do.

Your throat is your erogenous zone, which you might not know about yourself. You might also not know that the reason you are prone to sore throats, swollen glands, and laryngitis is that this is where you are most sensitive. Also, you are a picky eater and love the sensation of swallowing—and you can take that morsel with all the double entendre intended!

YOUR BEST-BET CAREERS

I'd say that whatever it is that you do, you're in it for the long haul. Changes of occupation are rare for TAURUS-Taurus decans, holding on as you do to commitments and responsibilities.

If you are currently deciding between career paths, you may want to note a couple of the fields where 1st Decan TAURIANS have made the grade. Money management is a natural for you; you do just as well with other people's bucks as you do with your own. When you say, "buy Sterling," I'm going to run out and buy the mine.

In the merchant trades, you could open up any kind of shop you desire. Say, why don't you put all those relics up in your attic on sale? Or start a repair store and talk to everyone else's appliances while you're earning your rent and then some.

Any career in the arts, preferably behind the scenes, will give your Venus a chance to go to work. TAURUS-Taurus men and women make the very best entertainment agents and producers. No fast-talking, cigar-smoking banter from you, just sheer persistence will make you a legend in the business while lesser players have fallen by the wayside.

There is also a theme of music in the life of almost every 1st Decan TAURUS. So, if you aren't feeling too shy, get those vocal cords in order. Your audience awaits you.

YOUR BEST-BET LOVE COMBOS

TAURUS-Taurus Man: Dear Mr. Bull, all of that Venus makes you a true romantic. You give the most thoughtful and useful gifts to your ladies. And that's how you treat them: like ladies. In lovemaking you can be forceful, sometimes unaware of your own physical strength. Still, you'll make up for it by taking lots of time to please the lucky lady whom you've chosen.

Because your tendency is to look for appearances, a result of your appreciation of natural beauty, you can also become the victim of the "wrong-choice" syndrome. I know you like to show off your woman, but dig below the surface, fellas. It takes a very special temperament to fulfill you. A pretty bimbo who can't relate to your classical music CDs is just worthless, isn't she?

Except for a match with another TAURUS, which could be a fatal locking of horns, you'll do well with most Earth signs. The pick of the litter for you, though, is the watery, womanly CANCER-Cancer, your preferred sextile. In fact, you'll be the perfect "modem" couple-nesting and cocooning at home together.

TAURUS-Taurus Woman: Your emotional strength can sometimes be too much for the everyday fellow to handle. You've probably been deeply drawn to men you thought were your equal and then found that your love life was in a state of perpetual upheaval.

Please stay away from ARIES and LEO men, unless you enjoy straining your beautiful voice during screaming matches. Neither the Ram nor the Lion wants to budge an inch for the maidenly Cow.

Thank goodness you aren't as hooked on "lookers" as your buddy mate Bull-Bulls. In fact, when given a choice between a G.Q. model and an achievement-oriented nerd, your heart will beat in the direction of Mr. Four Eyes with the bulging wallet.

He may not be the prince of other girls' dreams, but instant chemistry isn't everything you're after. You are not purely sexual. Rather, I would say, you are entirely sensual. Intercourse isn't the objective in a TAURUS-Taurus woman's drive.

What you want and need are long hours of touching and caressing from a patient, strong, earnest, devoted partner. For a serious sensibility, I would push a CAPRICORN in your direction. If things click the way I imagine they will, your joint checking account will show a high balance for the rest of your lives together. With his discipline, he'll get rid of any stubborn flaws you might have hanging on. Hopefully, some of your good humor will rub off on him!

DECAN PAIRS WITH TAURUS-TAURUS

TAURUS-Taurus	&		
		ARIES-Aries (3/21-3/30)	1
		ARIES-Leo (3/31-4/9)	3
		ARIES-Sagittarius (4/10-4/20)	2
		TAURUS-Taurus (4/21-4/30)	3
		TAURUS-Virgo (5/1-5/10)	4
		TAURUS-Capricorn (5/11-5/20)	5
		GEMINI-Gemini (5/21-5/31)	3
		GEMINI-Libra (6/1-6/10)	3
		GEMINI-Aquarius (6/11-6/20)	4
		CANCER-Cancer (6/21-7/1)	9
		CANCER-Scorpio (7/2-7/12)	6
		CANCER-Pisces (7/13-7/22)	9
		LEO-Leo (7/23-8/1)	5
		LEO-Sagittarius (8/2-8/12)	3
		LEO-Aries (8/13-8/22)	1
		VIRGO-Virgo (8/23-9/3)	8
		VIRGO-Capricorn (9/4-9/13)	7
		VIRGO-Taurus (9/14-9/22)	6
		LIBRA-Libra (9/23-10/3)	1
		LIBRA-Aquarius (10/4-10/13)	5
		LIBRA-Gemini (10/14-10/22)	1

LOVE SCALE SCORES

0 = Forget it! • 1 = Don't be a masochist... • 2 = Why bother? • 3 = Fun for one date. • 4 = It won't last! • 5 = You could do better! • 6 = Romance will fade... 7 = Great buddies! • 8 = Pure passion • 9 = True love. • 10 = Eternal bliss!

STARS OF TAURUS-TAURUS

April 21:	Anthony Quinn
	Andie MacDowell
	Elizabeth II, Queen of England
	Tony Danza
April 22:	Jack Nicholson
	John Waters
April 23:	Shirley Temple
	Lee Majors
	William Shakespeare
April 24:	Shirley MacLaine
	Barbra Streisand
April 25:	Al Pacino
	Ella Fitzgerald
April26:	Sheena Easton
	Carol Burnett
April 28:	Jay Leno
April 29:	Jerry Seinfeld
	Daniel Day-Lewis
	Michelle Pfeiffer
	Uma Thurman
April 30:	Willie Nelson
	Jill Clayburgh

SECOND DECAN OF TAURUS

5/1 - 5/10

"I'M MATERIALISTIC AND I'M INTELLECTUAL!"

TAURUS-Virgo	FIXED-Mutable	VENUS-Mercury

You are one of the more complex decans of the zodiac, a refined mix of earthy awareness and naive purity. This blend of an artistic Venus and a critical Mercury creates spinning wheels of thought that whirl inside you constantly. There is nothing slow or dogged about your moods, that's for sure. Haven't you noticed that people are always asking you what you're thinking?

I happen to have the insider's scoop on this decan because my daughter, Toniann, born May 5, is a card-carrying TAURUS-Virgo. I used to worry myself crazy about what on earth she was mulling over all the time. Finally when I turned to astrology and saw that she was just brewing up artistic and intellectual notions, I began to breathe a little easier. And sure enough, as an adult, she paints, models, and publishes children's literature, all to such a successful degree that she's been able to afford the secure and luxurious life-style so important to her decan. She also has the typical TAURIAN love for crystals and other beautiful minerals. If it comes out of the ground, Toniann can find a special spot for it in her home. Given the Virgo side of her decan, she hasn't completely cured herself of the fear of aging, though. I've never seen anyone take so many milk baths in my life! When it's birthday time again, I just send her another jar of cold cream and have done with it. Seriously, if you had my daughter's good looks, you'd want to preserve them too. And if you're a member of her decan, you probably have.

Returning for a moment to that silent, thoughtful side of yourselves, you Bullish Youths do have a way of mystifying other people. You are not what you seem and you can seem to be what you are not. The Fixed aspect of TAURUS is a dead giveaway to anyone who knows a shred of astrology.

On the outside you may appear slightly distracted, vaguely concerned about something, picking apart your surroundings with your MUTABLE/Virgo observations. On the inside, the planner in you is working away on some secret high-priority agenda. It's sneaky to pretend that you aren't really sneaky, isn't it?

Those born in the TAURUS-Virgo decan are usually self-avowed mimics. Quiet, easygoing in social surroundings, you are fully "in tune" and you may find yourself changing your speaking voice, depending on the person with whom you're talking. You adapt to your environment, even away from your home in the out-of-doors, much more so than 1st and 3rd Decans of TAURUS who always stick out like bulls in china shops. Not you, you blend right in. Not that you'll approve of everybody else's environments. Critical is no foreign attitude to you.

YOUR DARK SIDE

Have you ever been accused of being obstinate, selfish, or underhanded? Well, I hope you haven't been, because those adjectives far from describe your real problem.

Other people become confused about your true nature because of your tight lock on your inner self. Because you are always mulling over your various opinions doesn't mean that you are snobbish, but that is how it looks to others. The fact is that your dark side is so private, you don't even allow yourself to go in and air it out.

The explanation for this phenomenon is best revealed by the secret held in your twelfth house, which as I've mentioned before, is what you've brought with you from a past incarnation. Suffice it to say, without going into the sordid details of your previous incarnations, many of those that I have charted in the 2nd Decan of TAURUS have a "mean streak," which is beautifully masked.

The splash of Virgo in you can cope with compromise, but the TAURUS that is such a part of you never could and never will.

What we see on the outside is a man or woman who is agreeable, helpful, trooping along with the best of the rest. My insight tells me that this same you is having an inner struggle, forever wanting to have the approval of others but stuck with your own hard-edged opinions.

YOUR LIGHT SIDE

These dualities I've been describing, particularly your ability to adapt to environments, regardless of how you differ from them, are at the same throw of the dice, your saving grace. After living with your complicated self all these years, you could live in just about any circumstance. The more experiences you have the better your mind and heart are at processing so much that you do absorb.

You have an eye for detail, thanks to Mercury, and not so as you get a swelled head, yours is one of the smartest decans of the zodiac. Smart, and creative, I should add. Your mind runs the gamut: from common sense to esoteric wisdom.

And let's not forget your flair for ambiance. The materialist in you knows how to decorate a parlor like no other.

BOTTOM LINE FOR YOUR POWER

As you know, 2nd Decans have the potential to be the most balanced of their Sun sign. That's why you have been given so many complex ingredients to juggle—because you can handle it. Dump the private, mean side of you, and you'll knock down the biggest wall that stands between you and a golden future.

Use your Fixed planning capacity together with your Mutable detail magnet. Gather up all those shreds of information that you are constantly absorbing and go to town! You will never fail when you are doing what comes naturally, as: an *Organizer*.

BODY TALK

TAURUS-Virgo, or "Bullish Youth" rules two regions: neck and bowels. Aren't you thrilled? Where you have the strong, youthful look of good health on the exterior, your innards are all nervy! Unfortunately, being complicated doesn't occur just in your personality, it occurs in your person, physically. Usually, you Bullish Youths will compensate by becoming health and hygiene experts.

The information that you glean from authoritative sources can be put to good use, especially in the event of any belly pain that you may encounter. You'll rarely put anything in your body that hasn't been thoroughly analyzed first. That's what I mean by being a smart decan. Thank goodness that you're not a hypochondriac.

Back to the Bull's domain—the neck. I've heard that yours is very sensitive, yet you are so private you don't advertise it. Well, you should. Don't try to tell me that when you feel the stirrings of desire, that the little hairs on the back of your neck don't just stand up and holler with excitement. If you haven't experienced the bliss of having a member of the opposite sex nuzzle the private zone at the nape of your neck, you're of your missing out on an erotic adventure! Give it a try and you'll get butterflies in your sensitive tum-tum that feel good-good.

YOUR BEST-BET CAREERS

When it comes to those born under Venus and Mercury, as you are, the fields are wide open. This is a highly artistic decan and you're also a whiz kid at numbers. Not to mention the fact that you've got a Midas touch with money.

The downfall of many a creative soul is the inability to cope with the business of their careers. Not so with you. You are the optimum blend of sensual purity and mental clarity. We'll never find you living in a garret, nor will we find you merely content "just makin' money". You could become one of the next Michelangelos of painting, sculpting, or photography. Or combine your mathematical skills with your creative ones and consider the areas of graphic arts, design, music composition. A behind-the-scenes element there is perfect for the private you.

Your intelligence lends itself to planning and research, particularly in a domain where lots of details are available for organizing. Or, if you have the impulse, share some of your private, strong opinions with readers and write an editorial column in a newspaper.

One last suggestion: If you can tolerate the travel required, you would make the ultimate spy. You never forget a word that anyone says, and you blend so easily into the woodwork when you want to. Shall we start calling you "Mata Hari" or do you prefer "007"?

YOUR BEST-BET LOVE COMBOS

TAURUS-Virgo Man: Picky is the understatement of the day with you opinionated, private Bullish Youths. You'll wait a lifetime for your goddess if necessary. You do not pursue women very often; instead they flock to your side in droves. They're attracted to that hidden tough side. Females of the species can sense it for miles around. You'd get the same attention by putting a sign outside your house that reads *Not Available*.

No wonder you have a nervous stomach, you're resisting your natural drive to connect with the opposite sex! Don't you know that isn't healthy for you? Don't forget that you are a virile Bull, even if you are a "Virgin." What's so special about what you've got that you can't be open and generous with it? Especially when several candidates are ready and willing to show you what to do and where.

Of course, I'm referring to your fabulous mind, aren't I? Or am I? In any case, please indulge your needs and desires with a 2nd Decan CANCER, a CANCER-Scorpio. You'll have some second-degree opposition, but you can handle that. And you can handle her while she putters in the kitchen just for you. Since you both have tummy aches all the time, you can save money on Alka-Seltzer. How's that for good practical advice?

TAURUS-Virgo Woman: "When I make love, I can't make my mind shut up." If you've ever said or even thought it, then comfort yourself by realizing that it's a common pattern among women of your decan. All that retentive TAURUS in you won't allow you to let go, while your Virgo influence is busy thinking about cleaning up the bedroom after you're done. You're not much fun, are you?

Sure you are. You, like your male decan counterpart, are picky, but you're more active in your pursuit of the opposite sex. The dating game is a sport at which you excel and you don't usually fall for Mr. Wrong. Trust your instincts because they'll work wonders every time. And give yourself a little credit for holding on to your virtue until the time is right. There's no reason for any woman to hop in bed with someone who'll make her wish she had a V-8, is there?

So who's the fellow who will make you glad you waited? He's got to be mentally stimulating, have a great sense of humor, and make you feel completely at ease so that you can open up that private side of yours. As you probably recall, with your attention to details, I don't encourage bonding between those who are too similar. With you, however, I'll suggest an offbeat combo that might just do the trick. Take your earthy coordinate, a male VIRGO-Taurus decan. Try it; you'll see that your mind and your body will let go when you make love.

If it turns out you aren't making love so often, don't worry. You can still have the bedroom photographed in *Better Homes and Gardens*.

DECAN PAIRS WITH TAURUS-VIRGO

LOVE SCALE SCORES

0 = Forget it! • 1 = Don't be a masochist... • 2 = Why bother? • 3 = Fun for one date. • 4 = It won't last! • 5 = You could do better! • 6 = Romance will fade... 7 = Great buddies! • 8 = Pure passion • 9 = True love. • 10 = Eternal bliss!

STARS OF TAURUS-VIRGO

May 2:	Dr. Benjamin Spock	May 6:	Rudolph Valentino
May 3:	Peter Gabriel		Sigmund Freud
May 4:	Audrey Hepburn	May 7:	Eva Peron
May 5:	Toniann Stallone	May 8:	Alex Van Halen
	Karl Marx		Harry S. Truman

THIRD DECAN OF TAURUS

5/11 - 5/20

"I'M MATERIALISTIC, I'M ALSO MASTERFUL."

TAURUS-Capricorn	FIXED-Cardinal	·	VENUS-Earth

There is so much concentrated power in this decan, that if you haven't found yours, wake up and smell the coffee! So what if you're a little too intense for the rest of the population to handle? You get what you want. You rise steadily, progressively to the top of the heap. And there you'll stay. Your Saturn influence demands this of you, while Venus supports you in efforts that require your keeping your nose to the grindstone, oftentimes for many years.

As we've discussed previously, 3rd Decans tend to have fewer qualities generally associated with the Sun sign itself. You are an uncommon TAURUS. Less prone to holding your ground and winning at a stare-down, you're seen frequently taking that first punch. By the same token, you can overcome bullish rage long before it overwhelms you.

This is not to say that you're all sweetness and light. Most everything is serious business for you. You'll take the time required to polish off a project to perfection, and you won't waste a second on anything that seems to be too frivolous.

Might I add that you have a severe case of being the best. This ailment is rivaled only by your other curse: having the best.

YOUR DARK SIDE

The pitfalls of power are strewn across your path. They will tempt and taunt you as you move through life. The worst danger that you must confront is the threat of corrupted power. Yes, you have undeniable earthly force, but you may not always use it to just ends. Once you've exerted it, you may fall in love with its products. Greed, indulgence, immorality, and dishonesty are the demons to which you could fall prey.

The mode of transportation that you most often employ is Fixed. You move toward goals carefully, cautiously, with a never-ending focus on attainment. But, suddenly, without warning you'll jump course, dashing ahead in Cardinal style, mowing down whatever and whomever stands in your way. Like Muhammed Ali, or even "Rocky Balboa," as a TAURUS-Capricorn, you'll pummel your opposition. And the point is that not everyone who happens to be in your vicinity is your enemy. On the contrary, the person that you just cut to smithereens could have been your secret ally. You are suspicious in your darkest times, and that holds you back.

Your work ethic, one of your higher qualities, can sometimes delude you. You imagine that if you don't do something, it won't get done. On top of everything you're too hard on yourself, perfectionist that you are. Take a load off, every now and then, for gosh sakes. If you don't rub your own shoulders, no one else will get the hint.

YOUR LIGHT SIDE

The bright energy transmitted by Venus is found in your unquestionable warmth within certain relationships. You adore children and are uniquely patient with the elderly. You have deep-rooted respect for the greats of your industry, no matter what industry you have chosen. Wise and disciplined, you follow the examples of those you admire as long as they don't come into competition with you.

Saturn brings to your decan the favorable aspect of putting yourself to the test. This is the planet of "making it or breaking it," and your life, if lived fully, will never be humdrum. Events seem to occur as though they were planned for you. And, maybe they were.

BOTTOM LINE FOR YOUR POWER

The sole ingredient that you lack in your makeup is faith. Strive to believe that the world is yours for the asking and a whole new you will step out into it. Have faith that once you've achieved your success, no thief or whim of fate is going to take it away from you. The corruptible side of you will be vanquished, and you'll have the magic of Starpower. The magic lies inside of you, on every plain of existence you can be: a *Winner*.

BODY TALK

With 3rd Decan TAURIANS we'll see visible signs of TAURUS-ruled shoulders and Capricorn-ruled knees. The good news is that you have strong and perfectly proportioned shoulders. This region in many of you TAURUS-Capricorn men has made me gasp out loud. Women born in this ten-day period are blessed with a graceful, supple slope of the shoulder. You see, Venus has been kind to you, after all.

Now for the bad news. You guessed it. Bum knees. Sorry you guys and gals, but you are a breed of Bull/Goats. Can you imagine not having knobby, chunky, or scuffed-up knees with your heritage? Don't laugh. All of your intense struggles have to take their toll somewhere on your body, and those knee joints are going to take heavy beatings since you're always charging or scrambling for success. Brittle bones, calcium deposits, strained ligaments, and possible surgery may all be issues for you at one time or another. Do, by all means, spend time relaxing. You tend to put your health on a low-priority list.

While you're taking care of problem areas, exploit your positive features, those sculpted shoulders you've got. Flaunt those babies. Men, invest in an assortment of tank tops. Women, let your necklines plunge with off-the-shoulder cuts. Both sexes should always wear silk against your taut musculature. Strangers will literally materialize and start pawing at you. You think I'm pushing the issue? Not a chance. I know that even while you neglect your health, looking good is no laughing matter to you TAURUS-Caps.

YOUR BEST-BET CAREERS

There are definitely right and wrong choices you could be making that either do or do not support the talents with which you are born. While other TAURIANS are directed to serve out of a sense of responsibility in whichever capacity they are called to do so, you really aren't productive in fields where there isn't any room to grow.

You can climb to the heights of many an artistic career, but the experience must be packed with obstacles, or you'll feel that it was all too easy. How ironic, when others would give their horns to go big places fast. Not so with you. You'd much rather master each step of the way, on your own. It's almost preferable for you to enter a field that is initially completely foreign to you. I don't care if your whole family is in the carpet-laying, business, you go out and decide to become a professional athlete, even with your bum knees, and eventually you'll find yourself with an Olympic gold medal. That's the discipline of Saturn for you.

Start a piggy bank when you're a teenager and by the time you're in your forties you'll own the nation's largest investment firm. Don't ignore the lucrative, challenging real estate market. After all, you're double Earth, aren't you?

Or, take a tip from George Lucas (5/12), who developed new applications of technology in the film biz, and found himself, after years of tireless work, as one of the few power players around.

Whether you sit at a desk or dig ditches, you have to be physical in your work. Pounding the pavement or pushing a pencil or holding up your trophy—your body has to be as involved as your head.

YOUR BEST-BET LOVE COMBOS

TAURUS-Capricorn Man: You want the best and you're willing to stampede 100 castle gates to attain your princess. You're even willing to do so when she's someone else's princess. Might I suggest that you happen to be especially aroused if she belongs to someone else? Admit it. You inflate your sense of security by knowing you can win her away. You think this action makes you the better of the male species, don't you? Shame on you, you old Bully Goat.

On the other hand, there are some women who love being the object of two men's interest. Please, if this is a pattern you have experienced in yourself, watch what decan of woman YOU snatch from that unsuspecting other fellow. Better be sure she's worth your dastardly deed, lest you get her home and decide she wasn't the princess prize you imagined.

Be prepared to face the fact that once you've got her to yourself, you're not sure how to entertain her. TAURUS-Cap males aren't fiery, passionate lovers by nature, although I will give you credit for being quick studies, depending on who's doing the teaching.

Whether she is attached or not, when you do select a princess, make that maiden the daintiest one around, Ms. VIRGO-Virgo. She is your trine and a fellow Earth sign. You'll fall in love.

TAURUS-Capricorn Woman: Remember your power. Remember that you're a 3rd Decan, unusual and uncommon under any circumstance. You forget sometimes that your intensity can blow a partner out of the water. How many times has a guy said to you, "I'm just not ready for a relationship. Can't we just sleep together?" Wasn't he a tad surprised when you knocked him flat on his big behind?

Your Venus makes you intensely romantic and ready for deep connections with your men, while Saturn is constantly scolding you to get serious or move on. Poor little thing, what you really need is a man with a huge, um ... heart, that's right, a man who is emotionally available. You know where to find him, don't you? Right in the Water signs. Wait, SCORPIOS and CANCERS are excluded. Yes, I hear you. You're attracted to those signs. You like the challenge, and you think you can handle it. Wrong. You like the sex.

You love bodies in motion, especially yours with his. But how do you really feel when a CANCER male cries in front of you? Or when a jealous SCORPIO reads your diary? Weakness like that in your men is a turnoff, right away.

Compromise is the answer. Meet a cool and dreamy PISCES-Pisces. You may have to keep your fishing pole in the water longer than you'd planned to get him to bite. But once he does, he's a perfect catch that you'll have for keeps.

DECAN PAIRS WITH TAURUS-CAPRICORN

TAURUS-Capricorn &

ARIES-Aries (3/21-3/30)	4
ARIES-Leo (3/31-4/9)	2
ARIES-Sagittarius (4/10-4/20)	2
TAURUS-Taurus (4/21-4/30)	5
TAURUS-Virgo (5/1-5/10)	7
TAURUS-Capricorn (5/11-5/20)	5
GEMINI-Gemini (5/21-5/31)	3
GEMINI-Libra (6/1-6/10)	2
GEMINI-Aquarius (6/11-6/20)	1
CANCER-Cancer (6/21-7/1)	5
CANCER-Scorpio (7/2-7/12)	4
CANCER-Pisces (7/13-7/22)	6
LEO-Leo (7/23-8/1)	1
LEO-Sagittarius (8/2-8/12)	3
LEO-Aries (8/13-8/22)	3
VIRGO-Virgo (8/23-9/3)	9
VIRGO-Capricorn (9/4-9/13)	8

VIRGO-Taurus (9/14-9/22) 7
LIBRA-Libra (9/23-10/3) 3
LIBRA-Aquarius (10/4-10/13) 1
LIBRA-Gemini (10/14-10/22) 2
SCORPIO-Scorpio (10/23-11/2) 7
SCORPIO-Pisces (11/3-11/12) 7
SCORPIO-Cancer (11/13-11/22) 6
SAGITTARIUS-Sagittarius (11/23-12/2) 4
SAGITTARIUS-Aries (12/3-12/11) 3
SAGITTARIUS-Leo (12/12-12/21) 4
CAPRICORN-Capricorn (12/22-12/31) 5
CAPRICORN-Taurus (1/1-10) 6
CAPRICORN-Virgo (1/11-1/19) 7
AQUARIUS-Aquarius (1/20-1/29) 1
AQUARIUS-Gemini (1/30-2/8) 2
AQUARIUS-Libra (2/9-2/18)) 1
PISCES-Pisces (2/19-2/29) 9
PISCES-Cancer (3/1-3/10) 8
PISCES-Scorpio (3/11-3/20) 8

LOVE SCALE SCORES

0 = Forget it! • 1 = Don't be a masochist... • 2 = Why bother? • 3 = Fun for one
date. • 4 = It won't last! • 5 = You could do better! • 6 = Romance will fade...
7 = Great buddies! • 8 = Pure passion • 9 = True love. • 10 = Eternal bliss!

STARS OF TAURUS-CAPRICORN

May 11:	Natasha Richardson	May 16:	Pearce Brosnan
	Salvador Dali		Janet Jackson
May 12:	Burt Bacharach		Tracey Gold
	George Carlin		Liberace
	Emilio Estevez	May 17:	Dennis Hopper
	Stephen Baldwin	May 19:	Grace Jones
	Katharine Hepburn	May 20:	Cher
May 13:	Harvey Keitel		Socrates
	Stevie Wonder		Jimmy Stewart
	Dennis Rodman		
May 14:	George Lucas		

CHAPTER 5

GEMINI

MAY 21 - JUNE 20

First Decan	Second Decan	Third Decan
GEMINI-Gemini	GEMINI-Libra	GEMINI-Aquarius
5/21 - 3/31	6/1 - 6/10	6/11 - 6/20

Two GEMINIS once complained out loud to each other,
"Why do people always gossip about us? Who do they think
we are—a couple of paperback heroes?"

Sign:	Air · Thinkers
Symbol:	The Twins
Planet:	Mercury
Body Talk:	Arms & Lungs
Style:	Mutable

MEET THE MESSENGER...

Allright all of you GEMINIS, all three decans of you, listen to me. Those who populate this Sun sign move with the highest velocity of the zodiac. Like the Air sign that you are, like constantly changing wind patterns, you can't be second guessed. Your primary style is Mutable. You fly over hurdles, dig tunnels under walls, skip freely over a tightrope, anything to get you where you're going. Then, you'll change your mind right before you reach your destination and rush back to where you started.

Everyone loves to rag on poor Mr. or Ms. GEMINI, almost as much as they enjoy taking potshots at those show-off LEOS. They'll call you anything from "two-faced" to "flaky" to "flighty" to downright "schizophrenic." Now, some of these accusations do fit the bill every now and then, but the truth of the matter is that most everyone is jealous of you. You do things with such apparent ease and speed, you've just got us all miffed.

As to the question of whether you actually have a split-personality, as in a sort of Jekyll/Hyde or a Bad/Good conflict, I say that you can rest your busy mind on that subject. The reason that you are symbolized by the Twins is that you are two times yourself. There's just that much more of you to go around. You may have some other dualities, such as a separation between what you're feeling on the inside and what you show on the outside, or the big contrast between what you say and what you do. But that doesn't mean you're going to start cracking up into a Sybil full of different personalities. Let's leave that kind of thinking to the uninformed who love to gossip about you.

The real essence of GEMINI is more aptly defined by ruling Mercury, the Messenger. This planet influences your Airy substance via the spoken word. Yes, indeed, you're a talker. You'll talk all day until the cows come home. You'll talk to the cows when they do come home. And, if the cows never come home you'll just talk to yourself. That's why you have a Twin inside you, so that wherever you go you'll always have someone to listen to you. By the way, on top of being the pro at delivering speeches, you aren't a poor listener, either. That is, as long as the person talking can keep up with how fast you walk. See, I told you that you were a speed freak!

FIRST DECAN OF GEMINI

5/21 - 5/31

"I'M CONTROVERSIAL, I'M ALWAYS CONTROVERSIAL!"

GEMINI-Gemini	MUTABLE-Mutable	MERCURY-Mercury

I know what you are probably asking yourself. If one GEMINI is twins, would a GEMINI-Gemini be quadruplets? Well, yes and no. You are without a doubt able to do four things at once. You can practically be in four places at once.

You are Mutable-Mutable, in other words, an ambidextrous juggler. YOU are so multitalented and have so many diverse interests that I can't even begin to list them.

However, you are you through and through, no flip-flops of opinions, tastes, or viewpoints. A GEMINI-Gemini is a purebred, don't forget. Though your game plan may alter as often as Joan Collins (5/23) changes her hairdo, your belief system is a constant in this ever-changing world. You have clear, refreshing, new approaches that are well formed. Yes, your ideas aren't always accepted at first. But once you hop up on any podium, you can take over a crowd, almost as by storm. You shake and shock the very pillars of old established institutions and somehow succeed at converting your entire audience to your unusual point of view. And, with double Mercury as your ruler, there is no way that you haven't developed a strong point of view on five catalogs worth of subjects. The phrase "no comment" is one I suspect you've never uttered.

YOUR DARK SIDE

There is rarely a hidden strand of meanness in your fabric. You always mean well. But, hold on, don't go flying off and neglect to read what follows. You are by no means perfect.

You have a dangerous blind spot. You're speeding down the road, thinking of what you're going to do, what you did the day before, what you didn't do the day before, humming your singsong GEMINI-Gemini hum, and talking to yourself, naturally. Suddenly, seconds before the bloodiest head-on collision between you and a bulldozing freight train shatters the air, you screech to a jarring halt. You wipe your temples, exhale lightly, and forget that the near tragedy would have been your fault. How many times a day can you put yourself through such harrowing experiences? I can just imagine you now, shrugging your shoulders, waving away my concern. You're thinking, defensively, "Hey, I've got good reflexes." True, GEMINI-Gemini decans have superlative reflexes. But, haven't you ever heard the expression that sooner or later "your number is bound to come up"? I just pray that you are wearing your seat belt when it does. You see, the sobering reality is that way below the sparkling GEM-Gem that you are, there is an unconscious death wish.

YOUR LIGHT SIDE

There is no one stereotype of this decan. There are as many shapes and sizes of your potent double dose of GEMINI as there are species of winged creatures. What you all have in common here is that you are all human beings with a magical gift of flight.

When double Mercury and double Mutable influences interact in an Air sign, the result is a person who can almost defy the rules of gravity. When you are in your element, when you have found a purpose that speaks to all the gusto of your soul, you can take off to places and experiences that are simply never attained by ninety-nine percent of the population.

Also, a large portion of your talk is hot air. Yet, every now and then you hit upon a revelation that is inspired, and you speak with the voice of a winged angel, delivering to those who have been fortunate enough to hear an invaluable gift: the gift of understanding.

BOTTOM LINE FOR YOUR POWER

For goodness sakes, please try to keep a foot on the brake, at least when you get to the Stop sign at the corner. Work at listening to others, especially your "support" system buddies, your Taurus neighbors. And most important, don't be such a daring/erring air devil!

If you keep these instructions in mind, which for you with your Olympian mental abilities is not difficult, your address could always be a home on cloud nine. There is nothing unique about someone who is going places. There is something rare and fine about your ability to reach heights on easy wings, because you are always getting to places. And if you operate with an ounce of caution, you'll live to tell about it. Your ultimate aim is as: a *Communicator*.

BODY TALK

Not all Italians are 1st Decan GEMINIS, but all you GEMINI-Geminis must have a few drops of Latin blood in your veins. Why? Because no other two groups are as famous for gesturing when they talk. I figure you two must be related!

GEMINI rules the arms, and we'll never find you 1st Decaners moving yours aimlessly or limply. We're talking precise, powerful movements of both your upper limbs. With words tripping off your tongue, and those bold or hypnotic arm signals working in tandem, no one can get a word edgewise. Nor would they want to compete with your impassioned display.

Being the speed freak that you are, it's almost as if your whole body is vibrating constantly. Like anything else this has its positive and negative sides. On the one hand your vibrating arms are irresistible to the opposite sex. They're usually long, tapered, sinewy, velvet to the touch. You might not be aware of this, but your right and left arms usually perform similar gestures at the same time. Ever seen Clint Eastwood (5/31) do a double draw? It's as if he's packing two battery energized vibrators. That's what I call "making my day."

On the down side, you're going to have to watch that this part of your body doesn't talk too loud. Otherwise you'll find yourself with some of the typical GEMINI-Gemini injuries: broken arms, bruised elbows, sprained wrists. And do be careful what those arms lasso into your mouth. You're the last to realize that you are what you eat, and we don't want anyone criticizing you for being a walking garbage bin. Oh well, lucky you, you'll just vibrate off the extra pounds, won't you?

YOUR BEST-BET CAREERS

If your current profession doesn't offer you an opportunity to speak, orate, lecture, debate, or demonstrate, then you've missed out on your own in-born gold mine.

Second bests for you would be in the travel business, stunt flying, or safari leader. And, if the pace of those careers isn't top speed, you're bound to switch to something else to avoid your biggest employment hazard of finding yourself in a rut.

With all the newfangled technical computerization out there, a GEMINI-Gemini should never be out of work. Telecommunications, including all the intricacies of network programming, overnight express companies, and software packaging are right up your alley.

Despite the fact that you are a volatile and freedom-loving bird, do recall that flying solo all the time isn't healthy for you. You'd make an excellent manager of a branch office of any type, or a junior officer in the Air Force. With the right blending of personalities, a business partnership is your optimum means to financial victories. Stay away from handling money on your own. With you it goes as fast as it grows.

On that matter, please, if you are in the arts, don't try to manage your own career. Without prior counseling, you'll go on an interview and say something so controversial the media will bury you.

When all else fails, go to work for Ma Bell. You might even take over the entire company. Everyone who knows you knows you give great phone.

YOUR BEST-BET LOVE COMBOS

I could write an entire book just on the love life of this decan. Talk about leaving skid marks! It's no wonder that anyone who has even dated you once will never forget you.

GEMINI-Gemini Man: You are a charmer of the highest order. Give her a wink and, well...the rest is history. How do you do it? You know what to say to any woman, and when to say it. You do all the talking and she makes all the moves. And still, you can't get it into your head why she gets her feelings hurt when you move on to the next blushing rose.

I don't think that you 1st Decan GEMINI males are immoral, but I'd be hard-pressed to find one of you who had never at one time in your life had a series of bedroom romps. Like a male hummingbird, you vibrate from the bedroom of one to that of another to that of still a third. The question is: "How do you keep it up?"

Aside from the fact that you're supporting the economy with all those hotels and motels that you patronize, I'm sure not going to patronize that kind of behavior. Unless you are willing to openly admit to your love Victims that you are a confirmed bachelor, the day will come when you'll have to pay a huge price for all that fun. Your vibrator batteries will just run out and you'll long for the security you've sacrificed.

If and when the day arrives that you're saying the words "I do," you won't go wrong by saying them to another 1st Decan Air sign, a Ms. AQUARIUS-Aquarius. She is just as independent as you are, and she'll have lots of noble investment ideas for your money and your speaking abilities. Being the great social reformer that she is, you can bet she's going to reform you socially. Or else!

GEMINI-Gemini Woman: Thank God, you are not quite so cavalier as the men of your decan. Still, you know where and when to turn on all that sparkle to catch the eye of just about anyone who strikes your fancy. Problem is, your interest runs up and down just like the mercury in a thermometer!

When you first meet a new man, you are almost as aggressive as an Aries, pursuing him with your two-track mind running full throttle. You can't stay away, you call him hourly, you send him witty notes, you spend your entire paycheck and then some on the most lavish present he's ever received from someone he's only dated twice. Then, the second that he says the wrong word, or doesn't appear to be listening when you are expressing one idea or another, you go cold as an ice cube. Pretty soon he's making a hasty departure after being shown the door by your elegant arms pointing to the Exit sign. Too bad for him, because the chance to enter your romantic embrace offers most men an out-of-body experience.

When pogo-stick love affairs make you decide to stop acting like a female kangaroo, you will do well to open up your ears to your verbal compatriot, Mr. LEO-Leo. As long as you keep the compliments coming, he'll make you feel like a queen. Remember, you're Air and his Fire are so mutually supportive that you may never find yourself falling off this romantic high.

DECAN PAIRS WITH GEMINI-GEMINI

LOVE SCALE SCORES

0 = Forget it! • 1 = Don't be a masochist... • 2 = Why bother? • 3 = Fun for one date. • 4 = It won't last! • 5 = You could do better! • 6 = Romance will fade... 7 = Great buddies! • 8 = Pure passion • 9 = True love. • 10 = Eternal bliss!

STARS OF GEMINI-GEMINI

May 22:	Naomi Campbell	May 28:	Jim Thorpe
May 23:	Joan Collins		Jerry West
	Drew Carey	May 29:	John F. Kennedy
	Scatman Crothers	May 30:	Wynona Judd
May 24:	Bob Dylan		Benny Goodman
	Rosanne Cash	May 31:	Brooke Shields
	Queen Victoria		Clint Eastwood
May 26:	John Wayne		
	Sally Ride		

SECOND DECAN OF GEMINI

"I'M CONTROVERSIAL, I'M ALSO DISCRIMINATING."

GEMINI-Libra	MUTABLE-Cardinal	MERCURY-Venus

You are another one of the fortunate few decans that, as the saying goes, are "born under a good sign." You are lucky to others, and Lady Luck seems to follow you wherever you go. Well, almost anywhere. It is the combination of the energized Mercury, blending with a soothing, loving Venus, that usually keeps you in a healthy equilibrium. You balance between business and pleasure, creativity and common sense.

As fast as you move, and as unusual as some of your choices seem to be, you avoid many of the typical GEMINI jams. You instinctively know how not to rock the boat. You are the most diplomatic of all the decans, and rate high at being one of the most beloved of the zodiac. You have something to offer to everyone. You speak to the hungry homeless on the street and to the most exclusive, elite minds of academe. You are generous almost to a fault, giving time and energy and material aid to friends and strangers alike.

If this picture of you seems too good to be true, then perhaps I should point out one of the subtle flaws in your self-portrait. GEMINI thrives on change, and Libra works to establish an equilibrium. As a result, no matter how lucky and loved and successful you are, a part of you will always be in conflict. I've seen it over and over again with you Twin Balancers. At its extreme, the conflict can cause mental instability and physical illness. There are no easy answers to the basic puzzle that rests in your character. Knowing in advance that your life will always be switching from a stability you've sought to create to an open-ended quest for variety, will help you, at least, to be prepared for what lies ahead.

When you sink into a rut, I'll always encourage you to seek support from a friend or loved one, or from a professional counselor. Don't forget, your "backup" sign, the Earthy TAURIANS, can lend valuable "T.L.C." when you ask them. Asking for or accepting advice isn't always easy for GEMINI-Libras, especially because you're so good at giving it. Even though I'm not a member of your decan, my children always accuse me of this.

YOUR DARK SIDE

I've already mentioned some symptoms caused by the GEMINI-Libra conflict. What it boils down to is simply a case of astrological guilt. You are born lucky, you are almost handed opportunity on a platter. You are talented and motivated. But you don't believe you deserve it! You can't stand to see anyone else who is lacking, so you constantly give away everything you possibly can to make up for all of the good fortune you've received.

So, where does that leave you in the end? Broke, tired, and mad as hell. Stop and think about it. After all, you are blessed with a brilliant mind, as an Air sign. Leave some energy for yourself. Learn to be more selfish, especially when it comes to your brain power.

Most likely you're reluctant to face this problem, thinking, as I know you do, that charity is a virtue. I must warn you, though, that the ramifications of giving away all your power are self-destruction, anger, and resentment of everyone who "robbed" you.

Think of the two legendary stars, Marilyn Monroe (6/1) and Judy Garland (6/10). It's no mere coincidence that they were two women with similar decan. Judy, with her extraordinary voice, and Marilyn, with a sensual appeal that no other woman in our century has rivaled, were "lucky." Both had careers that took off without much personal effort. It could have been said, had their lives taken a different course, that they "had it all." What went wrong? Both were performers who gave their souls to their audiences. They took care of their men and their own children or strangers' children. But, both women lost track of their true selves, and turned to alcohol, drugs, and sex to fill up their emptiness. They gave away all their power and had nothing left over for themselves. That is why the selfless path alone can be a road to tragedy.

YOUR LIGHT SIDE

Okay, you can put your Kleenex away. I promise, no more scare tactics. Hopefully you will not go through any experience similar to what I have just described. And you shouldn't have to! Remember, you are born lucky. Don't forget that you are number one on everyone's invitation list. You're sharp, witty, a delight to have around for any occasion.

On a less superficial level, your thinking is a far cry from the type that is expressed in mere social chitchat. You can loosen the stickiest wickets of conflicts for others. Your Venus/Libra influence is your salvation, because it makes you artful in your judgments and full of affection for those you do judge.

Your lack of selfish ego, which as we've discussed can be your undoing, if held in check, can save you from wasting time with petty jealousy or indulgent competition. You know how to let go of whatever negative feelings are standing in your way.

An example I can't fail to mention is my dear friend Christina Crawford, a GEMINI-Libra from way back. Despite the fact that she suffers from a physical problem that causes her intense pain much of the time, she is constantly hopping on airplanes, dashing off here and there. She has committed her life to championing the children of the world who have been victims of abuse. Having now written two books on her personal experiences as a child of an abusive parent, she no longer sees herself as a victim, but rather a victor. She has matured into a beautiful, talented, philanthropic individual with an outgoing, gracious personality. On top of all that, she's got the dish on just about everyone in Hollywood. Between the two of us, we could gossip for years!

BOTTOM LINE FOR YOUR POWER

Practice doing something for yourself once a day. I'd suggest anything from buying a lottery ticket (which in your case should yield a winning number) to treating yourself to a form of fast physical recreation (something your decan often forgets). Or, why don't you go splurge on a couple of Jacqueline Stallone headbands? When you do take care of yourself first, you will be in top form to answer your higher calling. In giving assistance to others, you will always prevail as: an *Adviser*.

BODY TALK

The symbol of GEMINI is frequently depicted as a pair of Twins whose hands are clasped to each other. The Libra visual will sometimes show a pair of hands holding up items of equal weight, as in a human scale. So, naturally, with GEMINI ruling the arms and their extremities, the 2nd Decan gets domain over the hands.

Need I point out what's always been said about what you can tell by looking at the size of a man's hands? Use your imagination! With GEMINI-Libra men we often see wide, smooth palms with long, creative, and tapered fingers. You can draw whatever conclusions you want about the rest of his anatomy. What I will tell you is that whoever gets touched by those beautiful hands isn't going to do much complaining.

GEMINI-Libra women regularly have the type of hands other women spend fortunes trying to cultivate. Flawless, silky, perfect for showing off fabulous jewelry-that is if you haven't loaned out all your diamonds to your best friend who needed to impress a date. Men and women of this decan, haven't you ever been told you have "magic fingers"? I'm sure you have. I'll bet you keep them in immaculate shape as well. That must be why housework and gardening are jobs that your hands rarely touch.

In general you have such excellent health, and such an abundance of balancing energy, that you'll rarely have to do much to care for it. But don't take it for granted. As you get older, you may have to take up exercise or diet regimes. Because Libra rules the hips, do watch that your hourglass figure doesn't turn into a pear shape!

YOUR BEST-BET CAREERS

Any profession that predicates itself on luck or connections is a fine choice for you. Ever hear the old phrase, "it's all in who you know"? Well, you know more than your share of folks in many diverse areas. So it's an open game for you. If you can maintain your focus through the extra years of schooling, you will find yourself with a flourishing practice in law. Your success will be based on repeat business. Your clients will find they can't live without your daily advice. Even with the toughest cases that many a proven attorney has been unable to win, you have that smile of fortune upon you that gets the verdict you want. Not to mention a hefty commission to boot. Take a peek at the career of attorney F. Lee Bailey (6/10) if you think I'm exaggerating. Do, however, avoid getting pulled into politics, even when your winning all the votes seems a sure bet. You just don't have the egomania required for public office.

Members of your decan have excelled in psychotherapy, career planning, marriage counseling, and corporate personnel troubleshooting. Or get yourself a radio show where you solve callers' problems right on the airthat is your element, isn't it? Lest you neglect your artistic instincts, I'll recommend that whether or not you take it to a professional level, painting, drawing, sketching are appropriate ways to use your gifted GEMINI-Libra hands.

You may not have a knack for math, but 2nd Decans of GEMINI usually keep their net profits way up high. Even though you're fond of giving handouts, money somehow lands in your lap without your even asking for it. Thank goodness, because despite your altruism, you do enjoy an elegant life-styles long as you don't have to do the housework.

YOUR BEST-BET LOVE COMBOS

GEMINI-Libra Men: You make a very interesting puzzle for the matchmaker. On the one hand you require a constant change of scenery, or in other words, the freedom to explore new love interests with the frequency of dropping hats. On the other hand, you have deep feelings for each of the pretty flowers you've chosen to pick. So, every time you break a heart, it breaks your heart. It's your personal demon: guilt. When you move into a new relationship you're so bogged down with the details of how you did the last gal wrong, you inadvertently hurt the feelings of the new woman.

Then, to get your mind out of its muddle, you'll pitch all your energy into your body and its desires. In that department you can be lethal! Once most women have felt the magic fingers of a GEMINI-Libra man, they won't want to be touched by any others. They'll keep coming back for more of your surprises. Not that you're kinky, but you will try something new or erotic every now and then. Just enough to keep the bedroom, lively, without it turning into a warehouse for sexual devices. Sometimes you're just as happy to cuddle and talk. What woman in her right mind could push you out of bed?

In this respect you male Twin Balancers must find a happy medium between body and mind. So you have a choice. Either go to a monastery and preach about celibacy while you keep a handy supply of ice cubes nearby, or do what I almost always discourage, marry your own kind—another GEMINI-Libra. Then, when you're both being generous, you can spend your joint earnings on each other.

GEMINI-Libra Woman: Girls of this decan are notorious for getting themselves involved with strong, demanding macho brutes, and not being able to get out of the relationship. What do you mean you don't want to hurt his feelings? What do you mean he's really a sweet guy underneath all of his swaggering and swearing? Don't try to convince me that he's anywhere near intelligent just because he happens to have read a couple books. Knowing the type of guy you go for, they were probably comic books.

Some of your troublesome Twin behavior definitely finds its way into your love life, no doubt about it. One Twin wants a mental match of wits, whereas the other Twin wants a physical superior who'll let you know he's the boss. The romantic you wants to be pampered, whereas the flighty you doesn't even know how to take a compliment.

Because it is so hard for you to take advice, I'm going to present my suggestion very scientifically. GEMINI-Libras have MUTABLE-Cardinal style and Airy composition. The perfect mathematical match is a Fire sign whose mode is CARDINAL-Fixed, who is also a 2nd Decaner. Mr. "X" just so happens to be Mr. ARIES-Leo. Please, don't take my advice on word alone. Go out and see if science is right. Even with your verbal skills, I don't think you'll want to argue with me.

DECAN PAIRS WITH GEMINI-LIBRA

GEMINI-Libra	&	ARIES-Aries (3/21-3/30)	3
		ARIES-Leo (3/31-4/9)	9
		ARIES-Sagittarius (4/10-4/20)	5
		TAURUS-Taurus (4/21-4/30)	3
		TAURUS-Virgo (5/1-5/10)	2
		TAURUS-Capricorn (5/11-5/20)	2
		GEMINI-Gemini (5/21-5/31)	6
		GEMINI-Libra (6/1-6/10)	9
		GEMINI-Aquarius (6/11-6/20)	7
		CANCER-Cancer (6/21-7/1)	2
		CANCER-Scorpio (7/2-7/12)	4
		CANCER-Pisces (7/13-7/22)	3
		LEO-Leo (7/23-8/1)	9
		LEO-Sagittarius (8/2-8/12)	6
		LEO-Aries (8/13-8/22)	6
		VIRGO-Virgo (8/23-9/3)	2
		VIRGO-Capricorn (9/4-9/13)	3
		VIRGO-Taurus (9/14-9/22)	4
		LIBRA-Libra (9/23-10/3)	7
		LIBRA-Aquarius (10/4-10/13)	8
		LIBRA-Gemini (10/14-10/22)	7
		SCORPIO-Scorpio (10/23-11/2)	5
		SCORPIO-Pisces (11/3-11/12)	6
		SCORPIO-Cancer (11/13-11/22)	4
		SAGITTARIUS-Sagittarius (11/23-12/2)	5

LOVE SCALE SCORES

0 = Forget it! • 1 = Don't be a masochist... • 2 = Why bother? • 3 = Fun for one date. • 4 = It won't last! • 5 = You could do better! • 6 = Romance will fade... 7 = Great buddies! • 8 = Pure passion • 9 = True love. • 10 = Eternal bliss!

STARS OF GEMINI-LIBRA

June 1: Marilyn Monroe
Morgan Freeman
Brigham Young

June 2: Stacy Keach
Jerry Mathers
Dana Carvey

June 3: Tony Curtis
Scott Valentine

June 4: Dr. Ruth Westheimer
Bruce Dern

June 5: Kenny G
Marky Mark

June 6: Sandra Bernhard
Bjorn Borg

June 7: Liam Neeson
Jessica Tandy
Prince
Tom Jones

June 8: Joan Rivers
Keenan Ivory Wayans
Johnny Depp
Frank Lloyd Wright

June 9: Michael J. Fox
Cole Porter

June 10: Judy Garland
Linda Evangelista
Tara Lapinski

THIRD DECAN OF GEMINI

"I'M CONTROVERSIAL, AND I'M UNCONVENTIONAL!"

GEMINI-Aquarius	MUTABLE-Fixed	MERCURY-Uranus

The 3rd and last decan of GEMINI is a lone bird, a free flyer to the max. If you are born during this ten-day period, you rank as the most independent of all GEMINIs. This is not to say that you don't need other people. You do. But, only in frequent short doses. Then you're off and sailing solo again.

The power of Fixed Aquarius in speedy, Mutable GEMINI streamlines all of your actions. Though talkative, you're less wordy than other Twins. You don't waste your energy on tasks in which you know your talents will be lost. You have a brilliant sense of timing, sensing instinctively when to move and when to rest.

The planet Uranus brings to your decan two distinct traits. First, with Uranus considered one of the "newer" planets, your stride will always be in the forefront of your culture. You're hip to new trends, fashions, ideas, and lingo. Baby, you are one cool dude or dudette—like totally rad! You know what's "in" before the "in-crowd" catches wind; you'll take a pass on what's "out" while the rest of the masses are standing around looking like fools.

Second, Uranus is the planet of uncharted possibilities. Its presence in your decan interacting with mental Mercury makes you the ultimate opportunist. You are no stranger to the power of positive thinking. Remember, President George Herbert Walker Bush is one of your decan teammates. Having thoroughly examined his chart, I'm disappointed to report that I can't find one morsel of negativity. He is exactly where he is today because of his optimism. The only struggle he ever had was keeping his Mercury-ruled mouth shut when he had to play second fiddle as vice president.

You may not be seeking the presidency of the United States, but what you share in common with George is the 3rd decan GEMINI flux of attitudes going from good, better, to best. You just don't have time for the pain. Which is why, when everyone around you starts moping, you opt to make your way alone. After all, you aren't really along. There's two of you, right?

YOUR DARK SIDE

As a 3rd Decan, GEMINI-Aquarius can't avoid picking up invisible vibrations from neighbor Cancer. The emotional, watery, bluesy crustacean is like an alien from another planet to you. Well, the Crab is from the Moon, you know. You probably regard Cancer traits as completely foreign to yours. Little do you realize that you have been infiltrated by an alien invader who lives within your psyche.

That's right, my dear Twin Waterbearers, one of you is an emotional basket case and the other of you won't ever acknowledge it. As a rule, you have such disdain for any kind of negative feelings that you won't even allow yourself your own. Seriously, when was the last time you had a good cry? When did you admit that you were really ticked off about something?

The big question is when did you last feel deep love? Huh? Aha, gotcha! You're so accustomed to suppressing feelings that you've suppressed the high ones along with the lows. You can give affection, don't get me wrong. But, can you accept it? I'm afraid that flying as you do to such high altitudes, you've gotten some ice on your wings. You'll swoop down on opportunity without one ruffled feather in anticipation of the risk. Yet, you'll never gamble on opening up your own sensitive heart. This can be GEMINI duality at its worst.

YOUR LIGHT SIDE

Refer if you will to your call phrase, "I'm controversial and I'm unconventional." Though I worry about how you chain your negative side into a self-made prison, I can rest assured that your positive side will work overtime to compensate. You really are immune to what other people think. We'll never find you being duped or hyped by anything or anyone.

Isn't your motto "to go where no decan has gone before"? I thought so. Your whole life could and should be an adventure that very few will ever experience. What's more you seem to thrive on an element of danger, gliding through it unscathed. You'll always live to tell because telling is what you do best. Your flair for description is so lavish that you don't even need to take a camera with you on your travels. Your handle on language is so superb, that if you were forced to live on a deserted island, you would soon learn to speak to all beasts and other native creatures that inhabited it.

Although no one can influence you in your decisions, you have the supreme gift of persuasion. Go on, sell those ice cubes to the Eskimos. You could probably sell me my own headband. I'd never know.

BOTTOM LINE FOR YOUR POWER

Well, put two and two together, you know what you have to do. Your lesson in life is simply to be human. You must return to earth and feel your mortal pains, if only long enough to appreciate your superhuman potential. Once you've experienced your limitations, you are that much better equipped to defy them. Then you can employ your tremendous, unusual visions in sharing with others. The pictures you draw are of beauty and hope. Each pair of you refreshing, revitalizing Twins will never fail as a *Commentator*.

BODY TALK

GEMINI-Aquarius has rulership of what I call the three L's—Lungs, Legs, Lips. Now we've got good news and bad news about that. Let's begin with your least attractive feature, your legs. Plain and simple, you got skinny legs. Okay, maybe they're not skinny, maybe they just look that way because of those busy long strides you are always taking. Maybe they don't look so appealing because you give them so much abuse. Do you ever sit down, by the way? If, perchance, you've been given a nice set of gams, do take care to protect them. This is where you're vulnerable to a long list of unpleasant afflictions. In general, like most GEMINIs you *think* you are immune to illness. In fact, your decan is very delicate, though you'd never acknowledge it. I've got nothing against the power of mental healing; just don't ignore your body when it starts talking to you.

The good news is that just when your legs are ready to give out, your amazing lungs take over. If it were up to those two powerful bellows, you would be immortal. Boy, can you blow! What I mean is that you can blow out 200 candles on a birthday cake. That's it.

Last, and not least, when you pucker up your lips to blow, whatever it is that you're blowing, those lips are sure to be the softest, fullest, most beautiful set of smackers this side of heaven. Your smile is so irresistible you could literally charm a host of hostage-holding terrorists. And kissable? You bet. Want to play spin the bottle? I do!

YOUR BEST-BET CAREERS

Here's where we better not find you: at a conventional desk job. Sitting still will give you a nervous breakdown. You must be in a decision-making position where there's lots of risk involved. Otherwise, you'll be wasting all your Mercury, and don't want to do that.

For starter, let's talk aviation. As a commercial jet pilot you'll have a blast talking to the passengers from the cockpit about all the various climate conditions ahead. Taking that knack one step further, you could always research a travel guidebook. Your lists of hot spots will definitely be hot.

On the sidelines of the action you are the ultimate correspondent. In sports, military, and news fields you'll not miss a beat of exciting important info. In commodity trading your innate sense of trends will have you winning clients and commissions. Along those lines, you could open up any kind of establishment that attracts the chic crowds. From nightclubs, to restaurants, to hotels, to clothing boutiques, you'd make a mint!

A career in the arts might constrict your need for independence. With those lungs of your, however, you are a born natural at playing any of the wind instruments. Including your voice. The famed GEMINI-Aquarian, Paul McCartney (6/18) found endless success with his gifts of song.

When all else falls through, my suggestion is to get involved in a scandal, and then sell your story for millions. Isn't that the latest trend? And speaking of trends, you may pretend to scorn the materialists of our generation, but you need the bucks to support your unusual life-style and your romantic exploits as we'll soon see. Please, learn from neighbor Cancer about the wonders of savings accounts. They'll do wonders for you.

YOUR BEST-BET LOVE COMBOS

GEMINI-Aquarius Man: Before tearing you to pieces, I'll give you an out. More than any other decan of GEMINI, yours is a bachelor decan. If you have already admitted that to yourself, you can skip my analysis. Just be on your airy way. Don't complain the next time you get a telephone slammed down in your ear that Jacqueline didn't tell you what you were doing wrong.

For those of you who have not committed to a bachelor life, let me compliment you first on what a fab date you are. You'll take your lady out on the town, escort her to the most interesting locales, engage her with your vivid conversation. The wining and dining you know how to plan and execute will put her right where you want her in the palm of your hand. You'll be making all kinds of little innuendoes, possibly even coming right out and telling her what a great lover you are.

Okay, so you get her home, you get past the first kiss, which has probably already put her over the edge, and then finally, at the moment of truth, you freeze up. All of a sudden you realize you're with a woman who wants that gutsy, passionate, vulnerable, emotional man to emerge, and you are terrified. Of her, and of yourself. She'll think it's her fault and you won't convince her otherwise. She'll take a cab while you grab the telephone book to call up the next missy on your list, rationalizing that you didn't like the last one's old-fashioned attitudes, anyway.

Instead of having to perpetuate the sad cycle, you could exit the revolving door of women and enter the warm, positive arena of LIBRA-Libra. She may force you to do some of that soul-searching you fear, but she is the ultimate balancer. She won't judge you harshly for being afraid of your own passion. She'll teach you to let go of the chains on your heart and she'll steal it. And what you'll do to thank her is too racy for even me to describe. Use your controversial imagination, why don't you?

GEMINI-Aquarius Woman: All you bachelorette Twin Waterbearers, gather around to receive my hearty congratulations and my heavy scolding. You gals are heartbreakers, backbusters, and sometimes–shame on you–marriage splicers. Look, with all the agony men have dished out on us women for centuries, I don't really blame you. You misrepresent yourselves in the worst way. You can't help but say all those cute, coy, coquettish things that you know any man loves to hear. He's so strong, he's so handsome, he's so intelligent, he's so hooked on your line of verbal tease that he'll imagine himself ready to get you into bed within seconds.

Even when he finds out that you were feeding him a line, he can't overcome his desire to have you. You could sustain his pursuit for years if you wanted. Of course, the more he pursues, the less interested you are. How many poor fools do you currently have circling your house twice a day, anyway?

Now, don't fret, you haven't been condemned for life. If this has been a pattern for you, or anything close to it, and you do want to change, I'll find you a lad who'll get you to deliver what your seduction promises. He is even more unconventional than you and, knowing him, he'll probably send you off to an Awareness Group for Women Who Tease. He's a 1st Decan of AQUARIUS, the coolest of the cool. Like you, he too knows what's "in" and what's "out." And I mean that in more ways than one.

DECAN PAIRS WITH GEMINI-AQUARIUS

GEMINI-Aquarius   &   ARIES-Aries (3/21-3/30) 6
ARIES-Leo (3/31-4/9) 6
ARIES-Sagittarius (4/10-4/20) 6
TAURUS-Taurus (4/21-4/30) 4
TAURUS-Virgo (5/1-5/10) 3
TAURUS-Capricorn (5/11-5/20) 1
GEMINI-Gemini (5/21-5/31) 6
GEMINI-Libra (6/1-6/10) 7
GEMINI-Aquarius (6/11-6/20) 6
CANCER-Cancer (6/21-7/1) 3
CANCER-Scorpio (7/2-7/12) 2
CANCER-Pisces (7/13-8/1) 1
LEO-Leo (7/23-8/1) 7
LEO-Sagittarius (8/2-8/12) 6
LEO-Aries (8/13-8/22) 7
VIRGO-Virgo (8/23-9/3) 2
VIRGO-Capricorn (9/4-9/13) 3
VIRGO-Taurus (9/14-9/22) 4
LIBRA-Libra (9/23-10/3) 9
LIBRA-Aquarius (10/4-10/13) 8
LIBRA-Gemini (10/14-10/22) 8
SCORPIO-Scorpio (10/23-11/2) 3
SCORPIO-Pisces (11/3-11/12) 4
SCORPIO-Cancer (11/13-11/22) 3
SAGITTARIUS-Sagittarius (11/23-12/2) 2
SAGITTARIUS-Aries (12/3-12/11) 4
SAGITTARIUS-Leo (12/12-12/21) 2
CAPRICORN-Capricorn (12/22-12/31) 5
CAPRICORN-Taurus (1/1-1/10) 4
CAPRICORN-Virgo (1/11-1/19) 3
AQUARIUS-Aquarius (1/20-1/29) 9
AQUARIUS-Gemini (1/30-2/8) 7

LOVE SCALE SCORES

0 = Forget it! • 1 = Don't be a masochist... • 2 = Why bother? • 3 = Fun for one date. • 4 = It won't last! • 5 = You could do better! • 6 = Romance will fade... 7 = Great buddies! • 8 = Pure passion • 9 = True love. • 10 = Eternal bliss!

STARS OF GEMINI-AQUARIUS

June 11:	Gene Wilder	June 19:	Gena Rowlands
	Joe Montana		Kathleen Turner
	Jacques Cousteau		Lou Gehrig
June 12:	George Bush		Paula Abdul
	Anne Frank	June 20:	Danny Aiello
June 13:	Martha Washington		Olympia Dukakis
	Tim Allen		Lionel Richie
	Ally Sheedy		John Goodman
June 14:	Donald Trump		Cyndi Lauper
	Steffi Graf		Nicole Kidman
	Boy George		
June 15:	Waylon Jennings		
	Jim Belushi		
	Helen Hunt		
	Courteney Cox		
	Neil Patrick Harris		
June 16:	Stan Laurel		
	Laurie Metcalf		
	Tupac Shakur		
June 17:	Igor Stravinsky		
	Dean Martin		
	Barry Manilow		
	Joe Piscopo		
June 18:	Paul McCartney		
	Jeanette MacDonald		
	Carol Kane		
	Isabella Rossellini		

CHAPTER 6

CANCER

JUNE 21 - JULY 22

First Decan	Second Decan	Third Decan
CANCER-Cancer	CANCER-Scorpio	CANCER-Pisces
6/21 - 7/1	7/2 - 7/12	7/13 - 7/22

The question most asked by every CANCER is
"Why is a love affair like a high tide?"

Sign:	Water - Feelers
Symbol:	The Crab
Planet:	Moon
Body Talk:	Breast & Stomach
Style:	Cardinal

MEET THE PROTECTOR...

"I'M POSSESSIVE"

There are two things that everybody loves to tease Ms. and Mr. CANCER about, one being their "Moody Blue" personalities, and the other being their huge appetites. Both are true, but are far from describing the potential power of what may appear to be a non-obtrusive, homey, or even shy little creature.

Your symbol is the Crab. You have a protective outer shell that you never, and I mean never, let anyone penetrate. Inside you are private, emotional, brooding. Oh, but that exterior of yours can hide even the darkest thoughts.

You probably always look good and your surroundings probably look even better. That's because whether you live in a trailer or in a castle you absolutely require that your home resemble a womb! You like low lighting, soft and cushy furnishings, harmonious colors, peaceful protection from the storms outside.

No matter what your decan is, you are a Moon Child. The changes in the Moon, your ruling planet, affect you at every moment of your life. Like it, and like the force of water, you can exert an amazing yet undetectable power over others. As long as you can tear yourself away from the refrigerator, you have the ability to achieve all that you dream.

FIRST DECAN OF CANCER

6/21 - 7/1

"I'M POSSESIVE. I'M USUALLY POSSESIVE."

| CANCER-Cancer | CARDINAL-Cardinal | MOON-Moon |

If you are born in this 1st Decan of CANCER and you are not a whirlpool of interior emotions, then you must have some happy planet somewhere in your chart that saves you. With most of you "Moonies" I always find a man or woman who is constantly churning inside.

Your mode of transportation is Cardinal, don't forget, and you always move in extremes—that is, when you move. A Crab can sit in its little shell, mulling and fuming, and planning the perfect moment of attack. Then, at the second that others least expect, you explode into action, like a geyser shooting from the ground.

Your feelings tend to run in extremes, as well. When you're excited about something you seem to be running 1,000 rpm. When you're in love, watch out! You'll drop everything else and obsess about the object of your desire to the point of utter distraction.

You are a wonderful friend as long as you feel loyalty from those that you invite into your cozy, warm home. You love to feed the masses and your kitchen will usually be more seductive than your bedroom. Equipped with every new-fangled device from microwaves to automated carrot peelers, your kitchen is certain to reflect your passion for the preparation of whatever you're planning on feeding yourself and/or the rest of the gang. Let the guests beware, though. If they make a mess or, God forbid, refuse to eat what's on your menu, they're politely asked to hit the road. Personally, when visiting a CANCER-Cancer, I always bring chocolates.

Let's face it: You are a feeder, a feisty crustacean that sponges up anything edible, readable, watchable, have-able. That's why we call you: possessive.

YOUR DARK SIDE

All of the decans of Water signs are emotional, but yours wins the prize for being the most uncontrollable when it comes to your feelings. There literally is no stopping you when you enter the eye of the storm. Your anger is overwhelming. Your joy has no boundaries. Your sadness is as big as the ocean.

Not only do you turn away from help when one of your emotional attacks comes over you, but you also turn away from yourself, crawling deeper and deeper into your crab shell, until it all blows over.

To make matters worse, your ultra-sensitivity can pick up on other people's emotions. This simply adds to the waves of feeling inside you that you usually can't control.

Listen, there's nothing wrong with being in tune. When you're constantly stirred up, however, it's hard to get anything done. Some of the greatest endeavors of CANCER-Cancers have been blown to pieces because of emotional mismanagement.

YOUR LIGHT SIDE

Take a look at the power of the Moon and see if that gives you a clue about the type of influence you are able to exert over others. When you are on a steady flow, not being victimized by your strong emotions, your sensitivity allows you to become the ultimate persuader.

Your high values of home, family, and nurturing give you a sincerity that others can depend on. You thrive in taking care of the basic needs of loved ones.

Your possessiveness allows you to have great respect for what you do own—for the beautiful surroundings you try to create, the things that you choose to bring into your womb-like comforting world. And, most important, you respect yourself. It's that self-love that will save you every time your emotions go out of whack.

BOTTOM LINE FOR YOUR POWER

The first step in overcoming those emotional hurricanes of yours is becoming aware of them. Many CANCER-Cancers don't even realize what piles of mush they really are.

Once you face this aspect of yourself, you can begin to use your infinite reservoir of feeling for yourself instead of against yourself. If you combine your ultra-sensitivity with your ability to gain the trust of almost anyone, together with your need to nurture, that private shell of yours will start to open right up. Knowing how to give comfort to family and friends is a gift you possess. Use it! For yourself and for others you are: a *Caretaker*.

BODY TALK

CANCER rules the stomach, so with the 1st Decan there isn't a doubt about what part of the body expresses the inner you. We already know how much you love to eat, and logically we can assume that you are prone to weight gain. No, not in all-over chubbiness, just in that vulnerable spot that always threatens to turn into a potbelly, grow unsightly love handles, or ripple over your jeans.

Digestive illness will be the first on the list of those that bother you. Sorry, Charley, but your decan has almost as many sick days as the hypochondriac VIRGO-Virgo. Maybe it's not that you're really sick, maybe it's just that you'd rather be at home–fixing yourself a big plate of mashed potatoes and gravy.

This is not to say that all CANCER-Cancer born are paunchy. I've known many women with birthdays in this ten-day period who have the flattest, most gorgeous tummies around. Still, you better believe that these women had to work hard at trimming their middle. After stuffing themselves with pasta, they had to stay at the gym extra hours.

Whether you've beaten the bulge or not, you probably do have a chronic dialogue going on with your belly. When your attentions have been grabbed by a new love interest, others around you can almost hear the flapping of butterfly wings in your stomach. You love to have your tummy touched, rubbed, stroked. When it comes to this decan, the cliché holds: The quickest way to his or her heart is through the stomach.

YOUR BEST-BET CAREERS

Choosing a job that will last is almost as complicated for you as deciding what you're going to eat next. You are highly versatile and extremely proficient at whatever you do. The number-one criteria for you will be establishing an acceptable work environment. No matter how high the starting salary is, you can't abide a messy, loud, or chaotic atmosphere. Stay away from work that requires you to travel. Straying too far from home base makes a CANCER-Cancer crabby as hell.

Now, with those exceptions aside, the working world is your proverbial oyster. Being the sponge that you are makes you a quick study for a wide choice of professions. Your decan's knack for retaining details is a proven plus.

Careers in history, education, and science can utilize your capacity for remembering dates, names, facts, and figures. In medicine, you're sure to graduate at the top of your class. Just watch out that you don't become too emotionally caught up with your patients' conditions.

This decan yields the absolute best housewives and mothers. If "Domestic Engineer" is your current job title, you probably put all the other ladies on the block to shame.

Male CANCER-Cancers make superb chefs. Sometimes men of this decan are just as happy to tend to the babies and the household chores while wifey goes out to earn the bacon. Anything that is "home" related, from interior decoration to real estate, will allow your innate talents to put money in the bank. And, by the way, 1st Decan CANCERS love making deposits in their savings accounts almost as much as they love putting food into their mouths.

YOUR BEST-BET LOVE COMBOS

CANCER-Cancer Men: First of all, you love love. Second of all, you love sex. It's not that you're a sex maniac, it's just that you have as healthy an appetite for the opposite sex as you do for rich, plentiful plates of food. You are so proud of your male virility that the secret thought of getting a woman pregnant thrills you to no end.

Attracting women is no problem for you, not with your cuddly, cozy, charming demeanor. Once she's in your arms though, that's where you want her to stay. And, if by chance you've made the mistake of choosing an independent gal, or a fast-moving flirt, she is in for a tirade she may have never expected from one as loving as you.

Stick to your sextiles and you can't go wrong. With any TAURUS you will find a dependable, home-loving woman who basically wants the same things that you do. Do not, repeat, do not, marry a CAPRICORN. Her seriousness and your moodiness will make you two the last couple to get invited anywhere.

CANCER-Cancer Women: If more men knew more about astrology you would have every guy lined up down the street trying to propose to you. You are a devoted spouse, a sensual lovemaker, a fantastic mother, a topnotch homemaker. You are a catch and a half!

So what's the problem? Well, you are so womanly, so fluid and mysterious, and such a darned emotional merry-go-round that most men are downright scared of you.

My guess is that you find yourself attracted to Air signs, romantic or poetic types who can never provide you with the home and security you need.

My suggestion for you Moon Ladies is a male SCORPIO, particularly one of the 3rd Decan, a SCORPIO-Cancer. His sex drive and career drive will give you all and more than you'd ever dreamed you could possess.

DECAN PAIRS WITH CANCER-CANCER

CANCER-Cancer &	ARIES-Aries (3/21-3/30)	7
	ARIES-Leo (3/31-4/9)	5
	ARIES-Sagittarius (4/10-4/20)	7
	TAURUS-Taurus (4/21-4/30)	9
	TAURUS-Virgo (5/1-5/10)	9
	TAURUS-Capricorn (5/11-5/20)	5
	GEMINI-Gemini (5/21-5/31)	2
	GEMINI-Libra (6/1-6/10)	2
	GEMINI-Aquarius (6/11-6/20)	3
	CANCER-Cancer (6/21-7/1)	6
	CANCER-Scorpio (7/2-7/12)	7
	CANCER-Pisces (7/13-7/22)	4
	LEO-Leo (7/23-8/1)	5
	LEO-Sagittarius (8/2-8/12)	6
	LEO-Aries (8/13-8/22)	4
	VIRGO-Virgo (8/23-9/3)	8
	VIRGO-Capricorn (9/4-9/13)	6
	VIRGO-Taurus (9/14-9/22)	8
	LIBRA-Libra (9/23-10/3)	3
	LIBRA-Aquarius (10/4-10/13)	4
	LIBRA-Gemini (10/14-10/22)	2
	SCORPIO-Scorpio (10/23-11/2)	7

LOVE SCALE SCORES

0 = Forget it! • 1 = Don't be a masochist... • 2 = Why bother? • 3 = Fun for one date. • 4 = It won't last! • 5 = You could do better! • 6 = Romance will fade... 7 = Great buddies! • 8 = Pure passion • 9 = True love. • 10 = Eternal bliss!

STARS OF CANCER-CANCER

June 21:	Jane Russell	June 30:	Susan Hayward
	Juliette Lewis	July 1:	Diana, Princess of Wales
June 22:	Meryl Streep		Dan Aykroyd
	Kris Kristofferson		Deborah Harry
	Bill Blass		Pamela Anderson Lee
June 23:	Bob Fosse		
June 24:	Jack Dempsey		
June 25:	Carley Simon		
	George Orwell		
	George Michael		
June 26:	Pearl S. Buck		
	Chris Isaak		
	Chris O'Donnell		
June 28:	Mel Brooks		
	Gilda Radner		
	Kathy Bates		
	John Cusack		
	Mary Stewart Masterson		

SECOND DECAN OF CANCER

"I'M POSSESIVE, AND I'M ALSO SEARCHING."

CANCER-Scorpio	CARDINAL-Fixed	MOON-Mars

There are no two ways about it. Anyone born in this decan is bound to do things in big ways. When you combine the churning influence of the Moon with the outward, aggressive drive of Mars, you find yourself with someone who will always make a huge splash.

You are still a CANCER, but the Scorpion traits that color your decan allow you to come out of your shell more frequently than not. You avoid much of the CANCERIAN boohooing by setting priorities. Instead of giving way to the waves of emotion that overcome you, you're able to place those feelings on the back burner, so you're free to pursue any endeavor.

Scorpios are by nature planners and schemers, their Fixed style making them highly methodical. A CANCER-Scorpio uses that Fixed motion to conserve energy, breaking into a Cardinal pace only where and when it counts. Take a look at Nancy Reagan (7/6), our First Lady of the 1980's. Believe you me, she didn't get where she got by letting others do the planning. And Ron didn't get where he got all by his lonesome. Having a CANCER-Scorpio working behind the scenes for him set him way ahead of the game early on. Nancy's rule over Ron and his Cabinet was no secret and it certainly' didn't surprise me. If a CANCER-Scorpio isn't running their own show, they're certain to run somebody else's.

Most CANCERS love to eat and this decan is no exception. What makes CANCER-Scorpios distinct is their love of a lavish display of food. I know someone born during this period who asked for his bologna sandwich on a pewter platter when he was but a wee one. Yes, of course it was one of my three children, whom I've only begun to discuss. Would you believe he has always insisted on drinking soda pop out of crystal glasses?

YOUR DARK SIDE

Crabs of this decan have the sharpest claws and snappiest jaws of all CANCERS. Though you are not as punishing as a pure Scorpio, you express your intense emotions with behavior that can take others by surprise. And though you won't hold a grudge as long as almost every Scorpio, once you feel someone has treated you poorly, you cut them off without so much as a how-do-you-do.

You basically have too much energy and sometimes you make improper choices for channeling it. You do before you speak and think, then brood about what you may have done or said wrong afterward. Most CANCER-Scorpios rarely realize how greatly they impact the world around them.

Your worst pitfall is what I call "gettin' the spooks." A CANCERIAN will sneak up on you, and that Scorpio fascination with death or morbid thoughts hangs over you like a dark rain cloud you can't shake. At these times even your comforting cave-like home isn't a safe harbor for you. Unless you nip it in the bud, this unsettled state can cause you to make irrational choices, or say things you may later regret.

YOUR LIGHT SIDE

Your biggest lesson in life will be learning how to snap out of the jitters, and simply trust in your positive potential. Once you begin to handle your mysterious Moon changes, and give some focus to that Mars drive, your sensitivity can only enhance your effectiveness.

You have extrasensory imagination. You are able to come up with rare or unusual solutions to age-old problems. You are wildly creative and though you do not demand admiration, your peers usually think you're exceptional.

BOTTOM LINE FOR YOUR POWER

If you can simply accept that big things are always going to be happening in your life, and that you're always going to be experiencing strong sensations, then you might be able to relax and enjoy yourself. As the great saying of the 1960's went, "Go with the flow."

When you start swimming in the right direction, that is, when you know you're making the right choices, everyone around you benefits. Your achievement sets an example that brings hope to the less accomplished and is your way of expressing how much you need to give of yourself. This gift of hope makes you a nurturer of the highest order: a Torchbearer.

BODY TALK

Not as plagued by digestive problems as your neighbor, CANCER-Cancer, you still fuss over your body as if you were your own mother cat. CANCER has dominion over the breast area and Scorpio rules the genitals. So, this decan is often known as a regular "T & A" crew. Woman who are born CANCER-Scorpio usually are blessed with mammary endowments that other women can attain only through surgery. You are proud of your bra size and enjoy exposing your cleavage almost as much as CANCER-Scorpio men enjoy seeing it exposed. The torsos of these men are similarly well-developed and are similarly objects of pride.

Your overall health picture is generally well-balanced as we often find with 2nd Decans. Being Crab/Scorpion mixes, you've all been given a surplus of shell. In other words, you have natural built-in immune systems and defenses to common colds, flues, and other afflictions that can nail a less healthy person to the bed. When you do get the sniffles, it won't be because your body hurts, if you know what I mean.

However, CANCER-Scorpios are constantly being physically affected by the Moon. You will probably have a tendency to retain water, especially when the Moon is full. And any change in the Moon makes you horny as hell–an occurrence that appears every two and a half days. My prescription for you is several glasses of water a day along with a brisk cold shower whenever the Moon gets your temperature rising.

YOUR BEST-BET CAREERS

Whatever it is that you do, you must have an outlet for your imagination. You have the specialist's touch and the need to feel that your work efforts are appreciated. If your current profession demands too many mundane chores, you'll most likely end up at home in bed eating pastry rather than staying in the office feeling put upon.

A wise CANCER-Scorpio will choose a career that allows him or her an opportunity to be creative, while still being able to afford putting food on the table. Don't forget, your Cardinal style won't permit you to nibble Spam served off paper plates. Slumming it is for the birds.

In the arts, some choices for you that will fit this bill are illustration, fashion design, and architecture. With actors of this decan, we find many cases of pure magnetism. You probably won't have to work too hard to get those producers' doors open. And fortunately for you, your Scorpion suspicion keeps you from trusting phony offers.

Think about doing research in early childhood development. Your understanding of primal feelings, and your constant search for answers to basic behavior questions will both be tapped in this area.

Another option in which you're sure to triumph is restaurant and hotel management, especially when you own the joint. Knowing what a perfectionist you are, I know I'd make reservations there!

YOUR BEST-BET LOVE COMBOS

CANCER-Scorpio Man: I do believe that you are much more affected by every little thing she does and says than you ever let on. You hate being made to feel vulnerable by women and you usually do. Yet, you are so secretive about those inner feelings that half the time she ends up not knowing where she stands. A gal can think you worship the ground she walks on. But the minute she does or says anything to perk up that suspicious streak, she's history.

Your sexual drive borders on excess. We aren't talking about frivolous romps in the hay, either. You're into rock & roll when it comes to lovemaking. You love to bait the woman into bed with your quiet CANCERIAN seduction and then–BOOM–give her a roller-coaster ride she won't forget.

One celebrity example of this decan, Geraldo Rivera (7/4), makes a career out of seducing women on live television. That couch of his, the CANCER's den of comfort, puts his female guests completely at ease. Once he's got them charmed almost to the point of sedation, his little stinger flashes out, grabbing more hush-hush information from his guest than she ever planned to reveal. We can only guess what Geraldo's like in the bedroom. I've asked him several times if he wears silk pajamas to bed. Although he responds with a "No comment," we all know the real answer. Of course, he's got to wear something that feels good against his skin, and something that he can slip right off as he continues his seduction.

Incidentally, Geraldo has a power chart that's perfect for his vocation. With three planets each in two signs, CANCER and GEMINI–or what we call two stallions–his verbal talents are as obvious as the mustache on his face. As a CANCER, he understands deep levels of emotion, and with that dash of deadly Scorpio, he goes straight for the guts of the news. The secret to his success? He's cashing in on Torment Talk as he draws out other people's tortured pasts. He may try to keep his own tortured past always undercover, but as the cliché goes– it takes one to know one. I know for an astrological fact that he's had some real doozies of intrigues, ones that make getting hit with a chair by a neo-Nazi an everyday event. You can bet your bottom dollar that his numerous sexual exploits, if ever exposed, would make Sylvester Stallone look like a monk!

We usually find that male CANCER-Scorpios work and play with equal gusto. What usually redeems you from being a woman-aholic is that you are extremely monogamous. So, look for the same in your mate. A VIRGO-Virgo will never end up in anyone else's bed. And if you buy her lots of high-tech kitchen equipment, she'll keep a close eye on your diet. So what if her sexual drive isn't up to yours? Your passion is probably enough for the both of you.

CANCER-Scorpio Woman: Many of you ladies with strong maternal impulses marry long before you should, less for love than for security. Years later you sit up in bed hitting your head, saying something like "I could have had a V-8!" Don't be in such a rush to start setting up your nest. No doubt you are a true romantic, but you must consider the long-term picture before you plan the wedding reception. As I am constantly reminding myself and my children, divorce can leave the longest memories while marriage gives you the shortest visions.

CANCER-Scorpio woman needs an ambitious and also a sensitive man–one who will place her on the same level of importance as his work. Whether you believe it or not, you need to be in control. You like to do the seducing, and you do it like the sensual femme fatale you are. Keep up your guard against problems you may encounter with any of the Fire signs. Passion is one thing. Broken dishes are another.

You're safe with any of the Water signs, except your own–your chemistries would make life just too humdrum. For erotic adventures in mystery, and someone who can cope with you as the homemaker and you as the temptress, the hot ticket is a PISCES-Pisces. He's a bit of an oddball, but you are truly emotional soul mates. While he reminds you not to overeat, you can keep him away from his martinis.

DECAN PAIRS WITH CANCER-SCORPIO

LOVE SCALE SCORES

0 = Forget it! • 1 = Don't be a masochist... • 2 = Why bother? • 3 = Fun for one date. • 4 = It won't last! • 5 = You could do better! • 6 = Romance will fade... 7 = Great buddies! • 8 = Pure passion • 9 = True love. • 10 = Eternal bliss!

STARS OF CANCER-SCORPIO

July 3:	Tom Cruise	July 9:	Jimmy Smits
July 4:	Geraldo Rivera		Tom Hanks
	Ann Landers	July 11:	Giorgio Armani
	Abigail Van Buren	July 12:	Bill Cosby
July 6:	Sylvester Stallone		Kristi Yamaguchi
	Nancy Reagan		Julius Caesar
July 7:	Geraldo Rivera		
July 8:	Anjelica Huston		
	Kevin Bacon		

THIRD DECAN OF CANCER

"I'M POSSESIVE, BUT I'M ALSO DEMOCRATIC."

CANCER-Pisces	CARDINAL-Mutable	MOON-Neptune

Remember what I said about the 3rd Decan being the odd guy out? Well, you Crab/Fish blends epitomize the notion. You're just plain weird. Mysterious, off in your own land of dreamy dreams half the time, and right smack dab in the here and now the rest of the time.

Like your other pals who are also CANCERS, you're a nester, an emotional, possessive Cardinal creature who'd rather go first class or not go at all. But, having been born within the last ten days of CANCER, you are tinted by noticeable Piscean traits, and sun-kissed ever so slightly by LEO's pride. Neptune, as the ruler of Pisces, brings to your personality an element of disguise. This planet of illusion combines with CANCER's ruler, the Moon, and often produces a character that literally seems to change in. front of others. The Piscean motion is Mutable, wafting, alternating between impulsiveness and focused planning. What this all boils down to is that your entire being can be summed up by the word change.

Many CANCER-Pisces men and women change their looks so frequently that even close friends have trouble recognizing them from day to day. You tip the weight scales from highs to lows. You're usually over- or underweight, bingeing on culinary delights or living for days on a juice fast. Your opinions and tastes probably vary upon any given day. No matter what expressive words are coming out of your mouth, you're writing a whole other set of sentences in your head.

The escapist tendencies of the CANCER-Pisces Decan are legendary. But before you can run off and try to escape your planetary influences, listen to the quality that has you winning kudos time and time again. You have within all your watery changings, a drop of magic. Your presence sparkles in a room, an evening spent with you can sometimes be like a ride to heaven. You get yourself out of the most inescapable binds, and you thrive on helping others overcome their difficulties. For all your strangeness you tend to be one of the most popular decans on the block.

YOUR DARK SIDE

Your big problem isn't your crabbiness. Sure, dark or sour moods come over you, but they pass over as your ever-changing feelings turn to brighter thoughts. Your downfall isn't your fishiness either. Yes, you don't always tell the full story or you'll change the who-what-where-when's, depending on your fleeting fancies in telling the tale.

What is rampant within the CANCER-Pisces decan is pure, unadulterated insecurity. This is the demon that can throw off hopes and wishes and plans.

Your mind is always coming up with fabulous fantasies—dreams that are attainable. Yet the minute you go out to chase them you get cold feet worrying that you're not cut out for the challenge.

Insecurity can also make you work too hard. Trying to please everyone or worrying about what so-and-so meant when he said such-and-such is a complete energy drain on you. In love, your need for approval can get to be a pain in the tush!

Last but not least your dark side may delude you into avoiding your insecurity with superficial pick-me-ups. Alcohol, drugs, and casual sex are all known to be regular vices of your decan. Watch out for Neptune when the Moon is making you feel low...

YOUR LIGHT SIDE

The flip side of insecurity, taken in a positive sense, is vulnerability. You have an open, receptive quality that is permanently endearing. The fact that you are so rarely the same makes you equally entertaining to friends and acquaintances.

As a Cardinal sign, there is a lot you require for your stability and happiness. Yet, as a CANCER-Pisces, it is just as important for you to share the wealth. You are compassionate in the extreme and though you may not like to travel too far from home, you'll go to the ends of the earth for someone in need.

Again, astrology has mixed an unusual potion of magic in concocting your elements. Being a Water sign through and through you understand the quicksilver motion of water in all its potentials, the mysteries of nature. You believe in getting the impossible done.

BOTTOM LINE FOR YOUR POWER

Learn to take advantage of your own sailboat personality. Balance your creative fantasy life with that practical, crusty nature that is also yours. Throughout your continual changes there is a constant that is your fabulous instinct for safety.

In times of conflict you usually end up on the right side of the argument. When you or those whom you love are truly at risk your in born protectiveness will steer you into shelter until the danger is over. That's why you are always supreme as: a *Defender*.

BODY TALK

Whether you are having a lush or a lean year, as a CANCER-Pisces, you should know that you have an uncommonly high metabolism, which gives you the potential for having a great bod. Though your looks are constantly changing, with proper attention you males and females could be the mermaids and mer-men of the zodiac. We're talking about the type of figures people dream of–voluptuous bosoms or well-developed chests, narrow waists, and long, graceful legs.

Tummy aches, the CANCERIAN curse, shouldn't be too severe with your decan. If you are watching your diet with sensible nutrition, which, mind you, you don't always accomplish, your digestive functions shouldn't be an issue. Your Achilles' heel, in terms of physical ailments, is literally that—your heel. Your feet are supersensitive, the source of numerous bodily aches and pains. No laughing matter, here. At some points in your life your podiatrist and reflexologist could be your best friends.

Need I describe the erotic aspect of having your feet touched, or gasp—nibbled? I think you get the picture. Just in case you feared that you had a hidden fetish you can stop fretting. Comes with the territory; foot appreciation is a CANCER-Piscean characteristic. Pamper those two babies of yours and dig into your coffers for some extra change to spend on some luxurious house slippers.

YOUR BEST-BET CAREERS

My guess is that you need career counseling in the worst way. Unless you have made some serious sacrifices, you really aren't cut out for 90 percent of the jobs available at any given time.

You are not a team player and it's too dangerous for you to work alone. Remember, I warned you that you were weird! The solution here is for you to form partnerships, a one-on-one working situation in an unusual or creative field. Magic, ventriloquism, circus performing, especially when you're part of a duo, will all tap into your Neptunian charms. Having toured with the circus myself, I can assure you it ain't bad work if you can get it.

To capitalize on your defensive nature you might flourish in the fields of security and strategic defense. If you luck into the night shift, you'll really be in business; after the sun goes down all your ingenuity starts to flow.

One other area you might explore is the cosmetics field. Try developing new lotions to cure wrinkles. Use your charm demonstrating to others how to change their looks as often as you do. If fashion is your thing opportunity awaits you in selling or designing footwear. Some people try their hands at show business; CANCER-Pisces folks should step into success with shoe business.

Unless you have strong management behind you, be prepared to give up hopes of making it in the arts. Not that you don't have the talent. You have talent galore, but your native insecurity makes it difficult to survive during the periods that you are not receiving recognition. Not to mention the fact that because some of your ideas are so off-the-wall, the general populace doesn't always understand what you're doing. Probably you'll have several creative hobbies on the back burner anyway. Doing one thing at a time isn't part of your makeup.

Unless you are financially supported by someone else be careful how you handle your earnings. Though you definitely know how to save, you haven't a clue about how to spend. It wouldn't be impossible for you to blow all your assets in one fun night. Yes, I know, you usually like to spend your money on people you love, but what happens when you've tapped out your bank account on everybody else? You turn into a grumpy Crab, that's what happens!

YOUR BEST-BET LOVE COMBOS

CANCER-Pisces Man: If you've got your act together, you're probably used to women falling for you hook, line, and sinker. It's your sparkle, your mystery. While you're out in limbo land feeling sensual, you probably don't realize the numbers of women who are checking you out. Other fellows would kill for the ease with which you seem to pick up gorgeous gals, and sometimes the gals are ready to kill you once you have picked them up.

You seem to think that the unsuspecting new love interest is a mind reader while you forget that yours is constantly changing. You want her to be attentive when you want her to be and independent when you feel that things are getting too close. You want her to be as sexually active as you are, but God forbid she doesn't behave like the perfect lady. And when she does get fed up— which, believe me, can happen pretty damn fast—you're horrified and heartbroken that you've been left again.

One woman on the block who'll put up with your indulgence is a Ms. SCORPIO—any decan will do. This gal's sexual appetite can top yours. Plus, if your chemistry has clicked, she'll make you feel like you're the greatest he-man she's ever kissed. You both share a common bond in mystery and your love affair will be a deep, lasting one.

Overcome your urge to go moonlighting for other back-door entertainment. A SCORPIO woman will make you pay for your play and you'll end up feeling worse than a heel. Even though you're so great at covering your bases. A SCORPION has a nose for deception and a direct way of making you regret you ever thought about another woman. If you really must explore, do it in your fantasy life. I promise I won't tell.

CANCER-Pisces Woman: Like your male counterparts, you feminine CANCER-Pisces are initially desirable to the opposite sex. You're off into your own thoughts, looking enticing and unavailable. Or, as one female star of the decan, Linda Rondstadt, described it—you're matching to the beat of a different drum. Yes, you are a head turner as you glide through a room. Unfortunately, once you start to engage in conversation, most of your everyday Joes you become immediately stymied.

You are looking for someone as special as you and if you aren't doing it with any kind of sound advice, you're probably going through men like so much water, feeling inevitably dissatisfied. Because you are so unusual stick to your trines: only another Water sign will ever be able to speak your language.

If you are truly ready to settle into a loving and lasting relationship, I have the tip of the year. Do what I usually caution others against and marry your own decan.

A CANCER-Pisces man is just as offbeat as you and with both of your many mystic mood changes the two of you won't have a minute to get bored from too much similarity. You can make love passionately together or explore out-of-body experiences at the same time. Kick the bottle together, if that becomes an issue, or share a little love nest on a boat.

If two of your kind sounds all too exotic, you can always get hitched to a TAURUS. At least you can be confident that any money you earn will be in good hands. And, if you're ever feeling shaken or upset, he can sing to you, or even let you hold his teddy bear. How's that for romantic?

DECAN PAIRS WITH CANCER-PISCES

CANCER-Pisces   &   ARIES-Aries (3/21-3/30) 3
ARIES-Leo (3/31-4/9) 2
ARIES-Sagittarius (4/10-4/20) 7
TAURUS-Taurus (4/21-4/30) 9
TAURUS-Virgo (5/1-5/10) 6
TAURUS-Capricorn (5/11-5/20) 6
GEMINI-Gemini (5/21-5/31) 2
GEMINI-Libra (6/1-6/10) 3
GEMINI-Aquarius (6/11-6/20) 1
CANCER-Cancer (6/21-7/1) 4
CANCER-Scorpio (7/2-7/12) 6
CANCER-Pisces (7/13-7/22) 9
LEO-Leo (7/23-8/1) 4
LEO-Sagittarius (8/2-8/12) 3
LEO-Aries (8/13-8/22) 3
VIRGO-Virgo (8/23-9/2) 5
VIRGO-Capricorn (9/3-9/13) 5
VIRGO-Taurus (9/14-9/22) 7
LIBRA-Libra (9/23-10/3) 4
LIBRA-Aquarius (10/4-10/13) 5
LIBRA-Gemini (10/14-10/22) 3
SCORPIO-Scorpio (10/23-11/2) 9
SCORPIO-Pisces (11/3-11/12) 8
SCORPIO-Cancer (11/13-11/22) 8
SAGITTARIUS-Sagittarius (11/23-12/2) 5
SAGITTARIUS-Aries (12/3-12/11) 5
SAGITTARIUS-Leo (12/12-12/21) 6
CAPRICORN-Capricorn (12/22-12/31) 2
CAPRICORN-Taurus (1/1-1/10) 4
CAPRICORN-Virgo (1/11-1/19) 2
AQUARIUS-Aquarius (11/20-1/29) 6
AQUARIUS-Gemini (1/30-2/8) 3
AQUARIUS-Libra (2/9-2/18) 4
PISCES-Pisces (2/19-2/29) 8
PISCES-Cancer (3/1-3/10) 8
PISCES-Scorpio (3/11-3/20) 9

LOVE SCALE SCORES

0 = Forget it! • 1 = Don't be a masochist... • 2 = Why bother? • 3 = Fun for one date. • 4 = It won't last! • 5 = You could do better! • 6 = Romance will fade... 7 = Great buddies! • 8 = Pure passion • 9 = True love. • 10 = Eternal bliss!

STARS OF CANCER-PISCES

July 13:	Harrison Ford
	Patrick Stewart
July 14:	Gerald R. Ford
	Ingmar Bergman
July 15:	Linda Ronstadt
	Brigitte Nielsen
	Brian Austin Green
	Jesse Ventura
	Patrick Wayne
July 16:	Ginger Rogers
	Phoebe Cates
	Corey Feldman
July 17:	Donald Sutherland
	David Hasselfhoff
July 18:	James Brolin
	Nelson Mandela
July 21:	Robin Williams
	Ernest Hemingway
	Cat Stevens
	Jon Lovitz
July 22:	Danny Glover
	Alex Trebek
	Willem Dafoe
	Robert "Bob" Dole
	Aexander Calder
	Alexander the Great

CHAPTER 7

LEO

JULY 23 - AUGUST 22

First Decan	Second Decan	Third Decan
LEO-Leo	LEO-Sagittarius	LEO-Aries
7/23 - 8/1	8/2 - 8/12	8/13 - 8/22

When asked the secret to his success, a LEO once replied,
"I believe in strong comebacks!"

Sign:	Fire - Doers
Symbol:	The Lion
Planet:	Sun
Body Talk:	Heart
Style:	Fixed

MEET THE DRAMATIST...

Most people know more about the Sun sign of LEO than any other sign because LEOS are the attention-getters of the zodiac. They don't just enjoy being in the center ring—they require it. LEO is ruled by the Sun, born to step into the spotlight, to radiate warmth and energy.

As a Fixed Fire sign, LEO is predictably "on" all the time. Why, they're even putting out rays in their sleep. As the saying goes, "What you see is what you get." You don't wear a facade of any kind, you won't pretend to be anything other than a member of a royal class. There aren't any hidden, last-minute surprises with any of you Lions or Lionesses. I'm not suggesting that you are strictly superficial, it's just that you are so outgoing, you are consistently expressing whatever you're feeling on the inside.

Symbolized by the king of the jungle, you as a Lion are characterized by a regal posture, noble interests, lofty tastes, and by your commonly held belief that you are extra-special. If this sounds a little too self-centered for one as gracious as you, look again, honey. For all your personal power of presence, you by definition are egotistical.

Whichever side of the tracks you were born on, you believe you deserve the good life. Truly, in your heart you always feel rich. You appreciate being alive and thrive as an active participant. Thinking that you belong to the upper crust is just one of your tools for getting ahead in this world–something any LEO is more than capable of doing. With your sunny disposition, most others aren't even aware that you're stepping on their toes.

Whatever your decan, most of you LEOS are loud—you'll use any device to nab attention. With sound, sight, taste, smell, and touch, you'll play it all to the hilt. Now you can stop asking why your character traits are the most familiar of all the Sun signs. You asked for it—you got it!

FIRST DECAN OF LEO

"I'M PROUD. I'M EXTREMELY PROUD."

LEO-Leo	FIXED-Fixed	SUN-Sun

Take every stereotype you've ever heard about a LEO and double it. That's what you have with this 1st Decan, pure concentrated charm, energy, dignity, pride, heart, and ego. In your mind, and probably those of friends and family and coworkers, you are a star already. Most likely, others are usually catering to your needs, hanging on your every word, finding themselves going to bizarre lengths just to see your pearly whites gleaming in approval at their efforts.

How do you do it? What's a LEO-Leo's recipe for making every pursuit look like a stroll down easy street? What is the special method you employ to get others to carry the load for you? If you don't know, if you just seem to glide along on instinct, I'll tell you what you're doing.

You might not be conscious of your behavior because it isn't ulterior. What you do is out and out intimidation. You project yourself as some sort of divine being other individuals should feel fortunate to know, and fortunate for the mere chance to grovel at your feet. They're thinking to themselves, "What a jerk," but they just don't have the nerve to confront you. Remember the Emperor's New Clothes fable? The emperor was so flattered by the con-guy tailor, that he really believed his new suit of thin air was becoming to his own royal demeanor. As he paraded through the streets, not one citizen had the chutzpah to protest his nudity. It took the innocent child to call out without warning, "the Emperor is naked as a jaybird," for the cat to be out of the bag.

I'm not the first to use the example of the "streaking" monarch to illustrate the LEO-Leo mentality. It's important for you to realize that somewhere, somehow, sometime, someone is going to walk up to you and say, "Candid Camera," and you may be surprised that the snapshot of you is one of a mere mortal.

The rest of the time you can go back to your strutting, joking, primping, and posing for your audience and the effect will be sheer entertainment. We can bad-mouth you all we want, but we can't deny the fact that you give us something to talk about. To tell you the honest truth, if you put a halt to all your extroverted excess, we'd all be a little sorry. You know, better than I, that being king or queen isn't always easy, but someone's got to do it. And you LEO-Leos are elected.

And that's how you make your way very steadily into positions of power and influence, often by almost seducing others to pull strings for you. As a FIXED-Fixed mover, you usually have big plans for yourself. Though you're smart enough to realize there are steps you must climb up the ladder to success, you don't have an aptitude for little details-best leave those to the commoners who come to your assistance.

With double Sun and double Fire you're a warm-blooded creature seven days a week, four seasons a year. You love the beach or the swimming pool, not for cool dips or for sight-seeing, but for basking in rays, cultivating a perfect tan, and most of all, for showing off your royal physique. Tropical climates suit you best; don't forget that the jungle is your natural habitat.

This is a decan that I've been studying for some time. My son, Frank Stallone, born on July 30, is LEO-Leo all the way. Whether he is reading aloud from his writing, acting a role, or performing his music, Frank is always in his element when there's a group gathered around him. He is cheery and charming 24 hours a day. He takes disappointment in stride, and only when he feels that he has been criticized unfairly does he show anything but a smile. As to his love life—not that he tells me everything—he, like most LEO-Leos, suffers from an obsession with lineage. He wants to marry royalty. He doesn't care if she's pure Italian, or pure Polish, as long as she is pure something, and descended from nobility. Somehow, no matter how adorable his latest love is, Frank will find a relative five generations back who was a rotten apple. That's a 1st Decan LEO for you.

YOUR DARK SIDE

I bet all you LION-Lions are roaring over your bruised paws because I called you "self-centered." I just can't avoid nit-picking while I have you for an audience. I know you don't mean to dwarf your fellows. Basically, you are truly lionhearted in spirit, kind and noble in beliefs. Ninety-nine percent of the time your behavior is worthy of medals.

So, what happens during that scary one percent of the time when you are not at your best? You turn into a savage beast, that's what happens. Your temper, almost always easily controlled, goes haywire and all you can see is purple—the color of the royal crest and the color of royal, raving madness. You want to lash out and bite someone, don't you? Suddenly the world, your fabulous sunlit stage, turns into a blackened pit of emptiness, and you become terrifyingly lonely.

This is the price you pay for being the social center of the party. When the party's over and everyone's gone home and you have no one to entertain, you have to face the music by yourself and you don't like it. You turn into an old sourpuss, stomping about, throwing things, having a dramatic tantrum. On these rare occasions, you lose all control and transform from a pet pussycat into a demonic panther. Thank the dear Lord this only happens once in a blue moon!

YOUR LIGHT SIDE

I don't want to make my list of compliments too long, knowing as I do how you love flattery. We don't want to swell your head any more than it already is! Still, there's no getting around the fact that when you're good, you are great. You usually greet each day like a newborn, thrilling to new possibilities at hand. You are so willing to forgive and forget that you almost never hold a grudge.

When you're around the energy level just seems to rise. Your instinctive talent for getting attention not only serves your needs, it also entertains. When you are expressing a belief, it's usually a solid value, so that you are able to positively raise your listener's awareness.

In times of real crisis you can be an absolute lifesaver. Though you often shirk menial tasks, sitting on your comfortable throne until the unpleasant job is over, when lives are at stake you find yourself performing with superhuman power.

BOTTOM LINE FOR YOUR POWER

The only obstacle between attaining all that you know you deserve (and where you sometimes fall behind) is your exorbitant need for others. It's as if you don't really think you can be king or queen without your subjects. Learning to spend more time alone and knowing in your heart that you are as wonderful as all that attention makes you feel will quadruple your happiness.

With self-reliance achieved, you're back into all your social encounters outshining the brightest of competitors. You're a doer, the hottest of the hot. No matter what, you can't fail as: a *Performer*.

BODY TALK

Here are some handy clichés for you: LEO-Leos are all heart; 1st Decan LEOS wear their hearts on their sleeves. Heart is where the lion's den is. The heart and the circulation are ruled by LEO. So, with this 1st Decan, we find men and women with large, strong hearts. Free-flowing and vital circulatory systems give your skin a constant ruddy glow. You flush and blush easily.

How can we not notice the typical lush mane of a LEO-Leo? My guess is that you spend more money at the hairdresser's than at the doctor's office. Your hair should be your prized feature. Do you toss your lovely locks? Twirl long curls coyly around your fingers? Do you stock up on conditioners, blow-dryers? Do you suffer from mousse abuse? Don't worry if you've been finding yourself getting up hours early to fuss with your coiffure—you're only preparing to meet your public.

Getting back to the old ticker, let me caution that as healthy as most LEO-Leos are most of the time, any weakening in your physical status will be heart-related. Usually, when you do get sick, it's serious business. Don't take your hardiness for granted, and get regular checkups with a cardiologist. Even though you love attention you'll be a miserable wretch getting it in your hospital room. This decan of LEO hates being under the weather.

YOUR BEST-BET CAREERS

Any profession that comes with a built-in audience will keep your nose to the grindstone for years. You are a natural actor, though you'll probably want to change the lines to your own interpretation. Also, watch out for hamming it up. Other actors will constantly complain about your scene-stealing, even while they know you're the one who's bringing in the crowds.

With your popular appeal, running for public office can often land you the majority of votes. If politics is your bag, keep a constant eye on your staff; it's their abilities that will make or break your career.

Teaching and lecturing are good choices for you, no matter what your subject matter is. The sciences of botany and zoology can utilize your love for everything that grows under the Sun, your ruling planet.

The world's best salesmen and saleswomen are LEO-Leos. Even if selling cars isn't your notion of noble work, it's a pursuit at which you can really score. Before too long you'll own the dealership and be driving around in a customized Caddy.

In the event that you'd like to hold on to your earnings—hire a bookkeeper or investment manager to do it for you. Dealing with dollars can be your downfall. You need too many creature comforts to live on the edge of poverty—a constant threat for someone who loves to spend as much as you do.

YOUR BEST-BET LOVE COMBOS

LEO-Leo Man: You male lions may not want to admit this, but you'll date just about anyone who'll put out. You'll settle for a companion just to occupy the time it takes you to find that purebred aristocratic lady you believe you truly deserve. It's because you hate lonely times. You despise not having a dishy dame on your arm, or just someone at your side to gaze up at you in adoration.

I'm not suggesting that you're an impossible mate. On the contrary, the gal that you're courting is in for one romantic, glamorous affair. You'll go all out with thoughtful, expensive gifts. You'll wine and dine her right into your swinging bachelor bed. Once she's there you definitely make her feel as outgoing and uninhibited as you are. Lovemaking comes so naturally to you that it ranks up there with eating and sleeping in terms of daily requirements. Remember, performance is your forte.

And then, even though you had no intentions of marrying her, you feel sad when she breaks it off, realizing she's being used. Poor old lionheart, you get your little paws hurt, don't you? You usually don't even take the time to figure out where you're making your mistakes; you rush right out to find the next available lioness.

The other error men of this decan make is to stay in relationships that aren't working. You're too damn proud to admit that you've made a wrong choice. You take loyalty to the letter of the law.

To avoid this kind of a trap, you will probably fare well with an ARIES. As much as she loves to be bossy, you can channel her energies to let her be the power behind the throne. With the 3rd Decan of ARIES, ARIES-Sagittarius, her headstrong nature will be softened enough to dole out the compliments that you need to sustain your confidence. You'll learn from her independence, while she can benefit from your generosity of spirit. So what if you both have snob complexes?

LEO-Leo Woman: According to most astrologers, the females of this decan are extremely maternal. After many years of study I happen to disagree with that assumption. A LEO-Leo woman does not love childbearing or child-rearing. If she's made the choice to have offspring, however, many of her romantic choices will be based on her search for good genes for the children whom she hopes will grow up beautiful, rich, talented, and independent, just so she doesn't have to take care of them anymore.

As a LEO-Leo lady, you are much fussier about whom you'll date than your male decan counterparts. He's got to be handsome, rich, talented, and independent. And, he's got to adorn you with royal jewels, or good costume gems at least. He's got to think you walk on water, practically. When you enter a room, he's got to drop everything, and almost swoon when you open your mouth to speak.

Am I describing the impossible dream, or is there a guy out there who can satisfy your romantic, needy heart? Because you, by nature are loyal, a FIXED-Fixed Fire sign that can keep the flames of love burning for years to come, you do have a lot to offer to the right fellow.

You always look perfectly manicured, coifed, just plain gorgeous. But once you hop onto the mattress, you're not afraid to get your fur ruffled. You're tender and sincere when you make love–in front of a fireplace or under an open window while the sun sets. It's always emotionally dramatic when Mr. Right does get you going, especially when he tells' you how stunning you look in your lingerie.

With fabulous looks, great sex, a loving heart, ferocious pride, and the ability to entertain extravagantly, you can make many a bachelor change his ways. One of the bachelor signs—GEMINI-Gemini comes quickly to mind. You balance his Mutable nature, while he treats you as the glamour puss you like to be. Though he probably will be out traveling a great deal, it just gives you that much more time to go shopping preferably with his bucks.

Jacqueline Kennedy Onassis (7/28), a LEO-Leo as we mentioned earlier, was the perfect match for GEMINI John F. Kennedy. His political success was escalated without question by the beautiful, stylish, sophisticated first lady at his side. Her second marriage to CAPRICORN Ari Onassis wasn't of the same complementary astrological balance. However, it does say something about a LEO-Leo woman's sacrificing romantic fulfillment for the chance to sit on an even richer and more powerful throne than the one she came from, doesn't it?

DECAN PAIRS WITH LEO-LEO

GEMINI-Libra (6/1-6/10) 9
GEMINI-Aquarius (6/11-6/20) 7
CANCER-Cancer (6/21-7/1) 5
CANCER-Scorpio (7/2-7/12) 2
CANCER-Pisces (7/13-7/22) 4
LEO-Leo (7/23-8/1) 5
LEO-Sagittarius (8/2-8/12) 6
LEO-Aries (8/13-8/22) 6
VIRGO-Virgo (8/23-9/3) 4
VIRGO-Capricorn (9/4-9/13) 5
VIRGO-Taurus (9/14-9/22) 3
LIBRA-Libra (9/23-10/3) 9
LIBRA-Aquarius (10/4-10/13) 6
LIBRA-Gemini (10/14-10/22) 8
SCORPIO-Scorpio (10/23-11/2) 2
SCORPIO-Pisces (11/3, 11/12) 4
SCORPIO-Cancer (11/13-11/22) 3
SAGITTARIUS-Sagittarius (11/23-12/2) 9
SAGITTARIUS-Aries (12/3-12/11) 8
SAGITTARIUS-Leo (12/12-12/21) 8
CAPRICORN-Capricorn (12/22-12/31) 4
CAPRICORN-Taurus (1/1-1/10) 2
CAPRICORN-Virgo (1/11-1/19) 3
AQUARIUS-Aquarius (11/20-1/29) 2
AQUARIUS-Gemini (1/30-2/8) 5
AQUARIUS-Libra (2/9-2/18) 5
PISCES-Pisces (2/19-2/29) 4
PISCES-Cancer (3/1-3/10) 3
PISCES-Scorpio (3/11-3/20) 2

LOVE SCALE SCORES

0 = Forget it! • 1 = Don't be a masochist... • 2 = Why bother? • 3 = Fun for one date. • 4 = It won't last! • 5 = You could do better! • 6 = Romance will fade... 7 = Great buddies! • 8 = Pure passion • 9 = True love. • 10 = Eternal bliss!

STARS OF LEO-LEO

July 23:	Woody Harrelson	July 31:	Curt Gowdy
July 24:	Amelia Earhart	August 1:	Dom De Luise
July 26:	Mick Jagger		Jerry Garcia
	Carl Jung		
July 28:	Jacqueline Kennedy Onassis		
July 30:	Henry Ford		
	Frank Stallone		
	Arnold Schwarzenegger		

SECOND DECAN OF LEO

8/2 - 8/12

"I'M PROUD AND I'M VERY INDEPENDENT."

LEO-Sagittarius	FIXED-Mutable	SUN-Jupiter

Take all the charm so familiar in so many LEOS and add a heavy dose of fun-loving, free-spirited Sagittarius, and we get this fireball 2nd Decan. As astronaut Neil Armstrong, born on August 5, can show us, with these guys even the sky isn't the limit.

You dream up big plans, and you put those plans into action with swift and versatile maneuvering. Unlike the pure LEO-Leo, you aren't above getting down to some of the dirtier parts of the job. As long as you can incorporate an element of challenge into whatever you do, you'll solve problems that have confused a hundred others already. The part of you that is governed by Jupiter, the Sag within your decan, involves the need for expansion. You're happiest when the chase is on, when your talents and smarts are on the line. Unlike other LEOS, having it easy is just a big bore for you.

You play just as hard as you work—one of the secrets of why you are usually so successful at whatever you do. Your Fixed methods make you endearingly predictable to those around you. Still, the Mutable quality that's also in your decan gives you an element of surprise.

If you have what seem to be larger than life aspirations and nothing has happened yet to convince you that they're not just pipe dreams, let me give you a little reassurance. There is a pattern with many LEO-Sagittarius men and women where uneventful youths can lead to incredibly dramatic adulthoods. When you finally do take off, it is like a rocketship blast, taking you right into the realm of fame and fortune that you always knew in your royal-blooded veins was your rightful destiny.

You are the most resilient of all the decans—no storms can put out your fire. The hardship that may come your way early in life only builds the strength of your character. Once you've set your sights on a goal, neither hell nor high water can keep you down. LEO-Sags are walking power packs!

YOUR DARK SIDE

Being the activist that you are, caught up in your pursuit of better fortunes, you tend to overlook one important facet of life: your feelings. You neglect to take time out to examine your emotions of hurt, disappointment, resentment, and loss. You're so involved in the outward dramas that your inner life ends up sitting in the backseat.

So, what usually happens with this 2nd Decan is what is known as a delayed reaction. Out of the blue one morning, all those left-behind emotions come sneaking up on you and, wham!, you have to spend a week in bed, not knowing what in heaven has come over you. Everyone will walk around you on eggshells, helplessly trying to revive you to your normal enthusiastic demeanor.

What can be even more reproachable is that without even knowing it, you'll capitalize on their concern by manipulating them to take care of you. It can get so chronic that you'll quit your other projects, and fall into a pattern of dependence—the kiss of death for the Sag in you. While you freeload, no one will have the heart to give you the boot.

YOUR LIGHT SIDE

Without a doubt your biggest asset is your courage. Bravery is an adjective used frequently for all LEOS, and it falls with full force smack dab into your decan. The word fear doesn't even show up in your vocabulary. With the philosophical thinking that comes to you from your Sagittarian influence, you can literally reason away unfounded worries, saving yourself hours of wasted energy.

In the throes of real danger a LEO-Sag will almost get a rush of pleasure that he or she is being called upon to act with valor. With your ability to project power you can stop muggers and thieves dead in their tracks just by your presence.

As an attention-getter you don't go in for any cheap tricks or some of the other LEO decan ploys like posing and strutting. You go for clear, well-spoken oratory. Think of actor Dustin Hoffman (8/8), who seems inspired every time he opens his mouth to speak or makes a subtle gesture. As someone who requires attention, he gives all and more back to his audience. We're talking major chutzpah with this lion. Ever since his overnight-sensation film, *The Graduate*, Dustin Hoffman has told Hollywood where to put it. No one intimidates him! He's a star who delivers 101 percent of the time and gives the entire acting profession a dignified status. That's a LEO-Sag who'll be banking on the power of his decan for decades.

I'm not saying Dustin's personal life is always in the pink of things. Word is that he blows his lid at the most inappropriate times. Oh, well, as long as he keeps using all that stored up emotional energy for those magical film moments, we can hardly criticize him. After all, we aren't married to him.

BOTTOM LINE FOR YOUR POWER

All of you LEO-Sags could be living the charmed life every minute of the day if you could only attend to matters of the heart with the same verve that you do everything else. Learn to experience your feelings when you are in the moment instead of storing them up for a rainy day.

I promise you that if you take pains to balance your emotions against your fiery energy and courageous actions, you can achieve everything under the Sun. The universe will be your very own treasure chest. Oceans will almost part for you and mountains will fall if those are the goals you set. When you assemble all the inborn powers so that they work together, you'll become: a *Mover*.

BODY TALK

LEO-Sagittarians are a vision of physical grace. With LEO/Sun for vitality and Sagittarius/Jupiter for elasticity, strong hearts and lean thighs, you have the look and movement of professional dancers. Crossbreed a Lion with an Archer on Horseback and the babies are sure to be strong and limber all at the same time. You are nicely designed for sports-with stamina and competitiveness as ingredients of your horoscope.

You really don't have a vulnerable spot when it comes to health. Your heart is as steady as they come. You are usually moderate with food and beverages. Though you'll probably find yourself drinking socially, your LEO pride just won't let you become a sloppy drunk, and your Sagittarian independence will never allow you to become a slave to a bottle.

Similarly, you really don't have any one erogenous zone, unless your whole body counts. When you're on the move, your muscles are flexing and relaxing, or when you're prancing along in motion, you're turned on. And when you see another body moving with similar grace, your hormones start to flow. You don't mind being touched by that body either—as long as you're touched all over.

As resilient as you are, you can't become too confident of little things that may go wrong with your health. Don't run the extra mile if you haven't warmed up. Pulled muscles and thigh bruising frequent this 2nd Decan of LEO. Otherwise, count your lucky stars that you'll probably live in excellent fitness late in years.

YOUR BEST-BET CAREERS

Though most LEOS will dedicate themselves to one noble profession for most of their lives, you are not above doing a little moonlighting for extra dollars, or just switching gears midstream when the dice aren't falling your way. Tying you down to a life of academia would make you roar, even if it did afford you the opportunity to act as the authority figure you love to be.

As a mover, you're like the big up-and-coming one, the new kid on the block. You need challenge, diversity, irregular routines. You need an element of risk on the work front to keep your fearlessness in shape. You like a gamble–especially when it's with other people's money. Insurance sales and other speculative ventures will guarantee that you stay on your athletic toes. We know you love to convince others that you've got the tip of the day.

And speaking of athletics, you've got what it takes in performance and agility to score big in professional sports of any kind. Dance and gymnastics aren't out of the question either. Taking these fields one step further, many LEO-Sags have ended up in sports promotion and artists management. After all, whenever you are selling someone else—you're really selling you. As a 2nd Decan LEO, as much as you require attention, you don't want so much attention that you'll be at the beck and call of someone else—a situation you'll always want to reverse.

With the philosophical bent of Sagittarius in your decan, you could ace your way into a career in theology or religion. Giving a sermon on the mount is the perfect activity for any LEO-Sag, don't you think? Keeping vows of chastity might be difficult for you though, so stay with the looser sects, if you know what I mean. Even if this is not your chosen profession, you'll find that discussing existential issues is a part-time hobby natural to your personality.

YOUR BEST-BET LOVE COMBOS

LEO-Sagittarius Man: If you notice that most of your scores on the Love Scale are in the lukewarm range, I want to explain why. Especially you men. Your basic problem is that you don't take love that seriously. You love the physical part of love, that's for sure. But getting down to real deep emotions turns you into a jitterbug. You can ruin a perfectly good thing by suddenly trying out a new joke in the middle of ardent passion. And that's a surefire way to cool things off real fast.

You'd probably rather sing about love, preach about love, or just plain gossip about other people's love lives than actually be in love yourself. It always gets messy with you. You seem to be attracted to beautiful, dramatic women who do not enjoy sharing the spotlight with you. What you really need is a thoughtful, gracious belle who doesn't mind sitting backstage while you're out getting applause. You need a woman who'll take care of the bills, run the household, have her own career and hobbies, and who will still be fresh and ready to pamper you when you come home tired and hungry.

Because your blend is FIXED-Mutable, you'll find an excellent balance with a CARDINAL creature such as a LIBRA-Libra. She's a woman who will appeal to your philosophical tastes. Even when she's at the end of her rope with you, she'll never decide to leave you.

LEO-Sagittarius Woman: Why is romance like a chess game with you challenge-bound ladies of this decan? Is winning every match worth what you give up in terms of stability and long-lasting love? Well, maybe you haven't taken time out to examine the pattern that you seem to have set.

You love a high-spirited man, one who'll have a fast comeback to the many arrows of wit that you're always shooting out. You like your partner to be as ambitious and achievement oriented as you are; otherwise, there's no game of competition that you can play with him. And he'd better be as physically robust as you. When it comes to pulling down the covers, you like to get down to a real workout!

Ladies of this 2nd Decan of LEO aren't as vain as other LEO women. You're even something of a tomboy, preferring to spend your money on fast cars rather than new outfits. And cars can get expensive! Watch out for your inclination to hitch up with a guy's pocketbook without asking yourself if he's the one you'll want till death do you part. When and if the game stops being fun for you, you won't actually leave him, but you aren't above risking a little side action. As the saying goe—you have to pay to play.

If monogamy is on the top of your list of priorities, there is a nice way to solve your romantic dilemmas. Date and marry 2nd Decan Fire signs like yourself. These men are so familiar with your feminine wiles that they'll whip you into shape in no time. If you want ambition, the fiery ARIES-Leo won't fail you there. If you want fun and travel, Mr. SAGITTARIUS-Aries will have the agenda ready.

Lucille Ball (8/6) was a red-blooded LEO-Sagittarius woman, the royal queen of TV sitcoms. Talk about nerve. Lucy was never afraid to clown around. Why should she have been–that *ballsiness* of hers has earned her millions. She also wasn't afraid to hitch up with some very powerful men. She hit the jackpot not once but twice, first with Desi, the dream Latin lover, and then with Gary Morton, a prince of a guy. Lucy wasn't exactly the epitome of frilly femininity, and I'm not sure exactly what her men saw in her romantically. You don't think it was her incredible wealth and status, do you? Maybe they just wanted a woman who made them feel alive, and made them laugh.

DECAN PAIRS WITH LEO-SAGITTARIUS

LOVE SCALE SCORES

0 = Forget it! • 1 = Don't be a masochist... • 2 = Why bother? • 3 = Fun for one date. • 4 = It won't last! • 5 = You could do better! • 6 = Romance will fade... 7 = Great buddies! • 8 = Pure passion • 9 = True love. • 10 = Eternal bliss!

STARS OF LEO-SAGITTARIUS

August 2:	Myrna Loy
	Peter O'Toole
	Mary-Louise Parker
August 3:	Martin Sheen
August 4:	Louis Armstrong
August 5:	Neil Armstrong
	John Huston
	Loni Anderson
	Jonathan Silverman
August 6:	Lucille Ball
	Robert Mitchum
August 7:	David Duchovny
August 8:	Dustin Hoffman
	Esther Williams
	Hulk Hogan
	Andy Warhol
Augusy 9:	Melanie Griffith
	Whitney Houston
	Sam Elliot
August 10:	Rosanna Arquette
August 11:	Jerry Falwell
August 12:	Cecil B. De Mille

THIRD DECAN OF LEO

"I'M PROUD AND I'M VERY AGGRESSIVE!"

LEO-Aries	FIXED-Cardinal	SUN-Mars

With the 3rd Decan of LEO, I can finally use the cliché, "last but most definitely not the least." These lion/ram mixes are more Aries than they are LEOS. They want to be the king and they'll make sure you know that they're the boss.

If you have been both blessed and cursed to have been born a LEO-Aries, then you probably know what I mean when I say that you always get what you want. You are Demanding with a capital D. You are Daring, Driven, and almost Diabolical when it comes to achieving your aims. With LEO in Fixed motion, you are steadfast to your destination. You know how to pace that Aries/Cardinal impulsiveness. And if you do get a wild idea in your crazy brain, your ability to plan allows you to put it into action.

The word active can basically describe most facets of your life. The desire for grandness that can turn into delusions of grandeur for some LEOS is simply a channel for the Mars-given drive that characterizes your decan. You don't just dream of what you want. You build castles from sand and mountains from molehills, which in the end earn you bucks and recognition.

Unlike most LEOS, You don't need attention for attention's sake. What you do require is attention for deeds well done. If someone fails to comment on how tastefully you've redecorated your apartment, that person will not be invited back. In employment situations you don't give a damn if your superiors are impressed with your work. You want your bonus there and then, or you're out the door. Everyday flattery is spitting in the wind.

With all the emotional armor that you wear, you do have one vulnerable spot. Your love life can sap every ounce of your energy if you let it. While you're so busy winning awards in everything else you do, you seem to fail time and again at achieving a loving, stable harmony with one other person. Even though you are the last decan of LEO, you are still a dramatist, and the biggest drama for a LEO-Aries is in affairs of the heart. We're talking major soap opera! Whether you're making up or breaking up, it's constant fireworks with you.

YOUR DARK SIDE

Oh, how do I count the ways? Being proud and aggressive is almost an excuse for all the reprehensible little things you do. The fact that you thrive on competition means that inevitably you are hurting feelings, manipulating others, and being routinely inconsiderate of almost everyone else around you. Guilt just isn't a common emotion for your decan.

Yes, of course you push yourself ahead with a good deal of charm and political grace. You are, after all, a LEO. But the SUN-Mars combination in LEO-Aries often seems to exclude a moral conscience. Unless you work hard at being aware of this frightening shortcoming, you might be called the "hit and run" decan. You rarely take the blame for a defeat, whereas you're always claiming responsibility for a victory. When you have hurt someone else, be it lover, friend, or stranger, your response seems to be, "But I had to do it." At the extreme you'll lie, cheat, and steal, sometimes for minimal rewards.

Now, I hope you don't fall into the immoral trap that often, or ever. You still have to work on your lesser faults: impatience and greed. The list does go on, but I'll summarize by saying that your dark side isn't one to overlook. Thank goodness that you have shrewd powers of listening and observing. Let's hope you read with the same attention to detail.

YOUR LIGHT SIDE

What you may lack in ethics you make up double in pure smarts. You have the optimum blend of lofty LEO's broad-based knowledge and gritty ARIES' strategizing. This is one area where you are unusually modest. Your love of information may be self-serving, yet it happens to be exactly the quality that makes you so damn likable.

As interested as you are in furthering your multi-fold purposes, you are genuinely and deeply curious about other people and their cultures. Expanding your knowledge through literature, film, and travel is as important to you as expanding your bank account. Luckily for you they usually go hand in hand, as you tend to capitalize on almost every experience.

You are somehow able to extract the most intimate details from practical strangers. Talking to you can be a much needed relief for your friends and close relations. And, unlike many LEOS, you're careful as to how much you say about yourself. You're an excellent listener and you'll only dole out advice if it's solicited.

One of the positive aspects of your impatience is that you can't stand to see others wasting their energies. You have the ability to motivate the masses, to stir the spirits of those whose humdrum patterns aren't getting them anywhere.

With a life that's action-packed, and keen foresight that comes from a love of learning, you never make the same mistake twice—that is, if you'll admit that you do sometimes make mistakes.

BOTTOM LINE FOR YOUR POWER

LEO-Aries men and women are destined to leave their mark in professional arenas and on anyone who comes into their sphere of existence. You simply aren't someone to take lightly. If you can learn the higher lessons that have been laid out for your decan, particularly the lesson that not all means justify the ends, you will exceed your greatest ambitions. You will be recognized as an individual capable not only of accomplishing goals, but serving a greater good for all. You have the overwhelming strength of one who can make incredible strides and progressive changes. At your very best in your proud, dramatic, hard-driving style, your mode is as: a *Shaker*.

BODY TALK

With LEO ruling the heart and Aries in control of the head, You're just about all covered. From your nervous system to your cardiovascular network you are an excellent specimen of optimum health. You are able to put your body through rigorous pressure and come out unscathed. This decan is noted for long life spans, high tolerance to pain and discomfort, and brute strength. When you do get sick, you probably don't even realize it.

Do, however, check your blood pressure regularly. A LEO-Aries who doesn't need to sleep or eat or ever kick back can sometimes live for years without knowing his or her most vulnerable health areas. With the heavy regimen of activity that you put yourself through each day, that heart of yours is always working overtime. A weekly yoga class might be the perfect way to learn to mellow out now and then. Not that I worry about any serious health disasters with you. In this respect you're just born lucky.

What comes across to others is not only your tremendous energy, but even more so your physical confidence. Even women LEO-Aries will pose in a fighter's stance. The power that you exude just standing still attracts scads of admiring looks that you might not even be trying to get. So when you see a member of the opposite sex who interests you, stay right where you are. As usual, you'll get what you want.

And since you're such a control freak, you probably enjoy making love standing up. All you have to do is strike a commanding pose and the object of your desire does all the work, which I'm guessing is just fine by you, as long as you call the shots, right? Well, so to speak... .

YOUR BEST-BET CAREERS

When it comes to qualifying for high-profile, high-stress jobs in corporate big business, once again I'll say, you're born lucky. Particularly in marketing and sales, where your ability to outsmart the rivals is used to the utmost, you can find a happy, permanent working atmosphere. You thrive on the competition, you love the authority that you gain rising quickly through the ranks. Most LEOS earn well and spend poorly. Not so with you. A LEO-Aries is too aggressive to fritter away funds unnecessarily. At the same time, your LEO talents for drawing attention will get you fast notice from the minute you begin employment.

Your athletic nature can even lead you into careers where a fighting spirit is prerequisite, such as boxing and wrestling. I've hired several women of this decan for my teams, as a matter of fact. They love the performance aspect of the sport and they hate to lose. Which is all right with me!

Because the major fuel to your fire is information, which you constantly are absorbing, you make an excellent authority in history, politics, and law. If you elect to take a teaching position, do take care not to wound the feelings of a timid or wayward student. Sometimes your bite is as bad as your bark, if you know what I mean.

You are perfect as a skillful diplomat. Your LEO charm will have everyone bamboozled while you win every point of contention for your side. Sympathy for the opposition doesn't flourish in this 3rd Decan.

Many LEO-Aries folks are attracted to careers where fame is often a byproduct. It has to do with an innate understanding of how to make media work for you. So, even if you don't have a shred of artistic talent, your meticulous approach to business, combined with your need to be in the forefront of your generation, can land you a place in the sun in any of the fine and performing arts. You can stick a lump of clay on a wood crate and call it sculpture and pretty soon you'll be the talk of the town. With you it's simply a matter of will, and that's something that you're never lacking.

YOUR BEST-BET LOVE COMBOS

LEO-Aries Man: Has any outraged female called you a sexist lately? Well, if not, I'll have to do the dirty work, because in your heart of hearts, that's exactly what you are. You can't help fooling around, can you? Otherwise, how would you be able to uphold your reputation of getting everything and everyone you want? You'd like your woman in the kitchen rattling the pots and pans, while you're out on the prowl. And God forbid that she should try to play your game your way. The minute she even hints about having an outside love interest, you can't sleep, you can't eat, you think your life is over, you're ready to kill any man who would even dare to talk to her. My dear manly LEO-Aries, you've got a bad case of double-standard-itis.

When it comes to love you cannot have your cake and eat it too, something you get so accustomed to in other areas of your life. That's why you always seem to be in the middle of a chronic drama. During a business meeting at work, you have to leave the room to call the three women who are each independently preparing to sue you for all you're worth. And it's such a shame because you slept with two of them only because you thought they needed a little affection, whereas the third was almost your bride-to-be.

Often, when you tire of juggling girls like so many bouncing balls, you wind up in a relationship where your need for control is so fierce that the bedroom turns into a battleground. Oh, not that you're so turned off by a quick match of wits. *Au contraire*, you almost need combat to get in the mood to make love. A LEO-Aries macho male can make even the most defensive woman succumb to his every sensual wish.

My special love tip for any of you LEO 3rd Decans who have decided that you're tired of a diet of fast women and hurt feelings on both sides is: Meet and discover Ms. AQUARIUS-Gemini. This is a radical suggestion in that you have certain aspects that bring an ingredient of conflict to your union. However, her idealism will ennoble your character and her aloofness will always keep you on your toes. That little touch of Gemini in her decan will make her wild for you in the stack while you two one-up each other with verbal repartee. I think the expression is "tit for tat," isn't it?

LEO-Aries Woman: The male of your decan is bad in matters of the heart and you're even worse. As a royal LEO you've been a princess all your life and the Aries part of you makes you a terminal tomboy. You want to be treated like a lady, but you still want the freedom to go out and party down till all hours of the night. This is the dark side of your decan that has no conscience. It doesn't seem to faze you in the least that you have left a trail of broken hearts spreading out from state to state.

Remember the beautiful locket your first sweetheart gave you so very long ago? Probably not. Remember how crazy you were about your current beau when you first met him? Probably not. So soon you forget! That's your problem. When it comes to everything else under the sun you have incredible focus. With love you have a very short memory span. You're like a little girl in a candy store with eyes bigger than her stomach. Once you have every Joe, Dick, and Harry chasing after you, you don't know what you're going to do to get rid of them.

You probably don't create the dramas you incur with men. It's just that your strength brings out something primal in their behavior. You may tend to dominate in lovemaking, which often becomes what I call "athletic sex," making a weaker man unacceptable as an appropriate partner to you. Whether or not this is true in your individual case, I must stress that most women of this decan pride themselves in being excellent in bed. And they aren't just whistling "Dixie"!

Once in a LEO-Aries woman's life she usually gets her heart broken. It may be by a SCORPIO, or possibly by a TAURUS—the worst. Somehow, someone will hurt your feelings enough that you decide you'll do the hurting from now on. When and if you let yourself fall in love, you are intensely passionate and possessive. You demand fidelity from the man you do choose, and if you choose wisely you may even find yourself faithful to the right guy.

Please, dear God, make that man another Fire sign, and make him a 1st Decan SAGITTARIUS. He won't paw all over you. He may not even like holding hands in private. But once you pull down the covers, he's at your service. Literally! He'll love the fun and action that you love. His philosophical qualities will be a constant source of interest for you. As a gal who's used to getting what she wants, you'll find he pampers you without acting like a pushover. So, if anyone complains of not knowing what to get you for Christmas, ask for a SAG-Sag. That is, if you don't have one already.

DECAN PAIRS WITH LEO-ARIES

LOVE SCALE SCORES

0 = Forget it! • 1 = Don't be a masochist... • 2 = Why bother? • 3 = Fun for one date. • 4 = It won't last! • 5 = You could do better! • 6 = Romance will fade... 7 = Great buddies! • 8 = Pure passion • 9 = True love. • 10 = Eternal bliss!

STARS OF LEO-ARIES

August 14:	Steve Martin	August 18:	Patrick Swayze
	Earvin "Magic" Johnson		Robert Redford
August 16:	Madonna		Shelley Winters
	Frank Gifford	August 19:	Bill Clinton
	Kathie Lee Gifford		Coco Chanel
August 17:	Sean Penn		
	Robert DeNiro		
	Mae West		

CHAPTER 8

VIRGO

August 23 - September 22

First Decan	Second Decan	Third Decan
VIRGO-Virgo	VIRGO-Capricorn	VIRGO-Taurus
8/23 - 9/2	9/3 - 9/13	9/14 - 9/22

A VIRGO who was having a bad day placed a note on his desk and read, "I'm temporarily out of order."

Sign:	Earth - Attainers
Symbol:	The Virgin
Planet:	Mercury
Body Talk:	Bowels
Style:	Mutable

MEET THE CRITIC...

It's amazing that LEO and VIRGO who live right next door to each other are so completely opposite from one another. Where LEOS are all show, VIRGOS define pure modesty. Where LEOS sit on their golden thrones allowing the peons to grovel for them, a VIRGO can't bear to be waited on, preferring to serve rather than be served.

Though you're often quiet and thoughtful, you are rarely shy about expressing a personal point of view. You may not preach your opinions as loudly or brashly as a stubborn TAURUS, but you'll make damn sure to put your two cents in the record before the debate is over.

Mercury in VIRGO means mental organization. In contrast to fast-talking, breezy GEMINI (where Mercury reigns as well), VIRGO as an Earth sign uses Mercury to do meticulous, careful mind work. While GEMINIS command verbal communication, VIRGO is unrivaled in written communication. In school you probably won all the honors in reading, 'riting, and 'rithmetic. Unless, of course your service-oriented personality caused you to help all your school chums improve their grades and steal your thunder.

You are a genius at coping with zillions of boring little details and a complete devotee of order. You process, you analyze, you systemize. Let's face it— you're overflowing with gray matter.

Now, just because you score so highly with your intellect, don't start to fret that you're a total nerd. You can be fussy, finicky, nit-picky, critical of other ways of life, and sometimes even prudish. But you are not a nerd. Otherwise you wouldn't have earned the friendship and admiration of so many others. As irritating as some of your pet peeves can be to those who know you, your acts of giving are so impressive that your minor shortcomings are overlooked.

As symbolized by the Virgin, you truly are a purist-highly moral, wholesome, untainted, unwilling to be soiled by selling out to the status quo. VIRGOS are the boys-and-girls-next-door of the zodiac. You're Good with a capital G.

FIRST DECAN OF VIRGO

8/23 - 9/2

"I'M INTELLECTUAL. "I'M ALWAYS INTELLECTUAL."

VIRGO-Virgo	MUTABLE-Mutable	MERCURY-Mercury

All right, so if you've been doing your homework, which unless my name isn't Jacqueline Stallone, I know you've been doing thus far, you must know already that as a 1st Decan Virgo you have all the positive and negative traits of VIRGO in double force. You are the purist's purist. You are almost too good. You are almost too intelligent. You are definitely too critical. You could probably stand to take selfish lessons from your next-door neighbor LEO-Aries, who is clever enough to borrow some of your better qualities.

The potential power within you is obvious. You're smarter than the average bear. Your motives are never ulterior. As a Mutable-Mutable mover you have the ability to be flexible, to adapt to situations and problems that arise. In fact, your whole decan could be called the "Survivors."

And that's sometimes exactly where you get in your own way. You figure that as long as your mind is occupied, you'll keep getting the same paycheck every week, grumbling about how the system is generally unfair, but never coming right out and blowing your own horn. And then, because as an Earth sign, you are by nature an attainer, you become frustrated that you don't have the means to pay for all the finer trappings of existence that you really enjoy. VIRGO-Virgos may find themselves living Spartan lives, but believe you me, they hate it.

Now, let's talk about the purebred 1st Decan of VIRGO and sex. It is not true that all VIRGOS hate sex or even the mention of it. It is true that you place the act of lovemaking on a religious, spiritual level. A trivial romp in the hay is to you worse than being tarred and feathered. It is especially true for VIRGO-Virgos that you would rather die a virgin than sacrifice your body to someone with whom you do not connect intellectually. Hearing a brilliant idea spoken by someone for whom you care is enough to give you an orgasm on the spot—that's where your passion lies. And, if the object of your mind's desire tells you a great joke, your appreciation is enough to give back with tender physical affection. Usually, because you're such a hygiene fanatic, working up a sweat in bed only makes you worry about all the laundry you'll have to do. Oh well, just one more of those nagging details you're so used to handling!

YOUR DARK SIDE

As an individual whom I believe is basically composed of goodness, your dark side is not that dark. Rather, it is a hazy shade of gray, a space where your particular conflict is hidden to the untrained observer. Since I'm in the business of blab, I'll give it to you straight. You have a martyr complex. You do not relish suffering, you'll criticize whomever is dishing out unfair treatment. Yet, in your innermost self you believe that you were put on this earth to do good works and not to receive acknowledgment for your near-saintly actions. You sacrifice personal ambition for the betterment of others and then feel cheated. The only person who's cheating you is you.

Your given symbol of the Virgin, other times presented by the youthful Maiden or Lad, suggests your secondary limitation. Despite your already proven intelligence and your ability to solve practical and theoretical problems, you have a sometimes destructive blind spot. It is your native naive belief that others share your same values of goodness. You may be able to observe their shortcomings in character, but when they act with malice or ulterior motives, you react with total shock. In this way your perception of the world is unrealistic to the extent that you may feel chronically disappointed. So, you withdraw into your own environment where your innocence will never ever be tainted with the cold, cruel winds that blow outside.

Oh, yes, let's not forget your secret indulgence: vanity. You pray twice a day that you'll never wake up with gray hair or wrinkled skin. Though you're modest you do slave over your beauty regime. Trying to conceal the sin of pride now, aren't you?

YOUR LIGHT SIDE

Try to think of every book or theory that has been put forth about the power of the mind, its ability to heal, its capacity to transform the individual and society. Imagine then with double Mercury in your decan what limitless possibilities exist for you. Intellectual activity, knowledge, understanding, and truth are gifts you do not waste.

Waste is the great evil that you constantly seek to confront, in yourself and in others. The reason individuals of your decan are survivors is that you are unceasingly productive. Laziness, sloth, greed, and ignorance don't even appear in the VIRGO-Virgo dictionary. Above all, you will lament the waste of our greatest natural, national resource: our minds. Indeed, you probably were put on this earth as an example to others, to consistently remind us that mental flabbiness can be lethal.

Your critical impulse, which can annoy family members or co-workers, is truly an asset when expressed positively. You're able to spot and solve molehill problems before they become mountains. Being so aware of details, your meticulous analysis can unveil flaws in others, which serves to improve them. And you're no slouch on self-improvement, either!

BOTTOM LINE FOR YOUR POWER

The biggest task for any VIRGO-Virgo is to overcome the martyr syndrome. Just get over it! Modesty, when it limits the opportunities and recognition that you truly deserve, is no virtue. It's plain stupid; something you are not.

Claiming your moral, mental strengths will further you along the road to destinations that you may have only dreamed possible. You'll find a new kind of professional and emotional fulfillment that may feel so great, you'll even stop your fussing about the smaller, pettier issues that plague you. Once you have given to yourself, you're 20 times better suited to serve others. You will improve their quality of life and share with them your inner wisdom. You aren't a saint. But if you utilize the powers that have been bestowed upon you, you will become: a *Redeemer*.

BODY TALK

As you may have noted, VIRGO rules the bowels. There's nothing very sexy about that, is there? Not to be taken too literally, astrologers interpret this aspect of your chart to mean that your body acts to rid itself of waste. You are a cleanliness nut inside as well as out.

Your obsession with what you put into your body makes you the expert of the zodiac in nutrition. Now, I'm sure every once in a while you slip and throw back a few M&M®s, but you'll worry yourself sleepless that you've poisoned your purified digestive system. Nevertheless, all the fretting does serve a purpose. Your skin, hair, and eyes will most certainly shine with a startling, enviable glow. Your peers will all rush to the store to buy whatever products you're currently using.

I'm not here to embarrass my modest little 1st Decan of VIRGOS. So, please don't take offense when I congratulate you on your beautifully shaped posteriors. You've got cute buns and you know it, even though you rarely expose them for us to appreciate. If you think that I'm exaggerating what I've construed from astrological lore, you can test out my opinion. Go ask that someone special who saw you standing so demurely across the room what exactly it was he or she saw in you. If they don't respond that it was your darling, pinchable behind, they're not telling the truth.

You can also quit worrying about your health in general. VIRGO-Virgos may have martyr complexes but you rarely are sacrificed early in life. *Au contraire*, you're actually a candidate to become the next famous octogenarian. If you do tend toward hypochondria, rest assured that every little bodily ache or quirk you notice is more in your mind than in actuality. With the power of your thinking you're able to fight like hell any serious illness that might arise. Except for occasional bouts of constipation, or at worst a hemorrhoid or two, your decan earns a near-perfect medical rating. I'm confident that you're well acquainted with the purifying traits of healthful bran, in addition to all the various and sundry pharmaceutical supplies that you stock. Don't you just love Preparation H®?

YOUR BEST-BET CAREERS

There really aren't any professional options that are out of your league, because, in essence, you are a worker. You're dependable, resourceful, honest.

You enjoy tackling sticky, intricate problems that the rest of the crew has already clocked out to avoid. I would, however, recommend that you question whether your current employment offers you mental stimulation. If the answer is no, get the hell out of Dodge City before you get stuck in a rut that will only make you a nervous wreck. You must have a focus for your mental energy.

The skill with which astrology has blessed you can be perfectly used in writing, whatever the genre. As a journalist, you're able to organize the minutiae of the day into an exciting, coherent presentation. If you can be forward enough to ask for funding, you might write a book on any of your favorite subjects. A short paperback on diet or etiquette could be your ticket to success.

With double Mercury in your earthy Sun sign, you'll be a whiz in the physical sciences. From astronomy to human physiology to electrical engineering, you not only understand how all the tiny parts fit together as a whole, you are also able to communicate your knowledge through scientific writing and teaching.

Surprising though it may be to others who don't know you that well, your critical nature is not purely serious. Being Mutable means you are flexible, and nothing changes you more positively than a sense of humor, whether it's coming at you or from you. Careers in and around the world of comedy can be perfect platforms for airing your pet peeves with delightful details.

Whether you are male or female, you can rival any CANCER at housekeeping. "A place for everything and everything in its place" is your decan's motto. Your underlying sense of order combined with your Mutable flexibility makes you a superlative parent, and if you don't achieve widespread acknowledgment in a career, we can be sure that your children will usually grow up to be exceptional in whatever they do.

As a final resort a VIRGO-Virgo will always make an excellent nun or monk. With your subtle, smart wit you might just turn a dreary monastery into a chuckle palace. Remember, humor is divine!

YOUR BEST-BET LOVE COMBOS

VIRGO-Virgo Man: Heaven help the woman that falls for you and isn't completely perfect in every department. You won't dump her, you won't cheat on her, but you will make her life a living hell. You'll criticize her wardrobe, you'll point out the tiniest blemish on her otherwise fine complexion. You'll chastise her for her erratic eating habits, how she talks on the telephone too frequently for your liking. You'll think that her whole family should be sent to Siberia. Even though you'll approve of her earning a living, you'll ridicule most of her career choices.

So how is it that you manage to attract members of the opposite sex in the first place? The secret is so simple: you earn her trust. You don't court her with compliments, luxurious outings, and certainly not with romantic innuendo. You treat her with respect and genuine interest; you make her feel like a human being rather than a sexual object. Ingenious fellow that you are, you've just conquered centuries of most women's biggest complaint about men.

Once you have thus gained her deepest appreciation, she'll do almost anything for you, in or out of bed. If the truth be known you could get more women to comply with your physical needs than the bossiest ARIES. Thankfully your libido is not very strong; otherwise you'd stay in the sack all day while the ladies lined up outside your door. They just want to make you happy 'cause you're such a nice guy. So what if your moves are modest? So what if you'll only try the missionary position? It doesn't matter because your sense of duty is so developed you will never, never, roll over and snore before she's had her turn at pleasure. When a VIRGO-Virgo man says, "at your service," he means it.

When she discovers that you never liked her hairdo, or that you think she should improve her diction, her romantic stupor will pass. She'll face the reality that even while you are the most intelligent man she's ever met, you're also starting to sound like her nagging mother. At that point she will either take the next train to Brownsville or she will change you. And change you must if you ever want a chance at lasting love. You are made of double Mercury, you have MU-TABLE-Mutable motion, and you can ultimately rise above your pettier failings.

When it's time to put up the magnifying glass that you carry around looking at her faults, do it for another Earth sign. You'll do best with 2nd or 3rd Decans of TAURUS or CAPRICORN. My favorite for you is Ms. TAURUS-Capricorn. She'll share your perfectionist traits, and will warm up your surroundings with her love of beauty and humor. If you must marry another VIRGO, please let it be a VIRGO-Taurus. You need all the Venus you can get!

VIRGO-Virgo Woman: Before you start to criticize my description of your decan, especially the section on your dark side, try to remember the last time you had a relationship just because you were in love. I'm gambling here that many of you VIRGO-Virgo damsels are silently answering, "never." It's that old martyr complex that somehow in your busy mind convinced you to sacrifice your romantic ideals and settle for second best. Whether this is so in your case—and I hope that it isn't—I have observed that more 1st Decan VIRGO women marry or even date out of a sense of duty without asking themselves if they even like the guy.

Come on, admit that you want to please Mom and Dad by bringing home a suitable suitor, don't you? If he gets approval from your friends and relatives, you're so pleased that you stifle all your many dissatisfactions with him and label him Mr. Right. Wrong! In a worst case scenario you'll marry him just because he seemed as if he'd be a good provider, an honest man, a fine father. You'll grow old together in a kind of polite yet cold propriety where you never admit out loud that you can't even stand to kiss him, much less have sex with him. It'll be a wonder if you are able to bear him children, unless of course you close your eyes, hold your breath, and remind yourself that it's your duty.

This is why your decan has earned the reputation for being icebox women. In reality you are far from frigid. When you choose a partner who lights your mind, a cool current of electricity begins to spark. As a lovely, refined maiden, you certainly have no trouble attracting members of the opposite sex. Your semblance of virginal purity is a turn-on for almost every male personality. If only one of them is astute enough to find that special key to your heart, he'll be knocked almost senseless with the amount of passion that will emerge. You may not have experienced it very often, but I promise you that the tigress within can make one night with you, like a flight to heaven for that very fortunate guy. When he starts to call you "Angel," it's not because you were such a goody-two-shoes, believe me, honey.

With all the men who would jump at the chance to awaken you, the sleeping beauty, surely one of them can be your prince. You might just reign blissfully together for an eternity if he is a 1st Decan SCORPIO. For starters, he is a notorious schemer. He'll plot his pursuit of you with intense awareness of all the tiny details you hold so important. Being the secretive fellow that he is, he'll recognize your secret: that you're a little girl at heart. No doubt but that he's clever enough to treat you as such. His constant emotionally charged search for all of life's answers will supply you with enough food for thought to last a life-time. You may even end up matching his sex drive. If you don't, he'll just have to give you a little spanking, something I've heard VIRGO-Virgo girls tend to enjoy now and then. Don't worry, we all know with you it's just innocent fun!

DECAN PAIRS WITH VIRGO-VIRGO

VIRGO-Virgo	&		
		ARIES-Aries (3/21-3/30)	2
		ARIES-Leo (3/31-4/9)	1
		ARIES-Sagittarius (4/10-4/20)	5
		TAURUS-Taurus (4/21-4/30)	7
		TAURUS-Virgo (5/1-5/10)	8
		TAURUS-Capricorn (5/11-5/20)	9
		GEMINI-Gemini (5/21-5/31)	1
		GEMINI-Libra (6/1-6/10)	2
		GEMINI-Aquarius (6/11-6/20)	2
		CANCER-Cancer (6/21-7/1)	8
		CANCER-Scorpio (7/2-7/12)	9
		CANCER-Pisces (7/13-7/22)	5
		LEO-Leo (7/23-8/1)	4
		LEO-Sagittarius (8/2-8/12)	2
		LEO-Aries (8/13-8/22)	2
		VIRGO-Virgo (8/23-9/3)	5
		VIRGO-Capricorn (9/4-9/13)	6
		VIRGO-Taurus (9/14-9/22)	7
		LIBRA-Libra (9/23-10/3)	4
		LIBRA-Aquarius (10/4-10/13)	6
		LIBRA-Gemini (10/14-10/22)	3
		SCORPIO-Scorpio (10/23-11/2)	9
		SCORPIO-Pisces (11/3-11/12)	6
		SCORPIO-Cancer (11/13-11/22)	9

LOVE SCALE SCORES

0 = Forget it! • 1 = Don't be a masochist... • 2 = Why bother? • 3 = Fun for one date. • 4 = It won't last! • 5 = You could do better! • 6 = Romance will fade... 7 = Great buddies! • 8 = Pure passion • 9 = True love. • 10 = Eternal bliss!

STARS OF VIRGO-VIRGO

August 23:	Shelley Long
	River Phoenix
	Rick Springfield
August 24:	Steve Guttenberg
	Marlee Matlin
August 25:	Clara Bow
	Sean Connery
	Tom Skerritt
	Billy Ray Cyrus
	Blair Underwood
	Claudia Schiffer
August 26:	Macaulay Culkin
August 27:	Pee-Wee Herman
August 28:	Emma Samms
	Jason Priestley
August 29:	Richard Gere
	Ingrid Bergman
	Rebecca DeMornay
	Michael Jackson
August 31:	Van Morrison
	Chris Tucker
September 1:	Lily Tomlin
	Gloria Estefan
September 2:	Keanu Reeves

SECOND DECAN OF VIRGO

9/3 - 9/13

"I'M INTELLECTUAL AND I'M VERY MASTERFUL."

VIRGO-Capricorn	MUTABLE-Cardinal	MERCURY-Saturn

Forget what I ever said about 2nd Decans usually being the more balanced, conservative members of their Sun sign. VIRGO spiced with Capricorn during this period only makes all your personality traits that much more extreme. You seem to operate in two modes and you will continuously confuse others around you by the inconsistency.

What determines those two modes of behavior is whether you feel you are successful. When fast, mental Mercury is mixed with toiling, severe Saturn, you will either emerge as an excessive overachiever or as an abysmal failure. There doesn't seem to be any earth between those two states. When you feel that you are doing your absolute best in every department, from love to work to recreation, you adore the world and everyone in it. When you think that you've failed, even if it is at the most trivial pursuit, you're ready to write your will, throw in the towel, and check out. It shouldn't come as a shock that VIRGO-Capricorns have more nervous breakdowns than even, the most emotionally erratic Water sign decans.

But the news isn't all bad. The inborn need you have to excel intellectually will frequently propel you into positions of influence that other VIRGOS are simply too modest to occupy. The martyr complex isn't your cross to bear, thank goodness. Your mental powers are so obvious to others that even in your soft-spoken way, you'll attract crowds of the wittiest, most charming followers who'll be buttering you up for your approval.

Many VIRGO-Caps take forever deciding who they want to be when they grow up, following that Mutable pattern of changing approach and direction. Once you discover the pursuit that is truly right for you, however, you'll shoot straight to the top with a Cardinal velocity that you can handle. Fear of success is not your particular problem. Learning to take risks is, however, a lesson you may have skipped during your extensive education.

The foregoing can also apply to your love life. You may tend to have several relationships that fall flat on their face before the right guy or gal comes along. You'll no doubt blame yourself and conclude that you're a total loser as a lover. Not so at all. You just have to take the risk, and roll with the punches. As the saying goes, "You'll kiss a lot of frogs before you find your prince or princess."

YOUR DARK SIDE

In addition to some of the more typical VIRGO annoyances that haven't been left out of this 2nd Decan, such as your ultra critical views and worrying yourself stupid over hypotheses that are beyond your control, you also must contend with being your own worst critic and placing near impossible standards of success for yourself.

And those problems are minor! I do feel badly for all you dear Virgin Goats, but I must reveal to you that underneath your outward good humor, which you cultivate so successfully, is a morose strain of negativity. Remember Murphy who authored Murphy's Laws? Murphy must have been a member of your decan because only a VIRGO-Capricorn could have written, "If something can go wrong, it will." With your mind constantly assessing the potential damages, it's very hard for you to relax and enjoy life, even when you're operating in "success mode."

Very few others really know what shaky ground you walk on, because your pure ethics won't allow you to dump on a friend. So you walk around with bottled-up fears and woes, and nobody can come to your rescue unless you're willing to reach out and borrow a shoulder.

Just for good measure, I'll throw in one more pitfall that you can use your fine mind to analyze. Your decan is populated by intellectual snobs. You place the value of mental superiority so high that you may miss out on experiences with wonderful individuals who for lack of a better education, or a fancier vocabulary, somehow couldn't measure up to your taste. I'll bet you even had to sneak out to a bookstore where the salespeople didn't know you just to buy this book! Oh, yes, I know, you usually prefer to read the classics. That's okay, you can hide my book behind your copy of War and Peace, I don't mind.

YOUR LIGHT SIDE

Now that I've put you through the ringer, you're probably going to head straight to the nearest shrink to help you overcome your attack of astrological failure. Wait before you spend unnecessary dollars, something most VIRGO-Caps loathe. For every raking over the coals that you do to yourself, you make up doubly in goodness with your treatment of others. You'll walk a mile out of your way not to hurt someone's feelings. You may not spill your guts to anyone, but you'll stay up all night long with troubled friends listening to their miseries.

When it comes to problems of another your mind acts in such an integrated manner-evaluating the practical and emotional issues at hand. You'd qualify as a professional psychiatrist even if you'd never earned a degree.

Your constant effort to hide your internal gloom does have a positive effect, which is the peculiar VIRGO-Capricorn sense of humor. Not quite as pure or as innocent as VIRGO-Virgo, or as teasing as VIRGO-Taurus, yours is dark humor, slightly sarcastic and dry, but never spiteful. Remember, it's important to you to be masterful at everything you try, including your joke delivery. You make the perfect "straight guy," with those delightful deadpan expressions. It's his offhanded genius remarks that get all the laughs. Whether or not comedy is on your current ambition list it is one activity that you're successful doing even on a personal level.

VIRGO-Capricorn really translates as a young goat. You are a kid at heart, fond of puzzles, entertaining projects, treasure hunts, fascinating new scientific information. You love any kind of mental athletics, as long as you feel you're winning!

BOTTOM LINE FOR YOUR POWER

The prescription for happiness for VIRGO-Capricorns is so basic that you may have passed it by. Look in the mirror and tell yourself that you already are a super-success and you'll be amazed to find that those doldrum fears will vanish into thin air. Lighten up and give yourself a break today and every day.

Learn also to prioritize. You don't have to be masterful at everything; you do have to recognize your staggering talents in the few areas that are important to you. If you follow that advice, you'll see that failure transforms to victory with very little effort on your part. You won't have to blow your own horn, you won't have to bust your chops.

For your decan you just have to trust that you have it all and you will. With mastery and clarity of vision, you'll improve everyone with whom you come in contact as: a *Purifier*.

BODY TALK

You suffer from the reverse problem of VIRGO-Virgo's hypochondriac syndrome. When it comes to nagging little body messages, you're in a state of denial. If your children or spouse complain of mild cold symptoms, you dispatch them off to the doctor, *tout de suite*. But you have to be on your deathbed before you'll consult with a physician. That's how much you hate strangers touching you! You'll read up on diet and nutrition, you'll insist that your family eat three square meals a day, but you convince yourself that you are exempt from average daily requirements. You would go without eating for days just to prove that you're not giving power to food and then overeat for weeks with the same rationalization. Then, when you end up with stomach cramps or extra unwanted pounds, you can't imagine what caused them.

Remember you're the kid, the young goat? You may want to deny this, but unless you've been to dancing class lately, you're probably just a bit of a klutz. While CAPRICORN rules the knees, and VIRGO the bowels and posterior, I'm guessing that scraped knees and bruised butts are an almost daily occurrence for you. Admit that you once tried to ski down the expert slope before you'd ever tried the beginner run. I suppose for you to learn your lesson you had to take that spill down the mountain!

I could write a choice chapter on your prudish physical habits. One idiosyncrasy I must mention now is your sensitive, ticklish, delightful belly button. Yes, indeed, VIRGO-Caps have cute navels. How typical of you to hide your erogenous zone from public view. I have heard that when you and your true love go lint-picking it's like a religious experience.

YOUR BEST-BET CAREERS

Both of the other two decans of VIRGO approach most jobs with a sense of commitment and duty. Not so with your mix of Mercury and Saturn. There, are some professions that are beneath you, and you know it. Not only do you require mental stimulation, you also must have at least a degree of recognition for what you do. If you don't receive it, or if you're working too quietly behind the scenes, you'll never get over being self-critical. You have to prove your mastery at some juncture, so low-level desk jobs just won't keep a VIRGO-Cap punching the clock.

Speaking of time, your devotion to punctuality can lend itself to prominence in fields where scheduling, statistical charting, and transportation control are top activities. In commerce your position is usually second-in-command, keeping a sharp eye on everyone else's productivity. Speaking of understanding time and its cycles, I will predict that a VIRGO-Capricorn is bound to discover a new fail-safe birth control method, something that isn't as impossible as pure abstinence.

As I said earlier, you are the shrinks of the zodiac. Your powerful mind is always in the state of self-analysis, anyway, so why not let it earn you dollars with a career in psychiatry? So what if you have had psychological lows of your own?

As a purifier your intent should be to better the minds of those around you. Teaching and writing about self-improvement will also serve your need to give of yourself to society at large. Even if education isn't your profession, you may teach a class on the side for extra income. No one really knows where VIRGO-Caps' money goes. You don't deny the importance of a cash flow, and you can even be tightfisted lending it out. Certainly you don't have any trouble earning it, not with your masterful devices. But when it all comes down to "who has the bucks," you end up showing your empty pockets. For gosh sakes, you are a kid at heart.

YOUR BEST-BET LOVE COMBOS

VIRGO-Capricorn Man: If it weren't for the fact that you have such a good sense of humor, my analysis of you male VIRGO 2nd Decaners might inflict a serious inferiority complex on you. And that's exactly the point: though you really don't enjoy adapting yourself to just any woman, it's so important to you to feel successful that you'll put up aid put out just to earn a top rating.

Aren't women always gasping that they've never had a man like you'? Don't you just feel terrific when you're receiving a favorable review? What concerns me is that most of you men aren't really genuine in your pursuit. You may actually be better off staying single until the one who does make your heart beat and your temperature rise comes along. Otherwise, the whole time that you're earning the reputation for being a fabulous ladies' man, you're silently developing a disdain for the opposite sex. My advice to you is to quit trying to be the stud that you are not and wait before you leap into the next bed. You'll find that as a single fellow you're much happier reading your highbrow literature or seeing the latest new work of theater than trying to make any old gal think you're God's gift. It just doesn't cut the mustard—witty, warm, ambitious. you are; Tarzan of the Apes, you ain't.

So, give yourself time to meet the pure vision of your dreams who'll really appreciate all those fancy moves you've been practicing. You see, what usually happens with VIRGO-Cap men is that you harbor a mental image of the ideal woman, against which all other women can only fail. You may not criticize them outright, nag, or complain, but inwardly you'll be in a chronic state of disappointment. No one will ever measure up to that impossible standard. When your perfect other does walk in the door you're so love weary that you don't take a chance on her, and love just passes you by.

If you care to avoid that tragic fate, and if you can give up your silly efforts to be the greatest lover of the century, let's hope you find a 1st Decan SCORPIO. She will teach you lessons you can't learn in books, and still be intelligent enough to utter three-syllable words when you undress her. It's an astrological magical mix. And for all the badmouthing I've done to your decan, I will add that once committed, VIRGO-Cap men are masters at fidelity. A SCORPIO-Scorpio woman will take you for keeps.

VIRGO-Capricorn Woman: You've got one of the same nonproductive patterns as your male counterpart. You fall in love with the idea of love. Yet, when it comes to the serious business of maintaining a relationship it all becomes just too emotional for you. You find yourself becoming morose, moody, missing the old girlish, achievement-oriented you.

Or worse, some of you Virgin Goat-Maidens fall in love with impossible, unavailable men. You may have a deep, intense crush on a celebrity who is far beyond your grasp. You'll wish for suave, debonair knights in shining armor and in reality all the dudes you meet are duds.

Now, we've already established that VIRGO-Virgo women can be wildcats given the proper circumstances. I'm sorry to say that I can't give you the same hope. The adjectives prude, prim, proper hit 2nd Decan VIRGO ladies smack on the heads. At best you might risk being coyly playful in bed, but you'll never completely shake your extreme physical modesty. You don't mind sexual innuendo as long as it isn't being aimed at you. I bet you've even slapped a few cheeks for references that you weren't ready to accept. But stop feeling so failed— men go crazy for your unavailability. When and if some lucky guy gets you to turn off the lights and pull up the covers, your delicate touch will drive him wild.

Aside from living the single life, which may indeed be the path you'll choose, rather than sacrificing your "virtue" to Mr. Wrong, you can find another option in astrology. Try for a 3rd Decan PISCES. He's a tough nut to crack, if you know what I mean. It won't be easy to pin this dreaming, wafting man down but, after all, going after the impossible comes naturally to your decan. After you've reeled this male fish in, you'll be showing him off to all your ultra-smart girlfriends. They'll wish they could catch one, too!

DECAN PAIRS WITH VIRGO-CAPRICORN

```
TAURUS-Capricorn (5/11-5/20) ................. 8
GEMINI-Gemini (5/21-5/31) ..................... 3
GEMINI-Libra (6/1-6/10) ....................... 3
GEMINI-Aquarius (6/11-6/21) ................... 3
CANCER-Cancer (6/21-7/1) ...................... 6
CANCER-Scorpio (7/2-7/12) ..................... 7
CANCER-Pisces (7/13-7/22) ..................... 5
LEO-Leo (7/23-8/1) ............................ 5
LEO-Sagittarius (8/2-8/12) .................... 4
LEO-Aries (8/13-8/22) ......................... 6
VIRGO-Virgo (8/23-9/3) ........................ 6
VIRGO-Capricorn (9/4-9/13) .................... 6
VIRGO-Taurus (9/14-9/22) ...................... 8
LIBRA-Libra (9/23-10/3) ....................... 4
LIBRA-Aquarius (10/4-10/13) ................... 6
LIBRA-Gemini (10/14-10/22) .................... 4
SCORPIO-Scorpio (10/23-11/2) .................. 9
SCORPIO-Pisces (11/3-11/12) ................... 6
SCORPIO-Cancer (11/13-11/22) .................. 6
SAGITTARIUS-Sagittarius (11/23-12/2) ......... 2
SAGITTARIUS-Aries (12/3-12/11) ............... 3
SAGITTARIUS-Leo (12/12-12/21) ................ 4
CAPRICORN-Capricorn (12/22-12/31) ...... 7
CAPRICORN-Taurus (1/1-1/10) .................. 8
CAPRICORN-Virgo (1/11-1/19) .................. 7
AQUARIUS-Aquarius (1/20-1/29) ............... 7
AQUARIUS-Gemini (1/30-2/8) ................... 5
AQUARIUS-Libra (2/9-2/18) .................... 3
PISCES-Pisces (2/19-2/29) .................... 5
PISCES-Cancer (3/1-3/10) ..................... 7
PISCES-Scorpio (3/11-3/20) ................... 9
```

LOVE SCALE SCORES

0 = Forget it! • 1 = Don't be a masochist... • 2 = Why bother? • 3 = Fun for one date. • 4 = It won't last! • 5 = You could do better! • 6 = Romance will fade... 7 = Great buddies! • 8 = Pure passion • 9 = True love. • 10 = Eternal bliss!

STARS OF VIRGO-CAPRICORN

September 3:	Charlie Sheen	September 8:	Patsy Cline
September 5:	Raquel Welch	September 9:	Hugh Grant
	Jesse James	September 11:	Kristy McNichol
September 6:	Rosie Perez	September 13:	Claudette Colbert

THIRD DECAN OF VIRGO

"I'M INTELLECTUAL BUT I'M ALSO MATERIALISTIC."

VIRGO-Taurus	MUTABLE-Fixed	MERCURY-Venus

B y the time the Sun is nearing the end of its sweep across VIRGO and reaches the last ten-day period, its power is so diluted that many individuals born in this decan are rarely recognized as VIRGOS. You will more often seem to be characterized by Taurian traits: stable, solid, jovial. You can also pick up Libran influences in your creative life.

Don't think that you have escaped the VIRGO pitfalls altogether. Though you've cleaned up the nit-picking act established by the 1st and 2nd Decans, 3rd Decan VIRGOS have a vast reservoir of nervous energy that you've just become very clever at hiding. No one knows the extent to which you mull and ponder over this and that. You like to fiddle with ideas, take things or people apart and put them back together again. You're always asking the usually unanswerable question "why?" Thank the stars that you ask in such a sincere, loving way.

The blends of Mercury and Venus, combined with Mutable and Fixed motions, put you in an astrological position of good fortune. Forget the planetary lingo and just realize that your mix is all positive. You are emotionally evolved, in touch with your feelings without being a dishrag. You have good sense smarts and stay away from ivory towers. You are a happy realist with a deep appreciation for life. Even when events go awry, your perception of them leans to the interpretation that you just have another opportunity to learn something.

YOUR DARK SIDE

Somehow with your strong, zestful approach to experiences, while you're busy attaining more knowledge, you succeed at putting your nose where it doesn't belong. This is definitely not a trait for which we'd have you thrown in the slammer. Still, when you don't control it, others may tend to think of you as a bit of a busybody. Well, maybe a big busybody.

Prying and meddling into the affairs of others doesn't seem to hurt your overall popularity. What does happen is that you become responsible somehow for other people's problems. Once you've nosed around and gotten into someone else's dirty laundry they want you to help them do the wash.

A VIRGO-Taurus is spectacular at running his or her own life. Yet, you may sabotage all the excellent work you do for yourself by shouldering the woes of your friends and family. Give others a chance to learn from their mistakes and quit trying to be the cleanup crew incarnate. When you start to ask your regular list of "what-who-where-why's," stop for a moment and ask yourself why you're getting involved. When someone else asks you to climb aboard and help with their cause, use the popular retort, and just say no. Otherwise all your own plans and hopes will be put on the back burner, forever. You'll be tired and tapped out and you'll start moaning and groaning about every little detail that's been dumped on you. For the record I'll repeat: You brought it upon yourself.

YOUR LIGHT SIDE

As VIRGO "the" Critic, colored by Taurus "the" Trooper, you have been given a marvelous "Can Do" mentality. The goals you set for yourself are attainable and you usually have a workable plan to achieve them. When an unanticipated pitfall occurs, you are flexible enough to overcome it easily. There is an undying optimism about you that is neither false nor deluded.

Whether or not you choose an artistic career, which as you'll soon see is a perfect route for you, the arts will abound in your life. You lack the elitism of VIRGO-Capricorn so when it comes to appreciating the creative efforts of others you are a pure fan.

Also, being a *rubbernecker* doesn't have only its dark side. When push comes to shove, you will speak out against injustices that others are too meek to attack. You'll go to bat for the little guy and that's called being a hero in my book.

BOTTOM LINE FOR YOUR POWER

As long as you streamline your efforts, and focus on what you need to do for you, you'll have success every step of the way. VIRGO-Taurians do not have the reputation for being powerhouses. The secret of your decan is that you are. If you'll heed my advice and control your curiosity about the affairs of others, you'll be on your way to a lifetime of distinct achievement. Because of the good luck your birth period is graced with, abundance is your due. Riches and fame come to you for the right reasons because at your very best you are: a *Hero*.

BODY TALK

Breed a mindful VIRGO with a physical Taurus and the outcome is a youthful bull. If you want the visual of strength and eternal young looks, just glance at a picture of actress Lauren Bacall (9/16) at any age. What all of this decan shares with her is a hardy constitution and a superhuman immunity to anything that ails ya'. Where VIRGO-Virgos are paranoid hypochondriacs and VIRGO-Capricorns think that they're immortal, a VIRGO-Taurus has a healthy balance between those two attitudes.

You go to the doctor when you should. You watch your weight without indulging in fad diets or obsessive workout routines. The result is a look of natural beauty and fitness that makes your decan seem to have been born lucky. If you ever do incur a physical affliction, it may be located in your neck. That comes from your bad habit of sneaking peeks over everybody else's shoulder.

It's true. VIRGO-Taurians are body watchers. You're proud of your overall symmetry and love to compare yourself with the competition. In fact, many of you will meet your significant other out on the track or at the gym. You're not so modest that you'll deny yourself a good head-to-toe check of each and every one of the opposite sex that cruises by. Thank goodness you've already learned the expression, "look but don't touch." If you think that I'm suggesting you may have a tinge of the voyeur in you, you may just be right. Oh well, you're such a culture connoisseur, a little skin flick here and there can't hurt you.

YOUR BEST-BET CAREERS

Mercury for mental prowess and Venus for artistic appreciation means your most appropriate field of endeavor is art criticism. Write a review column or anchor a television show where you get to rate the greats of music, theater, film, painting, dance, or especially, literature. Your good-humored teasing won't bring you enemies, while your sheer intelligent taste will grab you a huge following.

In real estate and investment your talent for networking can put you at the top of the ladder. This is where being nosy does pay off. Knowing who's paying how much for what lets you ask your favorite question: "Why?" Then you make an offer they can't refuse.

Given your natural curious strain you may find your professional heaven in the theoretical sciences. You'll be experimenting and tinkering, deducing, inducing, and concluding to your heart's content. In nuclear physics, biological and genetic research, and animal behavior, many VIRGO-Taurus types have been honored with a Nobel prize.

Not that you have a problem with excessive worry, but in general you never need truly concern yourself about whether you have made the correct career choice. Like only a handful of other decans you will always gravitate toward making all the right moves. Also, as opposed to the other service-oriented VIRGOS, you make an excellent candidate for self-employment. Now don't get a swelled head; learning to delegate responsibility when you're in charge is still a big area for improvement for you. The phrase, "I'd rather do it myself" was coined by a VIRGO-Taurus, no question about it.

YOUR BEST-BET LOVE COMBOS

VIRGO-Taurus Man: I bet since I've said all these nice things about you already that you're waiting for the ax to fall. How right you are! You have everything going for you. You're charming, bright, suave, generous, romantic. You're strong, ambitious, usually heading toward success if not there yet. Why would any woman have to think twice about setting up permanent housekeeping with a catch like you? Why? Well, I'll be happy to tell you why. Because if you don't know every single little tiny detail of her every second of existence, you turn into an angry young Bully.

It's not so much about jealousy or being possessive. It's just your unquenchable need to know. If your loved one tells you that she's been out cheating on you, you're less upset than if she didn't tell you at all. If she somehow failed to mention a long-forgotten event in her past, you'll chastise her for hiding ghosts in the closet. For all your proven mental health, you can act like a real neurotic in the love department.

In the bedroom department you'll usually redeem yourself, thank God! You love to cuddle, kiss, and make-up. Unlike other VIRGO men, you don't obey all the rules of order. Nor do you mind working up a healthy sweat. After you accept the fact that a woman will eternally be mysterious to you and that you can't know everything about her, you'll relax into being a respectful teddy bear.

Please don't overlook a magical, mystical connection you could have with a SCORPIO. But SCORPIO women are so secretive, you protest. Take a dive into the cool waters of a SCORPIO-Cancer, a 3rd Decaner like yourself. You'll be surprised how refreshing her company can be. You both share an almost spiritual regard for the arts. If you don't actually go into business together, you'll still always be each other's soul partner. And when you want to take a few nudie shots of her, she probably won't mind at all–as long as you keep them for your private enjoyment.

I have faith that you're big on integrity, even if I don't have your exact dimensions in certain other areas.

VIRGO-Taurus Woman: It seems that with most decans astrologers are always cautioning: Don't settle for less, raise your standards, look before you leap, and so on. Now, you ladies of the 3rd Decan of VIRGO don't really need any of our advice. Mercury makes you analytical and Venus makes you romantic. Somehow you balance the two influences and never look at love through rose-colored glasses. When you commit you usually know what you're getting into and you do it for better or for worse. You may have a generalized cynicism about men due to one or two negative experiences that have rendered you extremely independent.

Your love life follows two routes. On the one hand you can opt for singledom, putting your industrious, inquiring mind to work, and forgoing the pleasure of companionship. As one VIRGO-Taurian lady, Greta Garbo (9/18) was known to say, "I'd rather be alone."

When you choose the second course, which is to find the ablest candidate for a union, 'til death do you part, you set extremely high standards for the man to whom you'll say, "I do." You are particularly aware of his capabilities as a provider. Some may call it "gold digging," but I call it "smart." If he comes with heavy credentials you'll offer in return a brand of feminine devotion that other men will beat down your door to try and find. You don't expect a free ride once you and he have taken the plunge. You'll cater and adapt and curtail everything you do around his needs. If he wants you in the kitchen rattling those pots and pans, you'll become a gourmet chef overnight. Let's say he prefers that you have a career of your own—no problem for you. Should he suggest you await him in the boudoir dressed in revealing lingerie, you're in the bed faster than he can say lickety-split.

As to your sex drive, you haven't been completely passed over by VIRGO prudery. That dash of Taurus in you does make you less inhibited than most VIRGOS. Still, you're no hot tamale. Maybe once upon a time, a fellow came into your life and got your blood to boil. You found yourself achieving a passion you'd never believed possible.

Unfortunately, that fellow didn't meet up with your detailed list of requirements. Instead of investing time and falling into a relationship that wasn't right, you probably moved on. Trust those instincts of yours you've got Mutable bounce-back ability, and a Fixed plan for where you want to be in life. As picky as you are, I can only salute you on your focus. My favorite saying, which I repeat at every opportunity to my children, is that there are two kinds of people in the world worth anything: those with commitments and those who want commitments. In marriage you get both!

I think a VIRGO-Taurus woman knows what I mean. And I also believe that a 1st Decan CAPRICORN can win her favors hands down. He'll make tons of money if it's the last thing he does. His volume of self-discipline outweighs that of any other man of the zodiac. His serious nature may not give you constant easygoing security, but if anyone can handle it, it's a woman of your loyalty. If he does get on your nerves briefly, just scoot over to your neighbor's and help her with her rocky marriage. Yours will seem like a dream in comparison!

DECAN PAIRS WITH VIRGO-TAURUS

VIRGO-Taurus	&		
		ARIES-Aries (3/21-3/30)	1
		ARIES-Leo (3/31-4/9)	1
		ARIES-Sagittarius (4/10-4/20)	1
		TAURUS-Taurus (4/21-4/30)	6
		TAURUS-Virgo (5/1-5/10)	6
		TAURUS-Capricorn (5/11-5/20)	7
		GEMINI-Gemini (5/21-5/31)	2
		GEMINI-Libra (6/1-6/10)	4
		GEMINI-Aquarius (6/11-6//20)	4
		CANCER-Cancer (6/21-7/1)	8
		CANCER-Scorpio (7/2-7/12)	7
		CANCER-Pisces (7/13-7/22)	7
		LEO-Leo (7/23-8/1)	3
		LEO-Sagittarius (8/2-8/12)	5
		LEO-Aries (8/13-8/22)	4
		VIRGO-Virgo (2/23-9/3)	7
		VIRGO-Capricorn (9/4-9/13)	8

LOVE SCALE SCORES

0 = Forget it! • 1 = Don't be a masochist... • 2 = Why bother? • 3 = Fun for one date. • 4 = It won't last! • 5 = You could do better! • 6 = Romance will fade... 7 = Great buddies! • 8 = Pure passion • 9 = True love. • 10 = Eternal bliss!

STARS OF VIRGO-TAURUS

September 14:	Mary Crosby
September 15:	Tommy Lee Jones
	Oliver Stone
September 16:	Lauren Bacall
	B.B. King
	Mickey Rourke
	David Copperfield
September 17:	Anne Bancroft
	Elvira
September 18:	Greta Garbo
September 19:	Jeremy Irons
	Twiggy
September 20:	Sophia Loren
September 21:	Stephen King
	Bill Murray
	Ricki Lake
September 22:	Shari Belafonte

Chapter 9

LIBRA

SETPTMBER 23 - OCTOBER 22

First Decan	Second Decan	Third Decan
LIBRA-Libra	LIBRA-Aquarius	LIBRA-Gemini
9/23 - 10/3	10/4 - 10/13	10/14 - 10/22

One LIBRA was overheard confessing to another LIBRA,
"Sometimes I feel bad. But I don't know when!"

Sign:	Air - Thinkers
Symbol:	The Scale
Planet:	Venus
Body Talk:	The Hips
Style:	Cardinal

MEET THE JUDGE...

"I'M DISCRIMINATING"

I like to refer to all you Librans as the "Cleanup Crew." Yes, it's true. Males as well as females of the 7th Sun sign are the handymen and washerwomen of the zodiac. Don't confuse yourselves with those overzealous nit-pickers born in Virgo. You see, when it comes to the fine improvements that you make in this world, my words are strictly complimentary.

Even the very sound of the name given to those of you born under the artistic, warm vibrations of Venus, is pleasing. "LIBRA" conjures up the image of free-flowing, peaceful airy climates in a Utopian world composed of goodwill and good acts, ruled by fair and loving creatures. In theory, you belong to that most ideal place, and the personality traits that you try to cultivate in yourself and in others are those that would be characteristic of individuals living in a perfect world.

Now, being the astute, mental Air sign that you are, you may have noted that I said "in theory." Your intelligence is of a kind that grasps concepts and broad-scoped abstracts that completely elude the feebler of mind. As discriminating as you are, you disperse with boring, extraneous details. Rarely do you get caught up with petty peeving like a certain neighbor of yours, whose cleanup act is performed more often with a mop and rag. Your tools are your well-recognized Scales, symbolizing to others your most positive attributes: honesty, fairness, justice; their opposites—dishonesty, greed, and corruption—are your public enemies. That's the dirt that you try to clean up.

What exactly you are always balancing isn't always clear, at least to others. Perhaps you are simply weighing all the positive possibilities and theories that you understand versus the practical and sometimes negative realities that you have experienced. In any event, once you have determined your answer, or made your decision, however long it has taken you in deliberation, you will stick with your conviction come hell or high water.

Remember, you are a Cardinal sign, one of the most disguised "sharks" of the zodiac. You go first class or not at all. You will knowingly step on toes if those toes are occupying steps on your ladder. Make no mistake about it, though you can be as loving and gentle as an evening breeze, anyone who comes up against you will receive a sound ramming on their head from your instrument of justice. Knowing how much you love laws, rules, and formalities, you probably have already procured a permit to carry your loaded gavel. You lady LIBRAS may have yours mounted on the wall for easy home access, while you LIBRAN men have yours conveniently tucked into your front pants pocket. That is what that bulge you males have there is, isn't it?

FIRST DECAN OF LIBRA

9/23 - 10/3

"I'M DISCRIMINATING. "I'M VERY DISCRIMINATING."

| LIBRA-Libra | CARDINAL-Cardinal | VENUS-Venus |

L et's talk about your VENUS, all right? In this 1st Decan of LIBRA, there simply is no escaping the powerful double influence that this planet exerts on you. Whereas VENUS in Earth, such as in Taurus, makes for an individual who beautifies surroundings and objects, VENUS in Air, which is your situation, creates someone who will eternally beautify thought. You know the old cliché that true beauty lies on the inside as opposed to the outside. Well, that notion only begins to describe the ideas of a LIBRA-Libra.

Don't get me wrong, I'm not suggesting that you are oblivious to pretty exteriors. Nor am I inferring that there's a chance that anyone would call you homely. On the contrary, most LIB-Libs are knockouts! When an ugly thought or word or experience enters your consciousness, however, your entire system becomes so unsettled that you have to retire to a peaceful, quiet spot and rethink the episode until it no longer pollutes your being. Don't you just hate swearing? Honestly, how often do you really use crude language? It would probably take a hideous circumstance to get you to even utter a four-letter word.

The key, as all you LIBRA-Libras surely must know, is: balance. You must forever balance on those Scales between your VENUS-Venus artsy, mushy side and your double Cardinal style that requires you to blaze your own trail into swashbuckling business and professional success. You need the parts of your life to be equal. For example, a thriving career will mean nothing to you without a flourishing love life. And there's a lot more that we'll talk about in those oh-so seesawing romantic dilemmas that torment so many of you in this decan!

YOUR DARK SIDE

The notorious downfall of most LIBRAS is simply the inability to reach a decision in matters of personal action. As usual, this tendency afflicts the 1st Decan most acutely. When it comes to judgment of others, of issues outside of yourself, no one can arrive at a verdict quicker and more decisively than you. But when it comes to important decisions that will affect you, there is a grave danger that you will get stuck in that process of weighing the alternatives for such a long time that opportunities pass you right on by.

Heavens to Betsy! Does this mean you can at times actually wimp out? Yes, sad to say, especially for someone like you who has been blessed with divine and powerful Venus in double strength. At the ultimate extreme of this negative bent, some LIBRA-Libras may risk sitting up on their fences trying to make a choice while not one but many opportunities fade.

YOUR LIGHT SIDE

From the moment of your birth to the last breath of air you inhale, you will be characterized most assuredly as a lover. Refer to the list of stars who populate this decan, and see for yourself how many matinee idols appear.

LIBRA-Libras shower love on friends and family with a seeming limitless supply. Your essence is pure; a potent core of love, harmony, peace, and beauty. You're the "Dr. Feel-Good" of the zodiac, with such highly developed social skills that you could rival any Leo at infinite charm.

Wait, your personality isn't just geared toward being a hit at a cocktail party. You also have an almost magical imagination, a perfect blend of artistic and logical thinking. When you do tap into your Cardinal rushes of ambition, you have the power to attract success as readily as flowers attract honeybees.

BOTTOM LINE FOR YOUR POWER

Using some obvious logic here, which is, of course, the LIBRA-Libra language, your most important objective is to get yourself off those mental Scales and into the heat of the action. Try not to be so judgmental; Don't spend your life balancing your thinking between what's right and wrong, just let yourself go! Follow the strong pulse of your instincts, which is usually so on target that you'll find yourself winning what you desire almost as easily as breathing in air. Not only will you achieve for yourself, but you will bring about positive results for those whom you love so genuinely. Whether you give unto yourself or unto others, your true power is as: a *Champion*.

BODY TALK

LIBRA rules the hips, so guess what? That's right, you men and women of this 1st Decan are pros at Hula-Hooping. You ladies probably wish you could calm your constant side-to-side sway. How many guys have gotten the wrong idea about your intentions just because you swished your hips accidentally in their direction? And you LIBRA-Libra gents aren't limp rags when it comes to thrusting yours back and forth, either.

With all that Venus of yours, it's no wonder that this decan is extremely fertile. So, of course, women are constructed appropriately for bearing children, and men similarly built to use hip motion to that end. Thank goodness both sexes are extremely discriminating in sexual choices. Otherwise, your whole life would be spent in bumps and grinds!

You probably do spend half your time thinking that you are completely immune to any illness, while the other half of the time you worry about all the ways in which you could suddenly drop dead. Surprise though it may be to you, yours is an extremely healthy constitution. Usually, you will integrate a heavy work load with ample R & R—something you require to maintain your desired equilibrium. You may also have a secret passion for gooey desserts that you devour in between healthful, balanced meals. While most LIBRA-Libras enjoy a caloric binge every now and then, and even more of you thrive in "hip" connection with a hot number of the opposite sex, I've never met a one who didn't love to sleep. Believe it or not, your expertise at napping has nothing to do with laziness. In fact, when arbitrating one of your many difficult decisions, you often find your best solutions just as you've laid your head on the pillow. Think about it, and see if I'm not right. Better yet, go sleep on it!

YOUR BEST-BET CAREERS

People who know you socially and consider you to be the ultimate in loving, thoughtfulness, and generosity, may not even recognize you when you are on the job. You're obsessive/compulsive, competitive, demanding, and aggressive. Sounds a little like your opposite, the Ram-rodding Aries, doesn't it? Although your sociability allows you to work with others much more harmoniously than the bossy Ram, your professional needs are quite similar. You like being in charge; authority makes you rebel. Nor are you strictly service-minded. Punching a clock and delivering work for someone else's profit will send you straight to the unemployment line.

Given all those prerequisites, a LIBRA-Libra is additionally versatile. You would fit in anywhere in the judicial system. We don't call you the judge for nothing! When you believe in your client's case, your skills as a litigator are extraordinary. Like your brash cousin Aries, you would inevitably rise to be the head of the law firm. Do consider both sides of the coin if you are contemplating a political career. Although your judgment of issues is excellent, your scrupulous ethics may soon be tainted by some of the sleazier methods now employed in most political arenas.

An interesting example of a LIBRA-Libra who had all the skills required for the office of president of the United States is Jimmy Carter (10/1). With his warm, genteel Southern manner, he seemed to emerge from nowhere and win the national vote. Once elected, however, he was unable to convince the country that he could put his beliefs into action. It is almost impossible for most LIBRA-Libras to be dishonest, and he was no exception. Unfortunately, telling the truth may have made heroes out of some, but all too often the victors in politics are those who know how to tell the country only what it wants to hear.

The need to "tell it like it is" or express your personal beliefs are only part of why you triumph in the arts. Whether in creative writing, theater, dance, film, musical composition, painting, you name it, you will most definitely "speak" your truths in ways that entertain, educate, and earn you an income. Where I discourage others from following an artistic path for dollars, I will insist that if you aren't in a creative profession that you pursue an avocation that uses your inborn sensitivity. Wasting Venus is a crime against nature!

On the college level, you're a whiz at instruction in the higher echelons of mathematics and history. A "Ph.D." is an apt addition to any LIBRA-Libra's name. Though you'll dish out heavy homework to your students, we can be confident that your grading policy will be squeaky clean and fair. No apple-polishing can get you to tilt your Scale! Wherever you do choose to go to work, please steer clear of this new trend in office romances. It's one of the perils of the trade for this decan. A soap opera on the job can short-circuit your power faster than you can fall for an attractive member of the opposite sex. As we'll soon see, that's where Cardinal velocity goes supersonic in all LIBRA-Libras.

YOUR BEST-BET LOVE COMBOS

LIBRA-Libra Man: The expression you probably like to use for women is that good old standby about not being able to live with them and not being able to live without them. With all due credit to your nature, I'd imagine that you basically adore the "weaker" (yeah, sure we are) of the species. A pretty face, a feminine touch, the sweet perfume of delicate skin, can send your thoughts into a whirl of romantic mush.

Not that you'll go for just any Miss. You are extremely choosy, so choosy in fact that many of your early picks are unavailable sex goddesses whose interest you've not yet earned. At the point where you finally have some interest that is reciprocated, you don't just fall for her. You dive into the love affair with so much fervor that the end result is oftentimes a crash landing. You hate feeling obsessive, you despise the fact that a mere female can exert so much power over you. So you may run the risk of feeling that all women are ball-busters. Little do you realize that it's you giving her that power.

If you must continue to put the fairer of the species (that we are...) up on a pedestal, put one of my decan up on yours. A SAGITTARIUS-Sagittarius is not going to misuse the power that you give her. She may require more independence than you'd like in your goddess, but she will always be honest with you. Her philosophical approach to life is the perfect match for your judgmental bent. And if your bedroom doesn't include another perfect bent of yours, I'd be very surprised. P.S.: You may appreciate the reputation she has for liking to ride on top. That's a position that LIBRA-Libra men don't mind placing their women in. It's a great way to improve your hip action, isn't it?

Just to illustrate what an excellent match 1st Decan LIBRAS and 1st Decan Sags make, I must mention that another certain-to-remain-nameless astrologer predicted that Latin dreamboat, Julio Iglesias and I would marry! Can you believe it? Even if we are astrologically suited, I wasn't about to hear him sing "To All the Girls I've Loved Before" to me. And he wasn't very keen on having me lump him in with all of my ex's. So, when we ran into each other, we both decided to call the whole thing off. Not that I wasn't tempted!

LIBRA-Libra Woman: Loving and lovable are only understatements for how extraordinarily, femininely affectionate you are. You adore kissing, touching, and cuddling as much as you require a peaceful, placid harmonious love life. Ah, but therein lies your conflict.

When it comes to picking out an outfit to wear, choosing a vacation spot, selecting what you want to eat, you give every option a thorough going-over before pronouncing your decision. That outfit is going to be smashing and stylish, the vacation spot a splendid paradise, and your entree an impeccable presentation. In almost every venue your discriminating mind is unleashed in full force. There is a huge gap in your thinking, however, a blind spot where all your wisdom seems to vanish into thin air. I suppose you've already guessed that it is in your romantic exploits that you turn into a major dumbbell.

A handsome male face, a manly arm around your waist, a deep-toned seductive voice, can all turn you into a babbling fool. Not only are you less than discriminating about his true qualities, you never seem to learn your lesson when he inevitably disappoints you. Catch him in a lie, or observe him behaving as an inconsiderate oaf, and you'll hop light up on your Scales. There you'll sit trying to balance his brutishness with all those cute and endearing come-ons that have bought your trust. You think that you can clean up his act, improve him, show him the light. Get a clue already, girl! These men don't change; only you can stop a cycle that will continue your entire life.

Remember your primary value: honesty. When a man tells you on a first date that you're the woman of his dreams and that he will be yours forever, just use your common sense. Don't let your beating heart and moist eyes distort his intent. He's just trying to get you into the sack. That's right, you are so naturally sensual, most men can't avoid using every trick in the book to get a taste of you.

If and when you're giving away more than nibbles, and want a lifelong love, I may have the answer to your dilemma. You need a charmer, a proud yet loyal romantic like you. You also probably will thrive where a man needs you to cultivate his better sides. The flawed but ultimately noble Mr. LEO-Leo could be just that man. Your soothing nature and his dramatic inclinations make for perfect balance. Don't trust his words completely, but do trust his actions. Turn out the lights and let Venus work her magic—on both of you. Even though you both love to sleep, I don't think that the sounds coming out from the bedroom will be just snores.

DECAN PAIRS WITH LIBRA-LIBRA

LOVE SCALE SCORES

0 = Forget it! • 1 = Don't be a masochist... • 2 = Why bother? • 3 = Fun for one date. • 4 = It won't last! • 5 = You could do better! • 6 = Romance will fade... 7 = Great buddies! • 8 = Pure passion • 9 = True love. • 10 = Eternal bliss!

STARS OF LIBRA-LIBRA

September 23: Bruce Springsteen
Julio Iglesias
Jason Alexander
September 25: Michael Douglas
Heather Locklear
Will Smith
Barbara Walters
September 26: Olivia Newton-John
Linda Hamilton

September 27: Meat Loaf
Gwyneth Paltrow
September 28: Brigitte Bardot
September 30: Eric Stoltz
October 1: Julie Andrews
Jimmy Carter

SECOND DECAN OF LIBRA

10/4 - 10/13

"I'M DISCRIMINATING AND I'M UNCONVENTIONAL!"

LIBRA-Aquarius	CARDINAL-Fixed	VENUS-Uranus

L et's return to my original statement that 2nd Decans are usually the most balanced of the entire Sun sign. This will hold true most definitely in the case of you "smoothies" born in the middle of the most balanced sign of the zodiac.

With Venus in charge of your never-ending creative side, and Uranus holding the reins on your practical, positive thinking, you are literally the happiest group of individuals under the sun. You attract success without having to race after it; you attract respect from other human beings and always seem to maintain a blushing modesty about your popularity. The Fixed style of your Aquarian influences keeps your Cardinal pushiness in check. Though some of your beliefs and practices are unusual, you are sensitive enough to know how not to ruffle feathers.

In fact, your presence is so pleasing, and your appreciation for the finer pleasures of life is so highly developed, you may find a lot of competition for your attentions. Well, it's not surprising. You offer refreshing, stimulating, sincere attitudes; you glow like a rare crystal with the joy of the universe. You're a precious and desirable commodity!

YOUR DARK SIDE

Your downfall, the real threat to your being the happy, peaceful, socializing, loving LIBRA-Aquarius that you are, is not so much in you, but around you. Remember, you are represented by the balancing Scales and by the Waterbearer. So, though you are choosy about whose act you're going to "clean up," you could empty that whole jug of water on some real losers.

My guess is that you are secretly attracted to dark, dangerous types. A natural tendency in astrology is for individuals to seek the quality that they most lack in themselves. Because you lack a dark side, you may unconsciously be looking for it in the friends you cultivate, the type of business in which you are employed, and even in your love life. You think that you can help the underdogs. You'd like to lend some of your goodness out, let others drink from your well of happiness. Wrong, my dear peaceniks. Wrong and sad.

Unless you have already become enlightened to this particular pitfall for you LIBRA 2nd Decaners, you may run the risk of trading all your precious powers for the hopes of rehabilitating someone who isn't ready to do the work himself. You'll find yourself with a fascinating, unusual throng of scum-bag friends! Being no dummy, you'll realize that you've been used and that, in a nutshell, is a common curse to anyone born under the most positive of all influences.

YOUR LIGHT SIDE

At this very moment, you're probably asking yourself, "Do I really let people use me?" And I'll bet that you are answering yourself appropriately, "Why, I suppose Jacqueline is right. I'd better do something to change that." Oh, okay, maybe you are using fancier language to express that basic idea. Lord knows you would never think or say anything just like anyone else!

At any rate, you are highly distinguished by your ability to accept criticism and then work to improve yourself on the deepest of levels. You are indeed progressive. Rarely will you make the same mistake twice. You don't pursue challenge for the sake of challenge alone. But, when you have chosen a pursuit that is difficult, you approach it with a special kind of joy that others find disarming.

There is also an indescribable quality in many LIBRA-Aquarians that magnetizes and charms beyond belief. Very different from that of the emotional stirred-up Water signs, yours is a look of ethereal, dreamy contentment. Why, it's almost as if you've just had a powerful orgasm, and you're in the afterglow of it, all the time!

BOTTOM LINE FOR YOUR POWER

When you have a guard up against those who seek to undo your goodness, you will find yourself in a constant state of walking on Air. Your popularity will then work for you instead of against you.

As you learn to channel your artful, individualistic talents toward the right ends, your powers will be as focused as the electricity that runs the international telephone systems. Your progressive ideas can change and improve the world as you bring about your greatest dream for global peace and happiness. On a huge scale or within your personal interactions you reign supreme as: a *Peacemaker*.

BODY TALK

As you recall, your symbols are the inanimate balancing Scales and the gentle human-bearing jugs of refreshing water. LIBRA, as we have already established, rules the area of the hips, whereas Aquarius has been relegated to the calves and ankles. How this translates in "lay" terms is that your graceful, mellow movements are both sensual and attractive. That aura of peace and your balanced pace can really trick others into thinking that you have been blessed with body beautiful. In reality, there are plenty of flaws that you've just become a pro at covering up.

For starters, you women undoubtedly retain water in certain places, much to your chagrin. They don't call them jugs for nothing! In both sexes of LIBRA-Aquarius, there is a good possibility that your posterior is, at least in your opinion, too big for its own good. I'll bet you are sick of getting pinched by greedy, hungry Crab claws. Disliking the flashy approach, both men and women of this decan are notorious for having all sorts of reductive cosmetic surgeries.

Privately, you may just want an excuse to meet a cute nurse of the opposite sex. Otherwise there's really no need for you to be dashing off to the doctor's office as often as you probably do. Being the balancer of all balancers, your approach is actually very healthy. You figure that you'd rather be safe than sorry. So, preventive medicine is a practice you don't shun. At the same time, you maintain moderation with your consumption of alcohol and gourmet goodies.

The best news of all is that the legs of most 2nd Decan LIBRAS are designed to be long, elegant, and limber. Your overall body tone should be extremely flexible. The better for all those unconventional positions you're known to achieve! Chinese splits, anybody? Attended any office meetings on a slant board lately? It won't come as any surprise to you that keeping up your supple elasticity requires that you have regular massage treatments. Well, they may be the closest thing you have to consistent exercise, as much as you probably dislike heavy workouts at the gym!

YOUR BEST-BET CAREERS

The most important issue for you to consider in the search for your perfect employment is that your brilliant talents not be exploited. Because of your warm, tolerant nature you could deliver innovative ideas to others for profit, while you toil away with little more than praise for your efforts. Make sure, no matter where you hang your working hat, that your superiors warrant the trust you give them.

With that criteria in mind, you might also want to make sure that your particular stamp of happiness is placed on any job contract you sign. Industries that provide enjoyment are excellent avenues for your spirit. Take, for instance, television sitcom writing or producing. Organizing charter air tourist flights to exotic destinations will earn you repeat business and allow you to exercise your vivid imagination. Or, put yourself in an artistic venue as a museum curator where you'll have visitors laughing while they learn.

With the Aquarian influence in this 2nd Decan of LIBRA, you may find that when it comes to employment you're at your best dealing with groups of people, as opposed to having intense little one-on-ones. In areas of social reform, especially in legislation, a LIBRA-Aquarian won't be afraid to take big risks for widespread, positive change.

Jesse Jackson (10/8) has established a whole new style of political rhetoric, hasn't he? With Venus and Uranus on his side, his eventual home might not be in the White House, but his career is far from over.

As the ultimate in peacekeeping, any LIBRA-Aquarian can score major renown in international diplomacy. On a less global scale, you're downright terrific in settling spats between neighbors.

Now, don't forget that your Cardinal style is best suited to positions where you do get a taste of public glory, whereas your Fixed methods allow you to work just as hard behind the scenes in research and planning. That harmonious balance actually makes you a fabulous career counselor, or corporate headhunter.

As with all LIBRAS, you need not turn up your nose at an artistic profession. Do, however, think twice before signing up with any fast-talking manager type who promises to make you a star overnight. Your success will be determined by your powers, not by those who try to influence you with theirs!

YOUR BEST-BET LOVE COMBOS

LIBRA-Aquarius Man: So far we've only been saying the nicest things about you Balanced Waterbearers, haven't we? Well, sure. You're nice, sweet, handsome, mellow guys, right? Of course you are, at least when your love life doesn't drop you on the hot seat. When it does, watch out! All that cool Air of yours can heat up to the explosive power of a hydrogen bomb. Or, at the other side of the Scales, your demeanor can be as icy as stinging sleet.

What can turn a happy, healthy bouncing boy like you into this ill-tempered monster? Your very own weakness for the unusual. That's right, you men in this 2nd Decan of LIBRA make choices that aren't just inappropriate for you, they're out-and-out outlandish! Admit that you have a passion for wild and uncontrollable women, don't you? Or what about that tendency you have for chasing after older gals—ones whose sexual appetite and experiences are more sophisticated than yours? As you get older this attitude might swing to the other side of the spectrum as you go plucking young, fresh daisies from flower beds long before they're ripe. Shame on you.

What is at the heart of these quirky customs is not so shameful. Simply understood, you are ridiculously romantic. Your unconventional choices are usually a result of sincere beliefs that you have fallen in love. Ironically, you pick the most unattainable women to love almost intentionally so that you can experience a sense of suffering when they inevitably reject you,

I say, get over it. After all, you're a sensible fellow and you know that strife on your insides can never be rationally ignored. When you outgrow your need to be the suffering poet laureate of the love set, you truly have all the makings of being the boyfriend of choice for just about everyone.

If you insist on weird, or still have to have a little roughing up, you'll probably do well with your own sign. And please, make her a 3rd Decan of LIBRA. She's out there all right, with a perfect mind-set for trying all those acrobatic positions of yours. Even trapezes aren't too much of a challenge for the two of you!

LIBRA-Aquarius Woman: With that ethereal, happy-go-lucky, spacey aloofness you occasionally exude, some men can mistake you for a bimbo. You may be fair-haired, but there's nothing dumb and blond about any women I've ever met in the 2nd Decan of LIBRA, one of the thinking Air signs.

As a matter of fact, you are extremely shrewd and have cultivated your aura of mystery to the heights of an art form. With Uranus coloring your decan, you will usually take advantage of any opportunity to snare the man of your choice. Playing dumb is just one of those handy tricks you've come to employ. Hey, more power to you. With your developed sense of justice, one of your favorite mottoes is "All's fair in love and war," and when you do care you'll go all the way to win.

Like your male counterpart, you too are capable of some unconventional choices in mates. Don't you get butterflies in your stomach when a man speaks with a foreign accent? Doesn't a tiny but tough scar on his face just thrill you to no end? Come on, I bet you love men with flamboyant mustaches. If he has a hint of a dangerous past you might just devote your whole life to reforming him. Do be careful not to fall into the role of Nurse Nightingale. Should he fail to mend his bad ways, you are even more likely to hand him walking papers faster than you can flip through the pages of this book to find out how low you score with him in the first place!

When you aren't romanticizing helpless derelicts and wasting all those clever feminine wiles of yours, you are infinitely capable of achieving blissful peace with the right guy. Your astrological solution lies in a double Mutable sign such as in the males of my decan. That's correct, a SAG-Sag is an adventurer of the highest order, and basically just as much of a mush as you can be. If you can curb his love of gossip, your private boudoir will be one juicy hot spot that the two of you can share, for a lifetime.

DECAN PAIRS WITH LIBRA-AQUARIUS

LIBRA-Aquarius (10/4-10/13) 6
LIBRA-Gemini (10/14-10/22) 9
SCORPIO-Scorpio (10/23-11/2) 6
SCORPIO-Pisces (11/3-11/12) 6
SCORPIO-Cancer (11/13-11/22) 4
SAGITTARIUS-Sagittarius (11/23-12/2) 9
SAGITTARIUS-Aries (12/3-12/11) 7
SAGITTARIUS-Leo (12/12-12/21) 7
CAPRICORN-Capricorn (12/22-12/31) 2
CAPRICORN-Taurus (1/1-1/10) 3
CAPRICORN-Virgo (1/11-1/19) 4
AQUARIUS-Aquarius (1/20-1/29) 6
AQUARIUS-Gemini (1/30-2/8) 7
AQUARIUS-Libra (2/9-2/18) 9
PISCES-Pisces (2/19-2/29) 6
PISCES-Cancer (3/1-3/10) 5
PISCES-Scorpio (3/11-3/20) 4

LOVE SCALE SCORES

0 = Forget it! • 1 = Don't be a masochist... • 2 = Why bother? • 3 = Fun for one date. • 4 = It won't last! • 5 = You could do better! • 6 = Romance will fade... 7 = Great buddies! • 8 = Pure passion • 9 = True love. • 10 = Eternal bliss!

STARS OF LIBRA-AQUARIUS

October 4:	Patti LaBelle
	Susan Sarandon
	Armand Assante
October 6:	Britt Ekland
	Carole Lombard
October 7:	John Cougar Mellencamp
October 8:	Jesse Jackson
	David Carradine
	Chevy Chase
	Sigourney Weaver
October 9:	John Lennon
	Scott Bakula
	Jackson Brown
October 10:	Helen Hayes
October 11:	Eleanor Roosevelt
	Luke Perry
October 12:	Luciano Pavarotti
	Kirk Cameron
October 13:	Paul Simon

THIRD DECAN OF LIBRA

10/13 - 10/22

"I'M DISCRIMINATING AND I'M CONTROVERSIAL!"

LIBRA-Gemini	CARDINAL-Mutable	VENUS-Mercury

Despite the fact that you are one of the stranger "mutts" of the zodiac, if you are born in these last ten days of LIBRA, you may also be one of the few true powerhouses around. With Venus for creative fuel, and Mercury for major brains, and just a touch of neighboring Scorpio's Mars for potent drive, your astrological constitution is the perfect makeup. Whether or not you will eventually achieve substantial success is, as always, up to you and what you do with your Star-given talents.

I like to call you LIBRA-Geminis "the multimedia" group, so skillful in so many areas that choosing exactly what hat you want to wear may be damned near impossible. We already have established that you, as a 3rd Decan are weird. Well, so what? You're also wacky, wild, and wonderful! You'll try any experience at least once just so you can sit back and weigh its value on your infamous LIBRA Scales. You never prejudge anyone or anything, and you fight prejudice as if it were your number one enemy. And yes, just to complicate the whole picture, don't ignore the fact that those Gemini Twins exist within you. They show themselves both in your love of verbal communication, and in the rapid pace that you, unlike most LIBRAS, are able to maintain for long periods of time.

You are also extremely impatient for a gentle Scale Balancer, aren't you, my charming Justice-loving Twin? You are generous to a fault both emotionally and materially, while you also can close both your heart and your piggy bank at a moment's notice.

As unpredictable as our nation's economy, you are never someone to be controlled by others. Just when your competitors think they have you beat, you bounce back with the most surprising new approach. Thank goodness that you consider the ramifications of your actions before you jump into anything—unlike certain Gemini types. However, you often find yourself the object of other people's wagging tongues. Don't let it get to you, you sensitive thing you. Just think like me and remind yourself that even bad publicity is publicity!

YOUR DARK SIDE

I've already hinted at two of your sorer spots. Don't think for a second that we can let those go by without a further investigation. Well, gee, haven't you figured out by now that telling people what's wrong with them is my favorite pursuit?

Now, don't get nervous, I'm only trying to soften the blow, knowing as I do how you hate criticism and/or argument—unless you're the one doling out the judgment. I am not suggesting that you're as weepy as, say, the Crab or the Fish, but you do get your feelings hurt on an almost daily basis. You can overreact ridiculously to mild statements of fact that you take personally. Let's say hypothetically that a stranger passes you on the street and points out that your shoelace is untied. You'll thank him politely and walk on, yet you'll spend the rest of the afternoon feeling misunderstood. You'll rationalize and fret and finally conclude that you had intentionally left that shoelace untied as a symbol of your individuality. If you ever see that stranger again, woe be to his shoelaces!

In professional situations this pattern can become even worse. You'll quit a job faster than a jackrabbit if you feel that you have been evaluated unfairly, In your love life you will actually choose a mealymouthed partner just to avoid a confrontation over your faults. What a pity that you've passed by potential loves who are more your equals in strength.

Second, any LIBRA-Gemini, as one of the "multimedia" group, has on one side of the Scales so many delicious and delightful and unusual talents, tastes, hobbies, interests, that the other side of you won't know what to do with all of them. You may be guilty of being a jumper, hopping into one pursuit only to bounce off toward another. Unless, of course, you've cultivated the fine art of juggling-and I don't mean tossing little colored balls into the air. Focus, planning, and patience are all lessons to which you will be constantly returning. Otherwise, your powers will be wasted and you may become the classic jack-of-all-trades, but master of none.

YOUR LIGHT SIDE

Even though you are a souped-up hybrid of influences, you will never escape your magnetizing Venus, which is your saving grace. As controversial as some of your behavior can be, your intentions always are born of love and goodwill. As much as you dislike having your feelings hurt, you would never openly brush up against anyone else's. I'm sure the great slogan of the 1960's, "Make love not war," was written by a LIBRA-Gemini.

Part of the reason that you are so hot on lovemaking is that the very act of creation is your driving force. Whether you are planting seeds in the garden, or watching newborn baby birds hatch, or bringing an artistic vision to life on canvas, you are always in your element. And your imagination isn't the only thing that's fertile, believe you me!

Your screwball sense of humor, together with your Mercurial traces, make time spent with you a super blast. Your friends may complain that they don't get enough of you, but you'll always make up to them in quality what you can't give in quantity.

Being a Balancing Twin doesn't just mean you'll have plenty of parts to your personality; it also allows you to have deep insights into human behavior in general. When you are in touch with your instincts you are capable of a form of ESP. In fact, dabbling into the supernatural could be one of your favorite hobbies, although I'd caution you against practicing professionally. God forbid you'd find out that you were unattractive in a past life! You see, you may be kooky, but you're pretty proud of being a good-looking kook, aren't you?

BOTTOM LINE FOR YOUR POWER

If you can only toughen yourself against the judgment of others, ever so slightly, you will discover that your greatness is for real, not at all dependent on the petty comments of those who are basically envious of everything you've got going for you.

Take that discriminating flair you have for style and expression, and make the big choice that is your worldly mission. Once you have decided what you want to be when you grow up, you can and wilt achieve it almost as if by magic. No matter what your specific choice is, the underlying purpose for this decan makes you the ultimate as: a *Creator*.

BODY TALK

Being born under a blanket of so many planetary forces, most LIBRA 3rd Decans are just as complicated physically as they are emotionally. Since you're so sensitive, I'd better start with the good news first for a change. The Venus/ LIBRA domination of the hips hasn't put yours out of proportion in any respect. You might even take the famous Cupid as your decan's look-alike emblem. Guys and gals alike will have the cutest, curviest, cuddliest figures around. That's why strangers are always making passes at you. To make you even more tempting, you probably also have those fabulous blushing Cupid lips brought to you by your Gemini strains.

So how do you like that? I hope you do, because you're not going to like my little lecture on your unfavorable features. Perhaps you've already worked hard to avoid yours, but astrological rumors say that your arms and hands have wills of their own. When they want to be flabby and/or grabby, that's exactly what they'll do. I've seen a few LIB-Gem men try to develop their upper arms with weight lifting and, well, I guess I could have given them A's for effort. You women probably try to disguise your funny, childlike hands with manicures, which results in little or no alteration. Just keep your hands in your pockets and they'll never know the difference!

As balanced and healthful as you try to make your diet and sleep regime, you may be experiencing bizarre medical problems such as chronic fatigue or mysterious headaches. Before you spend thousands of dollars on scads of specialists, do visit a neurologist. Nervous disorders run in your zodiac "family," but they are usually not serious. Within no time you'll be back to your familiar ways, jumping into this activity and that, traipsing your adorable bod to and fro. Formal exercise may not be your forte, but you'll still bum loads of calories in all your comings and goings. If you get my drift!

YOUR BEST-BET CAREERS

Telling you where you should go to work is almost as hard for me as it is for you to decide what your best professional assets are. By all means take my suggestions to heart, but don't pull a typical LIBRA-Gemini stunt by trying all seven at once. Pretty please.

Start with the media and see how far that will get you. Far, indeed, if you throw your energies into promotion, public relations, and publicity, particularly when your clients are in a creative field. Or just go out and sell yourself as an interesting, controversial personality. You'll end up on the talk-show circuit for life.

In communication you've got a whole menu of options. Your verbal skills are so plentiful that you're a shoo-in for teaching the classical and Romance languages. With all your human ESP, you could even communicate in unusual fashion such as with mime, or working with the hearing impaired.

We haven't really discussed how money affects the 1st and 2nd Decans of LIBRA, because money simply isn't a big issue for them. Sure, they're happy to have it when it is a by-product of work well done. Both the LIBRA-Libra gang and the LIBRA-Aquarians are temperate with spending. Not so with my zany 3rd Decans. You folks love making money not because you've invested it with any special status power, but because it's a game for you. And you play the game like the smart Venus-Mercury child you are. You'll score big in the stock market, either as a broker or for investments of your own income. What's more, if you can overcome any ethical reservations, gambling is a natural for you.

Second nature to you is a sense of style, so all the inroads to the fields of fashion and decorating are yours for the walking. Interestingly, You probably have a period or a theme that is your personal favorite, and you'll ever so flamboyantly throw it in whenever possible. In fact, any of you would make wonderful Jacqueline Stallone headband models if you're ever at a loss for employment.

Oh, one more thing. Should you truly want to settle into one responsibility for the rest of your life, you could always get a job posing on a podium as Cupid. Slap on a pair of wings, grab a bow and arrow, and no one will ever know the difference. If you do get caught, please don't tell them that it was me who suggested the impersonation.

YOUR BEST-BET LOVE COMBOS

LIBRA-Gemini Man: Maybe we should blame your naughty behavior on your close proximity to Scorpio, or maybe we should set you down and tell you to control yourself. I have never seen a man who gets as turned on as often as a 3rd Decan LIBRAN.

A woman's smile turns you on, her voice sends shivers down your spine, her smell makes you faint with desire. Inanimate objects turn you on. The evening news can even arouse your ardor. Pity on your wife or girlfriend who doesn't know when the next surge is coming! And what a tragedy should you suddenly turn to your old steady and not feel a familiar pulse in a familiar place.

Yes, it happens that just as speedily and without obvious reason that you fall for a dame, you turn your passion in another direction. What are we going to do with you and what are you going to do with yourself?

The problem and the solution are one: It's all pure chemistry and there's nothing to do but remain true to your feelings—as long as you make it perfectly clear to whomever is turning your love knob at the moment. Fortunately for the female species, you are as honest as you are horny, and that's the truth!

You are also a gentleman and would never act on impulses unless the feeling was mutual. That's why I'm going to refer you to one of your mutuals in the sign of LIBRA. We've just finished talking about how crazy she is for guys who are a little crazy. Ms. LIBRA-Aquarius will be nuts for you. If you get ensnared in a little controversy, she'll reform you immediately. Once the two of you get together she'll keep the peace and you'll keep the pace. A little horizontal exercise never hurt anybody, did it?

LIBRA-Gemini Woman: Ditto for you gals of everything I've just said about the hip-hopping men of this decan. If you think that the dreamy, sultry, hot moods you've been having lately are just a passing phase, let me ask you how long you've been feeling them. You probably drooled over big sis's boyfriends and panted over screen stars. Most LIBRA-Gemini girls have been swooning over the opposite sex since they were in their preteens. It's amazing that you don't keep a home supply of smelling salts!

What's even more surprising is that you'll be going gaga for guys way into your twilight years. Again, we can always blame next-door-neighbor Scorpio for spicing your decan with excess hormones, but little good it'll do to change your teenage heart. You're going to be a pushover for a handsome face forever.

Actually, you sweet-looking ladies of LIBRA's 3rd Decan can get yourself into even more trouble than the gentlemen of your set. Not only do you have true passion pushing you, you're also quite compelled to play the game to the hilt. You usually win the prize that you seek, but when you don't you'll retreat into a sulk that is vaguely reminiscent of Cancer the Crab.

To tell you the truth, you are such a love junkie that not many men will actually be able to stick it out for the long run with you. One guy who won't be put off is the stable and sometimes aloof AQUARIUS-Aquarius. His FIXED-Fixed style is the perfect compliment to your CARDINAL-Mutable mix. He may not want to make love as often as you, but in my opinion that's for the better.

On those rare nights that he has a headache, you can throw yourself into at least one of your ingenious projects. For instance, you could spend some time with your beloved children. You're a wonderful mom, by the way, as long as you can remember to schedule getting pregnant.

DECAN PAIRS WITH LIBRA-GEMINI

LOVE SCALE SCORES

0 = Forget it! • 1 = Don't be a masochist... • 2 = Why bother? • 3 = Fun for one date. • 4 = It won't last! • 5 = You could do better! • 6 = Romance will fade... 7 = Great buddies! • 8 = Pure passion • 9 = True love. • 10 = Eternal bliss!

STARS OF LIBRA-GEMINI

October 14:	Ralph Lauren
October 15:	Penny Marshall
	Sarah Ferguson, Dutchess of York
October 16:	Tim Robbins
October 17:	Rita Hayworth
October 18:	Jean-Claude Van Damme
	Sean Patrick Flanery
October 22:	Jeff Goldblum
	Christopher Lloyd

CHAPTER 10

SCORPIO

OCTOBER 23 - NOVEMBER 22

First Decan	Second Decan	Third Decan
SCORPIO-Scorpio	SCORPIO-Pisces	SCORPIO-Cancer
10/23 - 11/2	11/3 - 11/12	11/13 - 11/22

Two SCORPIOs tried to enter the Olympics. When asked which sport was their specialty, they responded in unison, "We're bedroom athletes."

Sign:	Water - Feelers
Symbol:	The Scorpion
Planet:	Mars
Body Talk:	The Privates
Style:	Fixed

MEET THE STRATEGIST...

One of the reasons that everyone spends more time picking on Aries, Leo, or dear old Capricorn is that those three overbearing signs are easier to criticize than the power-monger SCORPIO. We're all just too scared to come out and say anything insulting about the most truly volatile Sun sign of all. And well we should guard our words around the stinging tail of the Scorpion. Believe you me, I'm definitely going to watch my p's and q's when talking to you, both about your intense temperament and about your infamous sex appeal.

When Mars controls a Fire sign, such as in the case of ARIES, we can observe a flamboyant display of drive. When the same forceful planet takes charge of the Water sign SCORPIO, the result is an invisible yet mighty power that can overtake almost any other. With a Fixed movement pattern, you Scorpions will devise your game plan meticulously. You'll move toward your goals slowly and deliberately, as if you were stalking live prey. You may prefer to keep your ideas and plans under wraps. No matter which decan your birthday falls under, you'll have some secrets that you share with no one, and I mean no one.

By the same token, you are chronically seeking the secrets of other people. The magnetic power that you often exude seems to draw information out of others automatically. I'll bet that strangers are always spilling their guts to you and then complaining, "I didn't mean to tell you all of this!" You just always seem to have your feelers out for heavy-duty action. And though you may not be center stage on it, you will have more control of what's going on than the major players. As the searchers of the zodiac, most Scorpios have an insatiable desire for knowledge on every level. From spiritual and intellectual revelations, to psychic or scientific wisdom, to good old carnal knowledge, you want the edge on everybody else. You take the phrase "to know" someone in the Biblical sense, don't you now? Your aggressive Mars sex drive isn't mere bumps and grinds. When you get down to the business of making love, it's serious business. You elevate intercourse to the highest experience of your life. You put your heart and mind and body and soul into a union with another.

As long as you feel the devotional love of your partner, your active sexuality is always kept within healthy bounds. Should he or she stray from your beaten path, however, you will pull every imaginable trick in the book to seek your revenge. This is no laughing matter! Sex and death are your two favorite areas of interest; lovers, friends, and family alike tread lightly in your presence. Double-crossing you is like signing a suicide note—a major Stallone no-no.

No doubt you may already have an interest in the metaphysical sciences, such as astrology. You may have heard or read that together with Mars, Pluto is considered by some authorities to be a co-ruler of SCORPIO; actually, some astrologers take the position that Pluto is sole ruler of your sign. I haven't accepted either of those viewpoints for two good reasons. First of all, Pluto was only discovered in 1930. For thousands of years, astrology has done wonders understanding SCORPIO via the planet Mars. In that respect, I'm just an old-fashioned gal-astrologer!

Second, Pluto is slow moving and erratic, taking up to 20 years to move from sign to sign. It is a radical star, named for the dark, punishing god of Hades and connected to issues of death, revolution, and regeneration; at the same time, its impact on the personality of the individual is relatively weak. Though you SCORPIOS retain a fascination with things dark and strange, Pluto distracts observers from seeing the essence of your beat. That would be, of course, your active Mars aggression, the driving positive force inside you that you always try to bide.

FIRST DECAN OF SCORPIO

"I'M SEARCHING, I'M ALWAYS SEARCHING."

SCORPIO-Scorpio	FIXED-Fixed	MARS-Mars

I want to make one thing perfectly clear to you SCORPIO-Scorpios, born with all your intense influences in double force. I like you. I admire you. Remember the "support" system of the zodiac? I doubt that I would have to refresh the memory of your shrewd mind, but just in case you misinterpret my motives, I'll remind you that Sagittarius depends on SCORPIO for backup. So I wouldn't do anything to get any of your sign on my wrong side, especially not any of you born in this 1st Decan.

You've heard of "killer bees" haven't you? Well, you guys are what I call "Killer S's." That's right, the letter S is your emblem: for Superhuman, Strong, Scheming, Suspicious, Secretive, Stinging, Sexy, and, usually, Successful. There is nothing passive, lazy, or blasé about any of you. Your FIXED-Fixed style has determined the fact that you are never inconsistent. When you're good, you are beyond greatness. When you're bad, there ought to be a law against you!

No decan in the zodiac has quite your insatiable need to understand all realms of nature. No matter how many secrets of the universe you do uncover, you are still left with an emotional longing for more. No matter how much human nature is intimately revealed to you, you will never have a sense of enough. Your secret, felt so deeply way down in your watery, intuitive instincts, is an awareness that knowledge is power. So your double-double Mars drive sets you on a path for life, gathering little-known information that will aid and abet your cause. Very smart, Mr. or Ms. SCOR-PIO-Scorpio, very smart!

Probably from the time you were just a tiny baby Scorpion, you realized that you could influence others to do your bidding. As you grew up, this knack you have for cloaking your motives while still achieving your aims has probably been honed and tuned to perfection. Do not, however, in any way, shape, or form, take your strength lightly. A 1st Decan SCOR-PIO is the most likely to lash his or her tail out when provoked. Once you've stung someone, it becomes very hard to extract the poison you've released, and pretty soon, as we're about to find out, your actions will come back to haunt you.

YOUR DARK SIDE

I'd better add one more "Killer S" to your list, with a prayer that you won't seek revenge and write poison-pen letters about me, and an appeal to your hunger for self-understanding. The word is: Spiteful. That's right. Deny, boo, hiss me all you want. Still, you can't escape the fact that when someone or something has blocked your determined path, you will stop at literally nothing to punish your foe.

Though you are definitely morally developed and maintain strict standards for good behavior for yourself and for others, once caught in the fray you'll drop your code of honorable ethics and turn into a slithering, scummy snake. And you're very crafty in executing retaliation, aren't you? Why bother merely slapping someone's face for insulting yours? You'll lay an invisible trap, one that might take you months of planning, just so you can sting your enemy when he or she least expects it.

SCORPIO-Scorpios can hold grudges for life, not unlike your opposing sign, the, stubborn Bulls. However, where TAURUS will simply write off the one that has hurt them and hold on to the emotional resentment, you 1st Decan Scorpions are driven to seek revenge. What makes this pattern so scary is who you deem to be your enemy. How about the bully who kicked sand in your face and made you look like a wimp? You put sugar in the gas tank of his father's car, right? How about the teacher who told you that you'd never amount to anything? What did you do about that, hmmm? Something like spreading vicious rumors about her "'questionable" love life, I bet. I pity the person who got the job you were up for, as well as the guy who actually hired your competitor. And, last but certainly not least, I am shaking in my boots when I think what you would do if you caught the man or woman you loved cheating. You can make his or her life—not to mention the third party's existence—living hell. When a SCORPIO-Scorpio suffers emotionally, the whole world has to suffer along, or else!

YOUR LIGHT SIDE

Now all you angry 1st Decan SCORPIO guys and gals can lower your poised stingers, because the worst is over. As long as you are on guard against your dangerous pitfall, the rest of your behavior earns only top marks.

I can't even begin to describe your amazing endurance skills. Patience, persistence, and political savvy continually fuel your efforts. Though you will eventually live in the manner to which you want to become accustomed, you can abide a shoestring lifestyle when it is necessary to do so. You are an adaptive creature, which means you can go anywhere, anyplace, anytime, and find your niche.

Your ultra-sensitive SCORPIO-Scorpio radar draws you into areas that others are either too afraid or too unaware to go. You can unearth treasures that elude the most greedy digging hands because you use your calculating mind to go for the gold. Plus, the word squeamish is never included in your "S" list. You have the courage and curiosity to look at negatives as well as positives, which supports my belief that yours is the most realistic decan of all. With realistic planning as your hallmark, success is inevitable.

BOTTOM LINE FOR YOUR POWER

I strongly urge you to search within yourself for those spiteful, unproductive areas and to make a daily effort to fight the negative emotions that arise. Pin a note on the refrigerator that reads "no sour grapes on my diet." And, as long as you don't harbor resentment, there won't be a chance that those bad grapes you've eaten can turn into rotten wine. You'll be stronger and more able to pursue your heart's desires. The answers to mysteries that you seek will come to you as if by divine revelation. With knowledge only you command, you can command a greater and better planet Earth. Your secret purpose is a divine one if used for noble ends as: a *Discoverer*.

BODY TALK

Well, there's no use in my "beating around the bush," is there? SCORPIO rules the genitals, so no matter how delicately I put it, those of you born in the first ten days of the sign are going to have to accept the brunt of it. Luckily, this is one thing you won't lash out from hearing. Come on, you're proud of yours, aren't you? You male 1st Decans probably walk around alone in the house nude, just so you can glance down every now and then, in fondness and gratitude that your male parts are so beautifully constructed. Girls, you too! Admit that you spend more than a few pennies on getting the best bikini waxes in town on a regular basis. It's got to be all you SCORPIO-Scorpio women buying up entire stocks of peekaboo panties!

Seriously, you have been blessed with reproductive systems that operate optimally, inside and out. You men will rarely face bouts of impotence, while women may have to worry about how easily they can become impregnated. Thank God that most of you have developed an intimate knowledge of medicine on a "Jay" basis. Safe sex is an "S" that you will always champion.

Being the secretive specimen that you are, I've yet to put my finger on how you maintain your excellent health and stamina in all areas. Your exercise and dietary habits are erratic. You never seem to need sleep. You never appear to be affected by extremes in heat or cold. You are extremely suspicious of doctors, and figure you can treat any illness that arises on your own. And still, somehow, you look good and say you feel great. One day one of you will spill the beans and the rest of us will spend millions trying your methods.

I must remind you that we are speaking of the more general aspects of the decan. SCORPIO-Scorpios can end up with some nasty flesh wounds, especially when you've just used your stinger maliciously. One way or the other, someone or karma will sting you back with a yucky case of something, unless you're operating with your usual smart senses. Just don't get too cocky about your physical well-being, or about your prized jewels. And you know what I mean.

YOUR BEST-BET CAREERS

Without question, this is a career-minded decan. We've got almost a 100 percent employment rate among men and women of this group. You probably started working when you were in grade school and you will probably never retire. I suspect you knew very early what you wanted to be when you grew up, and have maintained a sharp focus in that direction ever since. Giving up is a foreign term to you, unless you discover that you are spinning your wheels and not taking over what ever field you've chosen. In such cases, you're perfectly able to switch gears into another Fixed path. For any of those options, take a look at professions where other SCORP-Scorps have scored.

Your Mars combative force makes for coups in both the military and in politics. In strategy and planning, you can successfully pull off the riskiest of campaigns. You are a born leader in that you don't mind delegating responsibility. If any of your underlings are unable to hold up the slack, you'll drop back and assist. No holier-than-thou attitudes from you, thank you very much. Holding a public office suits your private nature just fine—any skeletons in your closet will stay locked up for eternity.

As much as you may not require medical services for yourself, you are a superb practitioner of medicine, should you so choose. You can probably almost guess what I'm going to recommend as your specialties: gynecology and pathology. Looking in secret places is a habit you already have attained, so why the hell not? In the science laboratory you have a genius for genetics and you love to mix up strange potions in a test tube.

And for those of you truly thick-skinned Mars-Mars activists, you could go out and control the market in mortuaries. Anybody else would sweat bullets over a corpse, but your underlying curiosity in all of life Or death will allow you to deal with this delicate, difficult field.

Except for the dark-side issues that we've already discussed, a SCORP-Scorp belongs in a position of power and usually wields power with a fair and ethical grip. Stardom befits your magnetic, charged personality. So, if the glitter of show business has caught your eye, by all means follow the rocky road to achieve your fantasies. I would suggest producing or directing as opposed to acting for your best shots. However, if you have decided you want your face plastered across the silver screen, far be it from me to stand in your way. God forbid you'd try to prove me wrong just out of spite!

YOUR BEST-BET LOVE COMBOS

SCORPIO-Scorpio Man: Before I even begin to blast your love tactics, I'd like to know where you're hiding your scoreboard. I know you've got one stashed away in one of your secret hiding places. Oh, I hear you. You've lost count? For heaven's sake, have you no shame? Now, I'm not suggesting that you broadcast your conquests. You don't; however, you seem to think that there's nothing wrong with seducing one damsel right after another. We're talking numbers—high numbers.

You seem to think that giving her a night to remember for the rest of her life is quite enough. Haven't you gotten it into your mind that when a woman tastes a good thing she's going to want more? You're not the only one with an appetite, you know!

Well, at least you don't try to juggle lots of gals at the same time. You know that if one of your latest amours was two-timing you, you'd go out for blood. You also know that somewhere out in the misty sea of potential love victims is the queen of your dreams. You don't want to meet her too soon without having had time to sow your wild oats, or whatever it is that Scorpions sow. So, until you calculate that the time is right, you'll occupy the midnight hours with all the ladies-in-waiting. You may call it "fair play," but I call it playing havoc with the fairer of the species.

There isn't always a happy ending to the tale of the male SCORPIO-Scorpio, unless you are ready and willing to sacrifice passing pleasure for lasting love. If you commit to that transformation, of which you are fully capable, I'll pass you off as one of the greatest of all male catches. Loving, devoted, providing, erotic, even paternal. Don't get your head swelled by observing how many high scores you receive on the Love Scale, but do pay attention to the right signs.

If you have been suffering acutely from the syndrome I've described, I would be most pleased to see you with a 1st Decan CAPRICORN. Some of her bad moods will serve you right for your naughty past, while at the same time she'll only support your positive pursuits. Since you seem to like a little challenge, you'll enjoy chasing the Girl Goat around the bed. Once she gives in, she'll be just as eager to please you. Also, she's very big on "discipline." No harm in a little spanking, now is there?

SCORPIO-Scorpio Woman: I bet you feminine 1st Decaners have your own scoreboard, only one of a different sort than the proud males of your group. It's probably more of a "most Wanted" bulletin board, an assortment of past loves you'd like to ruin.

Let's talk about the time you failed an exam in school because every time you thought about you and Mr. Macho, and what you were doing with him when you were supposed to be studying, you palpitated too hard to concentrate. Let's blame that guy for your bad grades, okay? Or, what about the time that you and your male boss got playing kissy face over "lunch"? We'd better put him on the "No-Good" man list also.

Please, dear hormonal Scorpion lasses, consider for a moment that the trouble that haunts you is coming from your own overactive ovaries. You think with your passions and choose with them, and then blame everyone else but yourself for things not working out. And unlike all the other water creatures, you don't sit around and cry about it, you go out and zap those men just for taking advantage of their natural attraction to you. They can't help it if you are their dream-come-true version of the sexiest woman they've ever met in person.

You'll never not be sexy, but you can learn not to get swept up in the passions of the moment. You can learn to look a man who's made your temperature rise straight in the eyes and say, "I can't tonight, I have to wash my hair." Believe me, he'll respect you for it and you won't turn frigid overnight. If he is by chance a 1st Decan VIRGO, his curiosity will be as stimulated as yours. Waiting to consummate your mutual interest may pay off in a big way for both of you. He can analyze you while you get to the bottom of all his secrets. I guarantee that this is a match made in heaven. Would I lie? Well, maybe I get overly enthusiastic every now and then. But a VIRGO-Virgo man won't. Trust him, especially when he puts a diamond on your ring finger and asks, "Will you?" At that point, you can let your passions rip!

DECAN PAIRS WITH SCORPIO-SCORPIO

SCORPIO-Scorpio &	ARIES-Aries (3/21-3/30)	6
	ARIES-Leo (3/31-4/9)	7
	ARIES-Sagittarius (4/10-4/20)	2
	TAURUS-Taurus (4/21-4/30)	6
	TAURUS-Virgo (5/1-5/10)	6
	TAURUS-Capricorn (5/11-5/20)	7
	GEMINI-Gemini (5/21-5/31)	7
	GEMINI-Libra (6/1-6/10)	5
	GEMINI-Aquarius (6/11-6/20)	3
	CANCER-Cancer (6/21-7/1)	7
	CANCER-Scorpio (7/2-7/12)	7
	CANCER-Pisces (7/13-7/22)	9
	LEO-Leo (7/23-8/1)	3
	LEO-Sagittarius (8/2-8/12)	6
	LEO-Aries (8/13-8/22)	4
	VIRGO-Virgo (8/23-9/3)	9
	VIRGO-Capricorn (9/4-9/13)	9
	VIRGO-Taurus (9/14-9/22)	6
	LIBRA-Libra (9/23-10/3)	4
	LIBRA-Aquarius (10/4-10/13)	6
	LIBRA-Gemini (10/14-10/22)	5
	SCORPIO-Scorpio (10/23-11/2)	5
	SCORPIO-Pisces (11/3-11/12)	6
	SCORPIO-Cancer (11/13-11/22)	6
	SAGITTARIUS-Sagittarius (11/23-12/2)	6

LOVE SCALE SCORES

0 = Forget it! • 1 = Don't be a masochist... • 2 = Why bother? • 3 = Fun for one date. • 4 = It won't last! • 5 = You could do better! • 6 = Romance will fade... 7 = Great buddies! • 8 = Pure passion • 9 = True love. • 10 = Eternal bliss!

STARS OF SCORPIO-SCORPIO

October 23:	Johnny Carson	October 31:	Dan Rather
October 24:	Kevin Kline		John Candy
October 25:	Pablo Picasso		Jane Pauley
October 26:	Jaclyn Smith		Vanila Ice
	François Mitterand		Lee Grant
	Mahalia Jackson	November 1:	Lyle Lovett
	Pat Sajak		Larry Flynt
	Bob Hoskins	November 2:	Stephanie Powers
	Hillary Rodham Clinton		Burt Lancaster
October 27:	Theodore Roosevelt		
	John Cleese		
October 28:	Julia Roberts		
	Bill Gates		
October 29:	Richard Dreyfuss		
	Winona Ryder		
	Kate Jackson		
October 30:	Ruth Gordon		
	Henry Winkler		

SECOND DECAN OF SCORPIO

"I'M SEARCHING. I'M ALSO DEMOCRATIC."

SCORPIO-Pisces	FIXED-Mutable	MARS-Neptune

As the Sun sweeps through the watery Fixed sign of SCORPIO and comes to its second stop, here in this middle ten-day period, its rays bend to reflect on you some very distinct Mutable Piscean traits. Once again, my handy rule of thumb that 2nd Decans tend to be the more balanced of the bunch, just doesn't apply. Why, you ask?

Does your inquiring mind want to know? Well, it's because no matter how you stack your pancakes, Pisces is weird, dreamy, and lost in watery emotions, whereas SCORPIO is intense, focused, and highly charged.

Yes, Mars and Neptune are odd bedfellows, and their combined influences make you into a fish-basket case of contradiction. On the one hand you'll be intensely occupied, plotting your careful path to fame and fortune. At the other extreme, you'll be counting all the accessible exit hatches so that you can escape into your own world at a moment's notice. You can be downright selfish and single-minded in pushing your own campaign; you can also use the stinger on your tail to help someone in need. You haven't lost your SCORPION search for quantity X, that drive that pulls you away from other human beings. You've also picked up Pisces' love and compassion for all humanity, a democratic attitude that brings you back to the need for companionship.

To complicate your already complex picture, you are one of the visionary decans. A Scorpion/Fish breed can tune in to some unusual wavelengths, as you can imagine. Normally, your intuitive, sensitive powers can carry you right to where you want to go. Sometimes, you can be acutely psychic, almost to the point of scaring yourself. Morbid, dark thoughts may haunt you. But, if you read on, I'll reveal that special talent you have for slaying the invisible dragons.

YOUR DARK SIDE

The fact that you are two-sided isn't your basic problem, although the way you sometimes express yourself is. There's an old Native American proverb that says, "SCORPIO-Pisces speak with forked tongue." Get the message? You lie. You lie like a dog on the rug. Your Scorpion intensity is so set on achieving your personal goals that you use deception in the form of words to influence others to stay out of your way. The dash of Pisces/Neptune only makes your verbal disguises that much harder to unravel.

Sometimes you justify not telling the whole truth by convincing yourself that others can't handle it, or that they'll be hurt. Fiddlesticks! You're just covering up the fact that you'll use any means to accomplish your aims. At other times, you may have become so adept at lying that you don't even know when you're doing it. That's exactly when this pitfall becomes ultra dangerous.

When you stop knowing what the truth is, you short-circuit the secret current of your power. You begin to believe in frightening threats to your stability, and put faith in "psychic" messages. that only delude you. You'll be the victim of unrealistic fears that will only hold you back. What a tragedy for someone as rich in positive potential as you 2nd Decan SCORPIOS.

YOUR LIGHT SIDE

When your conscience is clear, when you feel you've been loving to your fellow human beings, and most of all loving and truthful to yourself, you can funnel from the universe a form of energy known as *I channel*. This is your special gift, the ability to tap into divine voices of ancient wisdom.

You may use this gift in being brilliantly creative, in answering some of the universal questions that you're always asking, or in a generosity toward other people. However you do use it, I can promise that it will come to you only when your intentions are honest. I know it sounds corny. Others can call it superstitious or too much part of the New Age doctrine. But I think you know what I mean.

It means that you have a magical ability to get things done or to attract love from mates and friends alike without much effort. Just "channel" your powers and let them do the walking! It's what the Eastern cultures refer to as "the path of least resistance." I refer to it as being astrologically blessed!

It is very hard for a SCORPIO not to scheme and calculate and fight the tide with stinger poised. Please, let your marvelous Piscean influence allow you to go with your own positive flow. Pretty soon you'll be lolling on a yacht with a bevy of beauties from the opposite sex surrounding you, experiencing inner and outer serenity, as you channel left and right. Why, I've even heard that the experience of connecting with your higher consciousness is better than an orgasm. You're one of the authorities in both cases, so I leave the conclusion to you.

BOTTOM LINE FOR YOUR POWER

You may always be tempted to manipulate the truth to suit your purposes. I ask you to do it sparingly. Remember that every time you tell a little white lie, especially to an innocent listener, you will set up a block against the brilliant insights that are yours for the asking.

Your psychic powers can bring you materialistic and spiritual wealth, if your intentions are loving. Have faith that good will happen and it absolutely will. No other human being will be able to conceive of the unique, individual creations that you bring forth, because at your height of heights you are: an *Originator*.

BODY TALK

Well, you'll be glad to know that SCORPIO's dominion over the sexual organs hasn't turned you 2nd Decaners into outright exhibitionists, although you will be sensitive in those areas, whether the sensations you feel are pleasurable or irritating. Your hormonal activity is not quite as pumped up, so to speak, as that of the 1st Decan of Scorpio, but it is erratic. You may go through periods where you can't shake feeling sexual at every second. Cold showers won't even cool you down. Then suddenly you'll wake up one morning and think your libido is gone for good. Even hot steamy bubble baths won't bring that drive back until it's good and ready.

Oh, but there is a secret spot that can fix your dilemma immediately, and it isn't between your legs. Your feet, ruled by the Pisces part of you, if rubbed properly, can bring lost physical ardor back in seconds flat. Or, if you're on an overactive binge, slap your little tootsies, and watch your sexuality mellow right out.

Scorpions, native to dry, hot desert climates, are always hungry for water, though they can sustain themselves on tiny amounts for long periods of time. Fish, on the other hand, will croak without abundant cold, clean H_2O. This tells us plenty about the health requirements of you Scorpion Fish. Your ailments will usually afflict your bodily fluids and can be detected by high fevers or shaking chills. You can almost always cure yourself with water, so keep a case of Evian in the fridge at all times, and whenever you start to feel puny just douse your feet in a warm foot bath. Pretty soon you'll be feeling no pain.

Avoid alcohol. You don't need it. No need to alter your natural high, which as we've already seen, is plenty juiced up all the time!

YOUR BEST-BET CAREERS

You Scorpion Fish probably resent authority and/or discipline, yet you do require it. You may prefer to work on your own, but being locked up in a room by yourself can make you stir-crazy. Therefore, I urge you not to opt for self-employment. Even in some of the following fields, which are far from conventional, I would hope that you were part of a team. When you feel support from others, you will naturally swim into a leadership position.

As a matter of fact, I'm praying for the next SCORPIO-Pisces doctor on a medical research team to come up with the cure to the dreaded AIDS virus. This should be the top priority of every health official in the world. If you have any interest in medicine, I urge you to apply your powers toward this dire need immediately.

If you are not scientifically oriented, but lean more toward creative vocations, do recall one of your key words-visionary. You will always come forward in the avant-garde of all cultural mediums, especially those that are visual such as painting, drawing, photography, and filmmaking. Lucky you, you won't have to search too far for artistic inspiration; all you have to do is channel it.

Speaking for those ultra-sensitive skills you have, let's talk about how you can earn bundles of recognition and cash with your inborn psychic abilities. Crime detection, whether as a detective out in the field, or as a medium brought in on a consulting basis, will tap your SCORPIO-Pisces talents. Knowing something about the art of deception, you are a human lie detector. Very few can fool you.

Professions based on studies of the occult could offer you an immediate practical application of your channeling gift. You've got a wide assortment of choices from aura-reading, to channeling, to numerology, to palmistry, to my very own passion for astrology.

My other lasting passion has been my friend and agent, Phil Palladino. Yes, that's right, a SCORPIO-Pisces from way back when. There's no chance in hell that I'm going to tell you how sensational he was in every single department. I may be a blabbermouth, but I'm no fool. Only a dopey woman would advertise her agent! But, what I can tell you is that his professional forte was as a personal manager. With his constant Scorpion searching, Phil never missed out on any business opportunity that would have benefited any of his clients. With his Piscean compassion, he was a major people person, giving out warmhearted articulate advice. I owe a large part of my success to Phil. He even incorporated his expertise in numerology into all marketing plans. He was a living example of Starpower, having used the gifts of his decan to the hilt. So if any of you SCORPIO-Pisces want to follow in his professional footsteps, you can see that you can't go wrong.

YOUR BEST-BET LOVE COMBOS

SCORPIO-Pisces Man: We've already covered some of your naughty tricks, particularly those that you use to manipulate the truth. Since I know you've probably already begun to mend your ways, I'm going to reward you by telling you how sensational you are in the bedroom. The word for you, when it comes to the opposite sex, is smooooooth. The males of your decan wrote the book on seduction. You are so expert at luring a woman into your arms that she won't even know she's being seduced. You could seduce an entire flock of Amish women with your eyes closed.

Even though you're still a secretive Scorpion and an evasive Fish, I have figured out what you use for bait. You know how to search for each individual female's individual weakness. Whether you act debonair, stage a conquering siege, pretend to be an innocent schoolboy, or just talk dirty, you are able to zero in on her particular fetish. Being so democratic, satisfaction of your mistress is your mission.

Having stroked your intense male ego, I must gently point out what you do not do so well. You hold on to your quarry as if she belongs to you. Just because you've made magic love to her, doesn't mean she's your captive. I think you get the idea, don't you? You should know. If you re-read the book you wrote on seduction, you probably will note that your first chapter is titled "Jealousy." A little jealousy is a tasty treat for a selective lady. However, a lot of jealousy can ruin relationship after relationship when taken to the extremes that you do.

You could seduce any woman of any decan, but until you've learned your lessons about possessiveness, far be it from me to point you down the aisle with anyone except Ms. PISCES-Cancer, who has got her own jealous streak. One thing's for sure, your powerful chemistry together may blow the roof off the house.

SCORPIO-Pisces Woman: If the men of this decan wrote the book on seduction, I wouldn't be surprised if the women edited and improved it. You are the femmes-fatales of the zodiac, the women to whom no man can say no. What is even more surprising about you unusual Scorpion-guppy girls is that you don't look like the stereotypical spider women who lure their male victims into their web. You look like "nice girls." That's your SCORPIO-Pisces deception all the way.

Once you get him back to your harmless-looking bachelorette den of iniquity, close the door, and give him one look, you transform into the sexpot of his dreams. By the time you barely graze his lips, he's yours for keeps. And that is exactly where you get into problems. Remember you have a Mutable libido; sometimes you want it and sometimes you'd rather channel your past karma for a high. And here you've got a worked-up man panting at your side every second and you don't know how to get rid of him. He'll become whiny and mopey and tell you that you don't spend enough time with him. You've transformed him into a wimp. I think that's fatale, don't you?

If you'd like to skip the sad ending that all those conquests can have, and move to one with a different consummation, you should face up to the fact that you need a real challenge. That's why I'm going to pair you up with your neighbor, something you know that I never do. A SAGITTARIUS man is no easy prey, and he'll make your jealous tendencies emerge like sensitive fish fins. However, you will never, ever get bored with him. He hates lying, so you can bet he'll be blunt if he ever catches you in the act. Bottom line though, is that you want your man to take control. That truth and two cents may just buy you romantic bliss.

DECAN PAIRS WITH SCORPIO-PISCES

LOVE SCALE SCORES

0 = Forget it! • 1 = Don't be a masochist... • 2 = Why bother? • 3 = Fun for one date. • 4 = It won't last! • 5 = You could do better! • 6 = Romance will fade... 7 = Great buddies! • 8 = Pure passion • 9 = True love. • 10 = Eternal bliss!

STARS OF SCORPIO-PISCES

November 3:	Roseanne
	Dennis Miller
November 5:	Vivien Leigh
	Art Garfunkle
November 6:	Maria Shriver
November 8:	Katharine Hepburn
	Courtney Thorne-Smith
November 10:	Richard Burton
November 11:	Leonardo DiCaprio
	Demi Moore
	Calista Flockhart

THIRD DECAN OF SCORPIO

"I'M SEARCHING AND I'M POSSESSIVE."

SCORPIO-Cancer	FIXED-Cardinal	MARS-Moon

Aren't you Scorpion/Crab mixes a lucky bunch? While SCORPIO's 1st Decan has hopped into the extremist slot, and the 2nd Decan has taken on the label of unusual, you 3rd Decan participants rate as the balanced, most evolved of the lot.

I would imagine that you are. Sprinkled by flakes of Sagittarian/Jupiterian optimism, grounded in SCORPIO/Mars reality, and stirred to feel only Cancer's positive moon-glow, it's as if you have three cheery twinkling stars hanging over you at all times. You have been able to lose the typical SCORPION suspicion of others; needless to say that with two kinds of outer "shell," one Scorpion and one Crab, you have a tough exterior that's hard to penetrate.

You are brimming with self-confidence, strength, and a special magnetic charm that you use selectively. With Fixed and shrewd preparation, mingled with a fierce Cardinal focus that requires you to succeed in everything you do, you are masters and mistresses of a destiny bound for fame and fortune, When you come from such a positive place, others rarely will stand in your way. Nor do difficult circumstances seem to upset you in the least.

As full of potential power as you SCORPIO-Cancers are, you may fall into a rut where you're spinning your wheels without really knowing it. You have what is commonly known as an "overachiever complex." It happens all the time when Mars interacts with the Moon. Add a little expansive Jupiter to the brew and what you are is hyperactive, inside and out. Your SCORPIO mind is always devising tactical plans, while your Cancer emotions are always swirling. Your possessive nature wants you to hold on to every victory you attain, while your searching self just wants more, more, more! As much as other people think you are the greatest, deep down you can be your worst critic. How many times have you said to yourself, "I could have done better"? Come on, you know what happens when nothing you eat satisfies you. You keep eating until you're a fat slob, that's what happens. Though no SCORPIO-Cancer would allow themselves to puff up like a blowfish, unless you become aware of your excessive appetite for success, you'll end up having to take a course at Overachievers Anonymous one day.

YOUR DARK SIDE

Perhaps I have exaggerated my previous concern about your overwhelming determination to be the best at everything. Do not, however, try to dilute my next warning, to any degree. As ultra-positive as you are, there will always be one sore, angry, vulnerable spot for at least one someone or one something.

You have, as a rule, very few enemies. But, when you pick someone to dislike, you sure know how to pick them. And you sure know how to bury them! This peculiar, nasty habit goes beyond any kind of reason. All your trusted friends and confidants will be asking you why you hate so-and-so so very much, and you won't be able to come up with one justifiable cause. You just do.

There is a karmic connection here that I'm not going to give away for nothing. That amazing topic is what I'll tackle in my next book! I will tell you, however, that SCORPIO-Cancers are always meeting up with loves and hates from past lives. When you set your eyes on someone who affects you the wrong way, it's as if he or she strikes a familiar chord of rivalry that you've carried in your soul for centuries. Whatever that person did to you in a past life could never be as bad as what you want to do to them in this life.

Don't laugh, and don't scoff at the principle that applies. Whether you lay stock in karma or not, you've got to confront this fatal flaw of yours. Your mission in life is to learn to conquer that ancient enemy with Cancer's emotional love, and not with Scorpion poison. Until you do, you'll keep swimming through an ocean of experience, on a universal trip to nowhere.

YOUR LIGHT SIDE

Say, that was a mouthful, wasn't it? Well, it was appropriate for me, to get fancy with words, just to honor your spectacular attributes in verbal power. Unless you have a strange block of Mercury in your birth chart, you deserve the highest praise for the way in which you express yourself.

The Moon's influence on your Cancer side allows you to speak with incredible force, with subtle wit, with compassionate eloquence and, of course, always with sexy SCORPIO seduction. I bet you've got a throng of pals who love to just sit and listen while you gab. Well, let's give a little credit to neighboring SAGITTARIUS for your gift of gab. Still, it's the power of your decan not to overuse this talent. You also know when to reserve your strong opinions—something most Sags never learn. Your claw/finger on the pulse of human emotions allows you to help others find what's really ailing them. When you care for someone, it is with a hundred and one percent of your being.

BOTTOM LINE FOR YOUR POWER

I suspect that the experience of feeling powerful hasn't eluded you; it comes to you easily and naturally. As long as you don't try to gobble it up all the time, you could be on a steady roll of one success after another. By stopping to applaud your own victories before chasing after the next, you'll be constructing a permanent ladder to the glory you seek.

As long as you don't fall down the steps by indulging in blind hatred of certain individuals who may cross your path, you will embrace the very best of yourself, and find yourself always at the top. You have a magical pull that makes you none other than: a *Charmer*.

BODY TALK

Once again I'd like to mention the positive influence you receive from my Sun sign, especially in the area of fitness. If it wasn't for your Jupiterian love of athletics, you SCORPIO-Cancer kids would be major pudgies. Your physical eroticism and kitchen kinkiness would otherwise have you bingeing out on gourmet orgies known only to the Roman emperors of days gone by. Let's thank the stars above that after you pig out, you *also* rush out to exercise your butt off.

I'm not saying it's particularly healthy, although it does keep your weight down. What it may also do is give you chronic stomach cramps, Just don't confuse them with your other vulnerable zone in the area of the reproductive organs. I'm sorry to say that the Mars/Moon mix in you SCORPIO 3rd Decans isn't the greatest for women's menstrual cycles. Even you men may experience a monthly low where your body feels like it's all tapped out. In fact, though both sexes usually operate on emotional highs, there might be one or two days a month when you'll turn into pure Crabs. They don't call it being on the "rag" for nothing!

In general, your health runs on a cycle. You'll go for years with nary a sniffle, only to get sacked one month with every flu bug in the book. I wonder if this has anything to do with your hyperactive tendencies, what do you say? Please, don't ignore the one "R" in the "R & R" package that is so important for your well being. Recreation isn't a problem for you, but Rest is. Learning how to sleep is something all you Scorpion Crabs could benefit from.

I've saved your best news for last. Plain and simple, no matter what shape you're in, your bod is sexy. In that respect you're SCORPIO all the way. And that Cancer possessiveness makes you very exclusive about who you'll let touch your private property. In this respect, I think there's some other decans of SCORPIO who could take some tips from you, don't you agree?

YOUR BEST-BET CAREERS

You've got a handle on your power and a grip on optimism. So it follows logically that professional success should come to you no matter what choices you make, right? Yes, and no. Yes, you're fabulously versatile. But no, you've got some reservations about how you'll spend your working energies. Being stuck behind the scenes is a problem for you, as is taking a lot of directives from authority figures. You need variety and freedom and, most important, financial compensation. You're a greedy little SCORPIO-Cancer, aren't you? I have noticed, however, that this decan hates to fly. Should your vocation force you to be jumping on airplanes all the time, you might end up a nervous wreck rather than a chronic overachiever. You can choose your poison, but I'd prefer for you to be the latter.

In any event, let's look at how you can corner the market in business and management. Very well, indeed, especially if you are in a trading capacity, as you utilize the shrewd twists and turns of your Fixed thinking. Stocks, commodities, and corporate kills could be daily dalliances for you.

With your verbal stings, and that magical charm you possess, you can't go wrong in any capacity as a political speaker, or speech writer.

You can also make technical writing as interesting as a juicy romance novel. I wish more of you would try your hand at saucing up some of the stale textbooks out there.

In the arts, you're still in your element with music and acting. Conducting a symphony orchestra would combine both of those abilities. Or, if holding a baton isn't your idea of success, you could hold the hand of another dancer, something I bet you SCORPIO-Cancers adore doing for show and for fun.

Don't forget the affinity you have for medicine and science, but do recall that you may be too emotional to perform surgery. Rather than electing to be a physician, you could find excellence as a hospital administrator, or a medical office manager.

The perfect profession for any Scorpion Crab is as a sex therapist. You'd be sending cured clients off in a state of sexual bliss while you jot down notes for the book you're going to write on the topic. You could make Dr. Ruth look like a nobody. And, being the Water sign that you are, I'll bet, as we're about to see, that you know everything there is to know about lubrication. We're talking about automobiles, right?

YOUR BEST-BET LOVE COMBOS

SCORPIO-Cancer Man: Even though you love women more than a stack of Crabcakes, you are extremely selective about whom you'll sting or claw. Well, good for you! So, while you wait for that special feminine someone, you'll just tease the rest of her species with your irresistible charm.

A male tease? "Who, me?" Don't be so coy, you know you get off on cruising a joint and turning every girlish face in your direction. Then when you do start a conversation with one of them, you can't help but stoke her hopes with clever, intimate innuendoes. For shame, you haven't got one single intention of ever seeing her again, have you? On those few occasions that you actually do find yourself locked in a physical, intimate embrace with one of your fawning females, you still can't resist being a tease. You'll prolong pleasure for hours just to see her beg. She'll be reduced to love-slave status, after you're done with her. Egads, man, you can be lethal.

Oh, but just wait till you get yours! That's right, when your perfect soul mate comes striding up to you, she's going to tease your hair on end. She is a VIRGO-Taurus, a Sextile/Opposition to you, and is she ever going to give you a chase. Deep down in both of you, you do have an overwhelming chemistry that just works. Follow her to the ends of the earth if you have to; she's worth it. She'll beautify the home that is so important to you and she'll be damn sure to hold on to your earnings while you go out and overachieve. What more can you ask?

SCORPIO-Cancer Woman: Half femme-fatale and half innocent Moon maiden, you'll be giving the men in your life a real run for their money. Yes, you're a tease, too, missy, as belle-ish as Scarlett O'Hara on a hot day. You thrive on male attention, and toy with sincere affections to an unlawful degree.

You should understand by now that the look you wear just says, "Come to me, my dah-ling," while your words are saying, "Get your hands off of me, you big brute," or "Get your dirty feet off the clean rug and get out of my house."

When a man looks at a SCORPIO-Cancer woman, he sees a seductress, a meal ticket, a mother, and a housewife all wrapped up in one. No wonder all the bonzos are bananas for you! If you really wanted to stave off his attentions, you'd have to tell him up front he's not for you, something you can't quite bring yourself to do.

Do be careful, though; you might just miss your karma's connection, that special man you've been waiting for several lifetimes to meet. He's mysterious, evasive, flirtatious, and creative. He never acts the big shot and is easy to overlook. He's a 1st Decan PISCES and he loves to go fishing.

If you haven't found him yet, buy yourself a ticket to the nearest pier and look for him in or by the water. You'll recognize each other from whatever past karmic experiences you've had together. The chemistry will be so passionate, just watch out that you don't maul each other right on the spot.

DECAN PAIRS WITH SCORPIO-CANCER

LOVE SCALE SCORES

0 = Forget it! • 1 = Don't be a masochist... • 2 = Why bother? • 3 = Fun for one date. • 4 = It won't last! • 5 = You could do better! • 6 = Romance will fade... 7 = Great buddies! • 8 = Pure passion • 9 = True love. • 10 = Eternal bliss!

STARS OF SCORPIO-CANCER

November 13:	Whoopi Goldberg
	Gary Marshall
November 14:	Prince Charles
November 15:	Petula Clark
	Sam Waterston
	Beverly D'Angelo
November 16:	Lisa Bonet
November 17:	Rock Hudson
	Martin Scorsese
	Danny DeVito
	Gordon Lightfoot
November 19:	Larry King
	Ted Turner
	Calvin Klein
	Meg Ryan
	Jodi Foster
November 20:	Bo Derek
	Sean Young
November 21:	Goldie Hawn
November 22:	Jamie Lee Curtis
	Mariel Hemingway

CHAPTER 11

SAGITTARIUS

NOVEMBER 23 · DECEMBER 21

First Decan	Second Decan	Third Decan
SAGITTARIUS-Sagittarius	SAGITTARIUS-Aries	SAGITTARIUS-Leo
11/23 - 12/2	12/3 - 12/11	12/12 - 12/21

At the divorce court, a SAGITTARIUS who'd gotten the raw end of the deal proclaimed, "A breakup isn't a failure. It's an experience!"

Sign:	Fire · Doers
Symbol:	The Archer/Centaur
Planet:	Jupiter
Body Talk:	The Thighs
Style:	Mutable

MEET THE ADVENTURER...

"I'M INDEPENDENT."

Y ou must appreciate what a thrill and a joy it is for me to let it all hang out and discuss what marvelous people we Archers really are. It sure is a relief to talk among peers! If you, like me, are born under the exuberant, jovial planet of Jupiter during the reign of fiery SAGITTARIUS, you probably enjoy blabbing as much as I do. We are by no means as verbally "promiscuous" as our opposing Mutable Air sign Gemini. However, the old saying that "loose lips sink ships" should be recalled by all SAGS on a daily basis. No matter which decan has claimed you, you will find that the ability to talk turkey will either earn you lifelong allies or permanent enemies. The area in which we can all improve is knowing when to keep our mouths shut. As we're about to see, some decans of SAGITTARIUS do it better than others.

If you contemplate all the positive properties of Fire, you will understand why our element, in its Mutable style, is considered the hottest of the hot, We warm hearts and homes, we heat up spirits when they're low. We inflame and ignite the minds of others through our fervent love of ideas. And, surprise though it may be, despite our reputation for bluntness, we're cornballs. We love clichés, and handy proverbs. I bet you would have never guessed!

Jupiter, the opportunistic planet of expansion, also thought to be a planet of "greater fortune," guides all of us ever onward through life. As we adventure along, always led by the scent of excitement or higher challenge, we gather treasures of experience. Like the flighty Geminis, we can sometimes move too quickly for our own good. But unlike any of the Twins, who would literally freak out if left entirely alone, we SAGITTARIANS thrive out in the open wilderness, galloping along solo. It's not that we don't like other people. On the contrary, we're often known among friends as true party animals. At the same time, we all have a chronic fear of confinement. Even writing that damn word gives me the willies!

If, for some reason, you find our symbol, the half-horse and half-human, with arrow poised, somehow unflattering, take another look. First of all, the Archer depicts us as the ultimate sportsmen and sportswomen of the zodiac. Come on, admit that life is a game, now isn't it? Whatever athletic activity has won your interest, you undoubtedly approach it with your total being. I truly believe that it was a SAGITTARIAN who coined the proverb, "It matters not if you win or lose, it's how you play the game." Of course, that's easy for us to say, because we usually win, right?

Now, notice a second, more subtle feature of our symbol. The arrow that we shoot points upward, which represents our positive, idealistic direction. We're mental adventurers, playing with lofty abstract concepts, following their trails to heights that only the wind can experience. Sure, some of our notions are off-the-wall. After all, we're sports oriented—bouncing philosophical ideas off others is almost as fun as a good game of spitball.

Finally, don't overlook the significance of our being shown as only one part human. This is what I've come to understand as our astrological handicap. If

Homo Sapiens are the most evolved in the biological chain, then the horsy side of the SAGITTARIAN nature, our animal instinct, is the wild, primitive force that unless tamed, can be our own undoing. If channeled properly, we energetic wild horses with minds of men or women can accomplish physical feats that seem inhuman. It's as if we have natural steroids built into our metabolisms!

My apologies to all you fellow SAGITTARIAN, but I'm going to spill the beans and give away our biggest secret. We like to play dumb. We have been fooling even the most astute astrologers for centuries. They've been describing us as direct, simple, straightforward types. Having been an extremist 1st Decan SAG for at least this lifetime, however, I'm going to set the record right. We are Mutable, and can alter our approach at the drop of a hat. We're complex creatures and as much as we despise being told we can't do something we want to do, we can't tolerate being given labels or pigeonholed. Having outdoorsy jock or jockette personalities is more or less a disguise for how brilliant we really are.

And "complex" is an ultra understatement when it comes to our emotions and our love lives. I will say that there are fewer Archers among all the zodiac's patients in psychotherapy. I'll also add that usually no shrink can figure us out. We do have the tendency to take on a sarcastic edge with anyone who tries to convert us to his or her way of thinking. To attempt to advise any decan of SAGITTARIUS in matters of the heart is a doomed mission. That is why we only ever find true love by trial and error. Never fear, we have plenty of heat-seeking arrows packed into our quiver. Romance to us is just a numbers game–sooner or later, ours comes up, so to speak. Unless we accidentally burn all our bridges by saying something rude, we are fully capable of winning jackpots of love. We're irresistible.

FIRST DECAN OF SAGITTARIUS

11/23 - 12/2

"I'M INDEPENDENT, I'M ALWAYS INDEPENDENT."

SAGITTARIUS-Sagittarius	MUTABLE-Mutable	JUPITER-Jupiter

I've given myself and all you other 1st Decan SAGITTARIANS the title, "Cheerleaders of the Zodiac." Instead of an umbilical cord, we should all come into the world with permanent pom-poms attached to our hands.

We are the enthusiasts of the world, high-spirited, spontaneous, flashy, flamboyant, just plain fun. We not only cheer for ourselves when we're out ahead in the race, we're the ones hollering the loudest for anyone on a winning streak. We don't like to lose, but a SAG-Sag is the first to march over to an opponent who has won, fair and square, to shake his or her hand.

We're bold, we're daring, and we are forever involved in zillions of projects at once. Take away our favorite instruments of play, our bow, arrows and quiver, and we would turn into nasty old mules. The fact is that we can balance more activities successfully than the most versatile Libran. Talk about multimedia, we're multidimensional. We can stick more into that backpack of interests we tote around than any bag lady on the street. We male and female double Archers of this 1st Decan are the original gypsies. We don't have the arrogance of the 2nd Decan, nor the luxury requirements of the 3rd Decan. Travel is our middle name. We'll go anywhere and anyhow, the more exotic and far-out the destination, the better. The more exotic and far-out the characters we meet in our journeys, the more tales we'll have to tell. We do tend to attract the "Klingons," if you know who I mean. But, once our entourage starts to look like too much of a caravan, we'll promptly dump the extra cargo and hightail it off in a different direction.

This gypsy mentality is the perfect mind-set for a SAG-Sag's excellence in the various "oral" traditions. We are the storytellers and yarn weavers of the planet. Some may think that we're gossips, whereas others might be offended by our somewhat derogatory tone, but we're really just telling it like it is. Oh, all right, we exaggerate sometimes. And yes, we're known to be blunt when push comes to shove. Still, try as anyone else might, it is near impossible to catch any of us in a malicious lie.

For example, let's say a SAGITTARIUS-Sagittarius is out having dinner somewhere. At an adjacent table, a complete stranger blows his nose loudly on the white linen napkin belonging to the restaurant. Any other decan observing this man would clear their throat and turn away. Not us, and not me. I'd lean over and say, "Boy, are you snotty!" Well, it's the truth, isn't it? Then, any fun loving SAG-Sag would laugh uproariously for having made the honest comment with a silly pun thrown in for good measure. The poor fellow glares defensively and stomps off. Finally, when we go to tell someone else about the incident, we might throw in a few extras. We might suggest that a wild brawl ensued, or that tables and waiters were knocked over in the fray. You see, a few harmless embellishments aren't criminal.

Unfortunately, we are driven by our forever expanding double Jupiter to constantly exploit any possible situation for even a bad laugh. When it comes to pointing out other people's faults, we never know when to stop. As cheery and good-natured as we can be, we can also get ourselves into some very serious trouble.

YOUR DARK SIDE

If there is one curse that has haunted me all my life, I'd have to say it's "bigmouthitis." Sometimes, I could just shoot myself with one of my own arrows for saying the most insulting things to people I truly like. I have literally lost important friendships because I blurted something out such as, "God, it's fabulous to see you. Wow, you have put on weight, haven't you? Oh, that's right, I did hear that you fell off the wagon." After realizing all too late that I've once again stuck my big horse hoof in my mouth, I'll offer the dear crushed thing a drink.

As loud as we SAG-Sags can cheer when we see others succeeding, we can boo, hiss, and stomp when we see anyone sitting on their butts, not fulfilling their potential. We'll take it upon ourselves to go up to complete strangers and utter our frank opinions unsolicited. No 1st Decan Jupiterite that I've ever encountered has fully mastered the art of diplomacy. Though we never intend to hurt anyone, we're notorious for trampling on other people's feelings.

Imagine, there I was with the entire royal family of England, all of whom were quite curious about their personal Starpower. So, I turned to Lady Mountbatten, the most dignified regal Aquarian you'd ever want to meet, and handed her a crystal, telling her loudly that it wards against venereal disease. The whole place became dead silent, horrified that I would bring up such a taboo subject. Well, planets were on my side that day, because, as luck would have it, Lady Mountbatten accepted my gift in good humor.

Nevertheless, that encounter could have resulted in my being banished by the court, an event that would have caused me severe upset. As everyone knows, hobnobbing with the Queen Mother and the princesses and princes is a delightful arena for hearing gossip!

With all humor aside, I strongly caution all SAG-Sags to travel with an appointed personal monitor who will clap his or her hand over your mouth when you start to commit a grave *faux pas*. The freedom with which we exercise our First Amendment rights is as overused as the freedom with which we spend money. Either way, it isn't easy to avoid those two pitfalls in this decan. It's always seemed to me that learning how to be polite and how to budget finances, both in one lifetime, is just too much to do!

YOUR LIGHT SIDE

I hate to resort to yet another cliché, though after all it is a habit of most SAGITTARIAN 1st Decans. So, for our defense, I'll employ a familiar yet truthful justification. No matter how much we ruffle feathers, no matter how wild and out of control we can become, and regardless of how bohemian our life-style can be, we are never, ever boring.

We zany Archers can walk into the dreariest affairs and liven them up in the blink of an eye. We can send just one zinging arrow of sarcastic wit into the center of the room, and pretty soon the whole crowd will be joining in on the fun.

But hold onto your hats, we are much more than just good-time Charlies. Don't assume that there isn't a serious side to our nature. Sure, we 1st Decan SAGs don't often express ourselves in emotional terms, but there is an intense, heartfelt desire that all Jupiter-Jupiterites share to ever expand our horizons. We are so philosophically hungry that we won't miss a chance to experience everything and everyone that we can. This is why it took me 40 years of studying astrology and practicing my theories on individuals from all possible walks of life, before I was truly ready to hang my hat on one approach.

Interestingly, though we can be obnoxiously impatient in the moment, we have an inner Sage living inside of us, who guides us in our adventures, always cautioning us against hurrying too fast. As Mutable/ Mutable creations, we do stop to smell the roses and reflect upon the world. In these quiet times, we own the market on wisdom; hence the name SAGITTARIUS, Wise One.

BOTTOM LINE FOR YOUR POWER

The need to learn with whom we can be frank, and with whom we'd better be quiet and pass the dip, is our highest challenge. I was frank with my first husband, Frank, and look where that got me! On the other hand, my children wouldn't be where they are today if it weren't for my ability to talk horse sense into them. We need to attain Discretion with a capital D, not always, as we've seen, an easy process.

Once learned, we simply have to trust in our own spirit of success. This decan tends to bloom later in life, or at least that has been my experience. It took me a few decades to find my magic touch, the special spark that is an everlasting flame. I'm damn proud of my accomplishments, and even prouder to have helped numerous others get their start. When we find our path, we SAGITTARIUS-Sagittarius men and women triumph always as: *Trailblazers.*

BODY TALK

Well, just look at us. Half-horse and half-man or half-woman, whichever sex you are, I hope you share with me the favored trait of SAGITTARIUS-Sagittarius: great thighs. I'm not bragging, although I am trying to get some mileage out of our two pillars of strength that get us all some mileage. From there it's all downhill.

Somehow, when Mother Nature was designing us, she was thinking along the same lines as those guys who used to design American cars. Remember the good old days for automobiles when bigger was better? Well, that is usually how an Arching Archer comes into the world, with big bones, big hips, and big appetites. They don't call us horsy for nothing! If any of you SAGITTARIAN

1st Decans out there have grown up petite, then you probably have a lucky planet somewhere in your chart. The rest of us can only rely on our inborn love of sports to keep us trim, a never-ending challenge if there ever was one.

As much complaining as I do about our natural propensity to expand, I'll praise our excellent health to the skies. It takes an army of flu germs to even make us sneeze. When we do get to feeling miserable, our positive constitution acts as a self-healing safeguard. However, sports injuries are common in this decan, especially along our spines. Being the gypsies that we are, we don't always take precautions for our health when we're out on long trips. My best advice to fellow SAG-Sags, when traveling away from home, is not to drink the water. Stick to wine and beer, or my favorite, fresh carrot juice.

Our ruling planet, Jupiter, in double strength for our decan (named for the god also known as Jove, who loved to drink and be merry) allows us to consume massive quantities of booze without appearing to be drunk. It can get dangerous. A typical stunt one of us might pull is to boast that we can drink any man or woman under the table and then walk a straight line. If you've been known to flaunt your immunity to alcohol, think again. Jovial we are, stupid we ain't.

Just in case any other decan reading this presumes that Jove has willed us an excessive appetite for the opposite sex, let me correct the fallacy. We love to talk about other people's kinkiness. We're actually almost shy in the bedroom ourselves, even with our silky smooth or muscular thighs as lures. If someone wants to seduce one of us, they'd better not go sliding their hands up our legs, without getting prior permission. The best ploy is to challenge one of us to a wrestling match and then let nature take its course. Both parties will soon come to understand why "thighs" and "sighs" sound so much alike!

YOUR BEST-BET CAREERS

Remember that dreaded word confinement? That is unquestionably the professional demise of any 1st Decan SAGITTARIUS. Routine is also the kiss of death in any job we tackle. Although the other extreme (i.e., unemployment) can cause severe emotional distress to every male or female bow-and-arrow-sporting Centaur.

I'd have to say that aside from my many marital blunders, I've been on perfect astrological target with my choices of vocations. Notice, please, that I refer to them in the plural. For one of our type to be completely satisfied with only one career is a rare occurrence indeed.

My first love, though not my earliest work experience, was astrology. Although the Water signs tend to dominate in the occult fields, it is our decan of fiery SAGITTARIUS that wins hands down when it comes to astrological predictions. We don't get caught up with petty details, but we do pay heed to important planetary trends. As you must know by now, I can only thank Jupiter for giving me the gift of excellent foresight, and for giving me the opportunity to make money using it!

In the early days, my revulsion at the thought of being cooped up at home set me trotting off with the circus. I would equally recommend any restless hearts among you to give Ringling Brothers a ring.

Or take our decan's penchant for gala productions and march straight over to the other glamorous big top–Broadway musical comedy. Nabbing lead roles is a cinch for any of us flamboyant ones. Do beware that you'll have to take orders from controlling directors before you make this your lifelong mission. As performers, we SAG-Sags tend to trailblaze off into our own genres. The Divine Miss M, Bette Midler (12/1), couldn't get arrested during her first years of struggling as a singer/ actress until she decided that if she "couldn't join em, she'd beat em" by doing her own thing. And look at her now!

With our flash, we can't help but strike gold, or at least gold lame, when we splash onto the fashion, beauty, and cosmetic scenes. Where do you think I got my inspiration for my versatile and fetching headbands? Right in my designing lst Decan SAGITTARIUS head, that's where. I pulled an even more original business caper some years ago, when I combined my knowledge of astrology with my flair for makeup application, by opening up a clinic that specialized in facial peels and cosmetic surgery. Every client who came in was analyzed from a decan perspective, and we never did surgery when planetary trends were negative. In fact, I was the first person to go public with permanent eyeliner, training facialists and doctors from all over the world in its process.

I've saved the best for last. Yes, I know all you similar-thinking SAG-Sags will guess what I'm about to say. Any profession that is any way connected with sports is a must do for this decan. From athletic players, to team owners or managers or coaches, we can't help but WIN-WIN-WIN. Growing up, I was taught boxing as my first sport. Then there was gymnastics, ice skating, and tackle football. Later, as an oldster, I threw myself into tap dancing and flirted with skydiving. You can use your imagination to figure out what kinds of wild sportswear I've been creating for these various pursuits.

I am most proud of my pioneering for women's physical fitness. Thirty years ago in Washington, D.C., I opened up the first women's gym in the country. As so often happens with our decan, I was way ahead of my time. I was ridiculed, told that my venture would never last, and literally laughed out of town. If I had crumbled under that derision, I would have never lived to see my dreams come true. Guess Who had the last laugh! Not only did I return to D.C. with Sylvester when he was honored for his contribution to fitness by the president of the United States, I was also treated as a royal descendant of the very city that had rejected me. By the time that I'd put a women's wrestling team on the sports and entertainment maps, I was getting invitations left and right to return to Washington to organize women's athletics. Fat chance! The stupendous success of G.L.O.W., my Gorgeous Ladies of Wrestling, was rivaled only by my Beautiful Women of Boxing, the very sport that got me punching as a kid. Victory is sweet, let me tell you. Or perhaps you already know what I'm talking about, being of the same mind-set. The challenge is the reward.

One further suggestion from my files of successful kooky ideas is my astrology/tarot board game, "Tell A Fortune" with my friend Daphne, as seen on TV. If we can make a game out of anything, we will. And why not? More Starpower to all of us, that's what I say. We SAG-Sags need lots of different ways to make money because we know so many more ways to spend it!

I do apologize for making this section rather self-congratulatory. It took me such a long time to learn how to pat myself on the back that I'm just making up for lost time. We are normally extremely modest when it comes to our accomplishments, unless of course, as in this case, we're talking among friends, right? Here's to us–happy hunting!!

YOUR BEST-BET LOVE COMBOS

SAGITTARIUS-Sagittarius Man: Did someone say hunting? Do I detect those ears of you male double Archers perking up? Unless you have cauliflower in yours, you've just heard your own mating call. You lads are notoriously on the hunt, always on the lookout for the damsels of your dreams, unsuspecting babes whose heartstrings you'd like to strum. I probably don't need to tell you that you pursue the most unavailable women you can find. Let's see, any older women you've chased lately? How about older and married? Or, how about older, married, and living in another country? Long-distance love is your favorite, isn't it?

Somehow you manage to drag home your booty after each hunt, no matter how difficult the chase. All your buddies are probably stewing in their juices, unable to figure out how you claimed your most recent prize. How do you do it? Simple, you have an infectious enthusiasm that even the most unavailable gals can't resist. You don't get them with steamy sexuality, nor with quiet machismo. You use your arrows of wit. Sure, sometimes you're too blunt. And sometimes when you get the girt back to your bedroom you don't know whether to play a game (of checkers with her or take her in your arms. Sorry to say, you aren't natural lovers. But, you can always learn. As the nerdy-looking SAG-Sag Woody Allen (12/1) once explained when asked how he got to be so good in bed, you can always "practice a lot—alone!"

You'll note that the men of the 1st Decan of SAGITTARIUS score lots of high marks on the Stallone Love Scale, meaning you've got lots of choices. However, I do want to beg you to overcome your fear that long-term commitment will limit your ability at marksmanship. Remember that once you've come home from your hunt, you'll have to do a little more than stuff her like a trophy and mount her bust on the wall, just so you can go out and hunt some more game. That is why I'm going to give Ms. ARIES-Leo your phone number. She'll cure you of being footloose and fancy-free. Ever been horsewhipped?

SAGITTARIUS-Sagittarius Woman: Once again we'll have to dig up some tales of woe from my archives to illustrate how unpredictable we feminine SAG-Sag ladies can be.

Basically, romance is an adventure for us. We hate to know the ending before the story has been told. And, that is how, over and over again, we mistrust our own instincts, jump into love affairs that are obviously risky, and wind up having to drop them like hot potatoes. I can't say that I ever married for true love. I can also testify that I never married for money. I did it for the sheer enthusiasm of it! I'd think, "Gee, a wedding to throw. What fun!" Sure, I had vague premonitions that he was going to want a domestic servant, but I thought that I could be the one goddess to set him straight. Wrong, wrong, wrong.

We 1st Decan women of SAGITTARIUS are so irresistible that men find themselves proposing to us on the first date. We shouldn't really blame the guys, now should we? We're the ones who don't know how to "just say no." Don't get me wrong, I'm not talking about being able to say no to casual sex. Yuck. As wild as we are in some areas, we are extremely private and possessive about our bodies. Oh, we talk a good game, flirting our way right into his heart, and, um, certain other strategic anatomical areas. But, before we'll actually prove ourselves, we have to have that silly ring on our fingers, which later turns out to be a Yoke around our necks, a chain to the dishwasher, and dirty diapers. Who, us, independent? Absolutely! By the time the honeymoon is over and hubby starts asking for his meat loaf, the nightmare begins. We 1st Decan SAGITTARIAN women won't actually ditch the dude until we've exhausted all possibilities, but we do have a saturation point at which time a divorce lawyer's phone number is a very handy item. A few cases of damp tissues later, we're back on our feet, ready to start the cycle all over again.

I want to caution all my gal friends of this decan not to go leaping off with any guy just because he chalks up a good score on the astrological Love Scale. It takes a very unique man to merit our long-term devotion, something we do have for the taking. We have some serious needs. He has to be nice looking, successful, understanding, progressive, loving, and patient. But he can't be overly demonstrative. We sporty SAGITTARIUS-Sagittarius women like to do our riding behind closed doors. If this man answers all those prerequisites and also happens to be, an AQUARIUS-Libra, a guaranteed match is just around the corner. This is a double Sextile chemistry that will get us to say "yes" even without a promise of matrimony. Once his Air starts blowing on our Fire—watch out! Not that I can vouch from personal experience, but there's nothing wrong with having high expectations, is there?

DECAN PAIRS WITH SAGITTARIUS-SAGITTARIUS

LOVE SCALE SCORES

0 = Forget it! • 1 = Don't be a masochist... • 2 = Why bother? • 3 = Fun for one date. • 4 = It won't last! • 5 = You could do better! • 6 = Romance will fade... 7 = Great buddies! • 8 = Pure passion • 9 = True love. • 10 = Eternal bliss!

STARS OF SAGITTARIUS-SAGITTARIUS

November 25:	John F. Kennedy, Jr.
	Christina Applegate
November 26:	Tina Turner
November 27:	Jimi Hendrix
	Bruce Lee
	Robin Givens
November 29:	Jacqueline Stallone
	Howie Mandel
December 1:	Bette Midler
	Woody Allen
December 2:	Gianni Versace
	Maria Callas
	Monica Seles

SECOND DECAN OF SAGITTARIUS

12/3 - 12/12

"I'M INDEPENDENT AND I'M AGGRESSIVE."

SAGITTARIUS-Aries   MUTABLE-Cardinal   JUPITER-Mars

Please, don't put yourselves on the offensive when I make the suggestion that you Archer Ram blends are the original fighters. The combined influences of Jupiter and Mars create an innate conflict in your personality.

Like any SAGITTARIAN, you have a wild, jovial spirit that is pure and contagious. But the overbearing need you have to dominate, brought to you by just a dash of Aries in this 2nd Decan, sets you on an almost perpetual warpath. Part of you, shown in your Mutable style, always wants the freedom to roam and ramble. However, that Cardinal part of you, ambitious and aggressive, acts as a guilty conscience, forcing you to stay put and establish your own dynasty.

As a result of these warring parties within you, you often express yourself in a combative, confrontational manner. It's almost as if picking fights is fun for you. I do have to admit that your audacious behavior can be rather entertaining to others as well. And, there are benefits to your complicated "M.O." Your unique brand of charm and intimidation earns you a level of respect from your peers that no other SAGITTARIAN can merit.

I can just see you all now, getting red in the face, putting up your dukes, accusing me of having led you astray by claiming previously that 2nd Decans are usually the most balanced of the sign. I'm not about to eat my words in your case and get myself on your bad side. As feisty as you are, there is a balancing agent within you that is your secret link to Starpower. You embody the very best attributes of the philosopher. You grapple with ideas and belief systems just as readily as you struggle to assert your opinions. You have extraordinary instincts that zero in on other people like flying arrows zooming straight for a bull's-eye. When you fight for a just cause, you have heroic ambitions, uncommon to many of us other SAG decans. Ultimately in life you are bound for a noble title, that of the Wise Warrior. That is, of course, if your flair for a flaring temper doesn't get you first.

YOUR DARK SIDE

Look, I've already put you through the ringer over your characteristic enthusiasm for striking up verbal duels with others whenever you can. If the truth be known, your combat mode can be very engaging, at least to me. There is an end result that can be personally devastating to you, however. So, please accept my analysis with my genuine concern for your well-being.

All of us SAGITTARIANS love a challenge, but some of us recuperate when we fail to attain our goals. Some of us don't, do we? Or should I say, do you,

you SAGITTARIUS-Aries gang members? You are the worst losers I've ever met. Admitting that you were wrong or that you made a mistake is harder for you than having a sex change. Listen, when I commit a typical SAG-Sag blunder by insulting someone needlessly, I suffer for days, blaming myself for bungling an opportunity at friendship. The only thing you guys fret about after you've decided to give somebody a piece of your mind, is that you didn't bury them for good.

You hate to lose in business and you're surprisingly tight with the bucks for a freewheeling SAGITTARIAN, aren't you? You don't like to lose in any competition of physical or mental strength, so much so that you'll assume the game was rigged if the winner doesn't happen to be you. Losing in love can cost you years. Frankly, from one blunt Archer to another, you can ruin your life by crying over spilt milk. What a rotten way to short-circuit the potential power so amply available to you.

YOUR LIGHT SIDE

Now calm down, the worst is over. As unruly as you are when things don't go your way, you are swift and surefooted when things work out. And the secret of why things usually do work out for you lies within those fabulous instincts of yours. Being half-human/horse and half-Ram, you've got a sense of smell that is out of this world. You sniff out opportunity before it even knocks. You sense disaster before it strikes. One whiff and you can size up your oppositions' weakness and strengths.

While the 1st Decan of SAGITTARIUS is excellent at seeing the future, I'd have to say that you 2nd Decans are even better at revealing it. Your Aries style of expression is always clear-cut, emphatic, forceful. You also have the noted SAGITTARIAN talent for calling the cards as you see them fall.

Sometimes you may even say something off the cuff, not even knowing how prophetic you really are. Later, you'll amaze others and yourself when your words prove you to be the prophet of the day.

Don't take this gift of yours for granted. As someone who will always be highly competitive, you can maneuver the odds in your favor with everything you do. You can also prepare yourself for failures that you may have to experience, and realize that your gains will always outweigh your losses.

BOTTOM LINE FOR YOUR POWER

Taking this ability one step further, once you accept the fact that the success of another doesn't take away from your success, you'll stop expending energy for useless spats. You'll unleash an unbridled power for achieving major coups. With your knack for confrontation, you can instill enthusiasm in those who have grown sluggish or lazy.

No matter what you undertake, you breathe fire into your pursuits. That's why you are unrivaled as: an *Igniter*.

BODY TALK

If only my publisher would let me, I'd just skip over this section. You Centaur/Archer/Ram beings live too close to home for me to sleep easily once I've laid it on the line here. I'll be as gentle as I can, which as you might assume, is a tough chore for me. For the love of Jove, one of your planetary rulers, I've got to get you 2nd Decan SAGITTARIANS to realize that you are not immortal. Your health isn't even astrologically that good. It's very simple: you're excessive. You play too much and you play rough. You take off with tons of gusto in the beginning of the race, and then burn yourself out before you cross the finish line. Instead of resting or taking a break, you'll trot on over to another track and push yourself further into exhaustion.

Okay, so you're hyper. Well, so am I. But I go to the doctor when I should. Not those of you born under the decan of SAGITTARIUS-Aries, you don't believe in doctors. Admitting that you're not feeling well is as difficult as admitting you were wrong about something. The stars have not been overly generous with you when it comes to overall fitness. You've got hands that are always getting broken, sprained, or bruised, a susceptibility to upper respiratory and other lung ailments, and a tendency to get headaches.

Expanding Jupiter and bossy Mars make it very hard for you to say "no thanks" to the pleasures of wine, food, and song. Even though your love of athletics helps to control weight gain, and keeps you from becoming a sloppy drunk, you will have to watch those temptations all your life.

As a consolation prize, you can comfort yourself with your eternally heightened sense of smell. You probably are highly attracted to certain people because of their personal scent, and repulsed by others for the same reason. Being a connoisseur of perfumes or colognes, you usually surround yourself with delicious fragrances at all times. Often, members of the opposite sex will follow the enticing, seductive aroma that wafts from you. I realize that you'd much rather have been given a body perfect, but smelling good covers up your physical flaws, How's that for positive thinking?

YOUR BEST-BET CAREERS

At last we come to an area in which you high-strung, arrow-slinging, ramrodding folks are indomitable. Independence and aggression may sometimes work against you in personal interactions, but on almost any work scene you are a powerful force. Both men and women of this decan can handle rough, rugged conditions and high levels of job stress. The only barrier you'll face is having to act as a subordinate to another's authority. You'll move up the chain of command so rapidly, however, that the years spent at the beck and call of someone else rarely take their toll.

As the Wise Warrior you can combine your love of travel with your fighter's instinct by joining the Peace Corps or overseas branches of the Red Cross. Also, combining your philosophical bent with your sports fanaticism, any of the Eastern martial arts will win you scores of black belts. From kung fu to karate to judo, you've got a wide arena to choose from.

One reason that you're always banging up your hands is that you are the classic busy beaver on any building project. Hammering nails or driving power equipment are skills that can land you careers in fields such as construction, engineering, real estate development, and architecture.

Of all the millions of little boys all over the world who dream of growing up to be firemen, it is rightfully the SAG-Aries ones who should pursue fire fighting professionally. Okay, if any of you female Archer/Rams want to blast your hoses on leaping flames, be my guest. After all, it does lie within your decan potential. But don't overlook the rigorous, adventurous demands of equestrian-related work. Horse racing, polo, ranching, wrangling, and roping are all fields for you to excel in.

Even though you have a highly competitive streak, and even though several SAG-Aries types have made big names for themselves in front of the cameras, I wouldn't urge you to throw yourself into an acting career. As much as you hate to lose, you will find yourself suffering something awful every time you miss out on the tiniest of roles. However, a behind-the-scenes position in producing, theatrical set and costume designing, or film promotion, will make you a happy camper.

Where you are not natively artistic, you have a remarkable appreciation for the creative talents of others. In fact, one of the few spending indulgences you'll allow yourself is in arts and entertainment. Otherwise, that Aries influence in your decan places a tight fist on your purse. With your prophetic talents you usually can foretell the shifts in the stock market before they happen. All in all, you are a "sense"-ational bargain hunter. Which is why, if you are at your wit's end for want of employment, you could always hire yourself out as a professional shopper. That way you could fight with the sales clerk to your heart's delight, and earn money while you're doing it!

YOUR BEST-BET LOVE COMBOS

SAGITTARIUS-Aries Man: If ever there was a lack of self-awareness as to how you come across to the opposite sex, it is in this decan. You seem to imagine yourself as a type of Casanova, a galloping gourmand of the female species; you haven't a clue as to why you are always getting your face slapped. It's because you are inconsiderate, a bad listener, and insensitive. Yet, you have convinced yourself that you are every woman's dream date. Well, dream again.

Maybe as a kid you watched a lot of old romantic movies, the kind where Bogart, swarthy and feisty, ends up winning over the dame in the final frame of the film. Unfortunately for you, it is rare that the scenarios you enter have such pat endings. In this day and age, the appeal of being called "toots" and "babe" and "sweetheart" has gone out of fashion. The playful tough guys that you Archer/Rams can be are just too damn rough, physically and verbally. If I believed that you just didn't like women, I'd say to hang it up, and nail up a

Bachelor sign on your door. As it is, though, your natural zest for life seems to peak around the ladies. You have some serious learning to do before you're ready to be the romantic hero you fancy yourself to be.

Start with realizing that kissing and touching a girl can't be approached with the same ardor that you have when you duke it out with the boys. Then, wash out your garbage mouth with soap four times before you scare off a lady with too many four-letter words. Finally, try to meet a lovely Ms. AQUARIUS-Aquarius. Even when you do stumble back into your brutish ways, her aloof cool temper won't flair. She'll have several campaigns to save the world in the works, just enough to keep her busy while you're out on your independent ventures. A fight may arise as to who gets to sleep on top. But, you enjoy a couple of rounds in the ring every now and then, don't you?

SAGITTARIUS-Aries Woman: Compliments, first of all, to all the girls of this 2nd Decan of SAGITTARIUS, for rarely letting a man run your life. You, unlike those of us in the 1st and 3rd Decans, usually restrain your enthusiasm for marriage proposals and the like, as you heed the voice of your instincts telling you "this guy's a loser."

However, there are a couple of idiosyncrasies common to female Centaur/Rams that may not be quite so self-preserving. If and when you decide that the fellow is Mr. Right, you could knock him out cold before he has time to slip a ring on your finger. You can be extremely boisterous. Over a dinner date, off on an outing, or in bed during an "inning," you are a far cry from a demure, quiet, retiring type, that's for sure. I would say that the word unladylike is fitting, wouldn't you? Just be careful that your need to win a philosophical match of wits, or even a physical contest of strength, doesn't intimidate the poor guy.

The fact is that you are a very energetic, ambitious woman, not made for any old so-and-so. You're a thousand times more industrious around the home and with children than I am. And, except for a hint of the dominatrix in you, your Jupiter/Mars sexual appetite should be a delight for that special "hungry" man. Whoever makes your heart skip a beat should be able to beam with pride that he's conquered your interest. The one fellow who has pride to spare, and a congeniality that will bring out the best in you, is a LEO-Sagittarius. With so much trine and Fire action, I'd say the two of you won't even have to spend money on central heating.

DECAN PAIRS WITH SAGITTARIUS-ARIES

LOVE SCALE SCORES

0 = Forget it! • 1 = Don't be a masochist... • 2 = Why bother? • 3 = Fun for one date. • 4 = It won't last! • 5 = You could do better! • 6 = Romance will fade... 7 = Great buddies! • 8 = Pure passion • 9 = True love. • 10 = Eternal bliss!

STARS OF SAGITTARIUS-ARIES

December 3:	Daryl Hannah	December 9:	Kirk Douglas
December 5:	Walt Disney	December 10:	Dorothy Lamour
December 7:	Larry Bird	December 12:	Frank Sinatra
December 8:	Sinead O'Connor		Dionne Warwick
	Jim Morrison		
	Sammy Davis, Jr.		
	Kim Basinger		

THIRD DECAN OF SAGITTARIUS

12/13 - 12/21

"I'M INDEPENDENT AND I'M EXTREMELY PROUD."

SAGITTARIUS-Leo	MUTABLE-Fixed	JUPITER-Sun

As the Sun makes its third and final stop in the Sun sign of SAGITTARIUS, we come to yet another unusual and highly magnetic 3rd Decan. With Jupiter as your dominant ruler, you are ever the explorer, wanderer, and adventurer.

However, your Leo shadings have instilled within you a love for noble pursuits, as well as a love for the attention that you get for those pursuits. The Sun, as a part-time influence, acts to draw positive energy toward you from, others something you probably appreciate already.

Being on the border of serious Capricorn, you haven't escaped the rigid discipline of Saturn. Where other SAGs approach everything with equal gusto, you Cardinal-Fixed movers are very selective about where you'll put your focus. As a natural entertainer, you rarely commit the same brash verbal no-no's that we 1st Decans do so regularly. Nor do you swashbuckle your way straight into an argument in the fashion of the 2nd Decan SAGS. You somehow manage to be honest and diplomatic at the same time. Lucky you!

So, what makes you unusual? Well, I was almost inclined to call you the happiest decan of the zodiac—gregarious, charming, achievement oriented, expressive, proud, filled with wonderful and original ideas, free, usually blessed with tons of opportunity and good fortune. But, every time I ask one of you Centaur/Lion breeds how you're really feeling, you respond with a smirk rather than a smile. Doesn't look too happy to me, that's for sure! At the heart of this discrepancy is a 12th-house complication, where you've stored some spooky quirks. What results is basically a split between your public and your private personalities. Let's examine the latter as we discuss the negative ruts that can limit anyone born into this potentially powerful decan.

YOUR DARK SIDE

Listen, all SAGITTARIANS are sarcastic. We never mean to hurt feelings, it's just that if we see an opportunity to get away with oral murder, we will. We're all a bunch of mischievous Archers. However, that private side of you 3rd Decan of SAGITTARIUS does tend to be seriously cynical. Although you won't just blurt out a derogatory comment toward another, I know that you're thinking it. And my guess is that you mean it.

That's why, even though you surround yourself with fond admirers during most of the hours of the day, you probably prefer the solitude of your own activities to the company of others, whom you basically don't respect. Or, why you might find yourself moving from one social group to another, being the restless type that you are. Yes, I'm sorry to say, but you have a mild superiority complex. Let's throw in a dose of excessive vanity, and see if we push any of your buttons.

You keep your faults extremely well hidden, but every now and then you probably expose yourself–long enough to tear someone else's ego to shreds. Come on, haven't you told yourself on several occasions that 99 percent of the rest of the world is a bunch of poorly attired idiots? And haven't you, once or twice, accidentally blasted someone to bits for being an incompetent nincompoop? You're probably nodding in agreement at this very moment, at the same time as you're reminding yourself that the person you blasted was an incompetent nincompoop.

Look, I don't really care if you'd prefer to sit back and scoff at your fellow human beings, but it doesn't seem to be productive. Especially when you've got so many other great things going for you.

YOUR LIGHT SIDE

You know one of my favorite words, and something that I believe separates the true champs from the "wannabes," is the word commitment. This is something that you're not short on, by any means. No matter what your true feelings about someone are, once you've given him or her your word, you'll honor that promise until your death.

Added to that, your Jupiterian love of trying new experiences, and that Sunny/ Leo knack for style both give you a distinctive touch in whatever you've chosen to do. I'll bet you have a fabulous, unique way that you articulate your language. I'll bet you have a special walk that is your very own.

All of us SAGITTARIANS are clotheshorses, but you guys and gals are the only ones who have truly good taste. You've probably been making fashion statements since you were in designer diapers. Last, and certainly not least, the one group of people that you do not scorn, is your family. SAGITTARIUS-Leo men and women revere their elders. This is where you show true Lion's pride.

BOTTOM LINE FOR YOUR POWER

I do hope that you'll take my words of criticism to heart, and get to work at ridding yourself of that chip on your shoulder. At the same time, don't completely lose your self-confidence. That would be like throwing the baby out with the bath water!

You can actually capitalize on your cockiness by combining it with your sincere concern for serious issues. That public you, who knows how to draw attention with the greatest of ease, can spread a sense of joy and truth, which is in fact your highest Archer Lion quest. Your mission, should you decide to accept it, is as: an *Entertainer*.

BODY TALK

All right, don't get smug. You part-Human, part-Horse, and part-Lion unusual types just got lucky in the body department. You got strong hearts, strong and supple thighs, and a proud, athletic stance. Are you happy now? There is something unusual about you physically that happens but once in the zodiac, and it happens to have happened with this 3rd Decan of SAGITTARIUS. You have moles! You got it, these blemishes, otherwise known as beauty marks, usually occur in spades on those with gorgeous bods and excellent health.

If for some reason, your body is mole-free, you probably have some other sort of skin sensitivity. Maybe you experience an overgrowth of hair, in certain places. Whichever has happened in your individual case, the occurrence may cause you undue worry. Get over it, you've been given priceless permanent health as a reward. Besides, moles are kind of cute.

For unknown reasons, you SAG-Leo boys and girls are excessively prudish about your bodies, despite the fact that you can be such showoffs in other areas. But, if you had your druthers, you'd rather be looked at than touched, wouldn't you? You also don't really enjoy sports as much as the rest of us horsy types. Being wise and vain, however, you'll keep up a, strict regimen of diet and exercise to preserve what nature has been so kind to give you. My astral gossip tells me that Jane Fonda (12/21) never really liked working out, but found that it was the one thing to save her from pigging-out like a madwoman. What a smart cookie she's been, convincing us to buy her books and tapes, thinking we'll end up with her perfect figure. She's sure gotten the lion's share of profit on this venture. Hmmm, I wonder where her moles are?

YOUR BEST-BET CAREERS

You want the constant challenge that every SAG requires, but you consider yourself to be above so very many professions that your choices fall into a fairly narrow vein. Primarily, you can't go wrong with any of the entertainment fields, whether you own the spotlight or you're running the show. I think Steven Spielberg (12/18) has taken his independent pride to the level of pure genius. My riding cap is completely off to him for giving the world the very best in film production and direction.

Because of that highly developed sarcasm we've already discussed, I'd definitely suggest political satire as a haven for professional success for this decan. Whether as a cartoonist, or as an impressionist, you'll be able to ridicule politicians all under the guise of entertainment. Or, if you'd like, jump into the political game yourself. You'll put that wicked, wry sense of humor to work, making what could under other circumstances be boring speeches. Given your sense of honesty, when you say, "Read my lips," you'll keep campaign promises.

We haven't forgotten your fondness for philosophy, nor your admiration for the greats of yesteryear. Teaching the works of Socrates, Plato, and Hippocrates will give you an opportunity to plug your heroes.

And not to overlook that developed sense of personal style, I'd love to see some of you trying your hands at jewelry design and sales. Harry Winston, the jewelry czar, ain't got nothing on you!

Some of you may want to ask how this decan fares with money. Generally, I should respond, "don't ask." You have as high an earning potential as any SAGITTARIUS, but your creature comfort needs and tastes are those of the aristocracy. Fortunately, you tend to attract wealth in your marriage partners, the very topic of our next section.

YOUR BEST-BET LOVE COMBOS

SAGITTARIUS-Leo Man: Well, naturally, as a guy who thinks he's Mr. Brilliant all the time, you're going to be mighty hard to fix up. In your heart you believe that most of the women you meet are not good enough for you. Oh, but you do have one vulnerable area that I will now bring to your attention. Since most of you bow-and-arrow-carrying Centaur Lion mixes grow up with a deep love and respect for parents, you guys tend to have "Mama" complexes. Your mother probably adored you, told you that you were the greatest, washed and cleaned and cooked just for her baby boy.

Consequently, every female you date has to measure up to the supermom who reared you. And watch out if she has maternal inclinations. You'll tumble off your mount for a girl who bears even a remote similarity to Mommy. If she happens to love the role of maid, chef, financial manager, and kiddie chauffeur, you experience a type of love obsession, and you'll propose on the spot. Unless you warn her from the beginning that you can be a major slob, and a major snob, and that you don't handle money well, you'll find yourself out on the street before the honeymoon's even paid for.

Fortunately for you male SAGITTARIAN 3rd Decans, you have incredible personal charm and noble honesty. And, because of the combined planetary vibes from Jupiter and the Sun, together with your very specific needs, you usually marry but once and for life. I hope when you do that she will be an ARIES-Aries, a bossy, competent woman all the way. When you misbehave she'll just turn you on by saying, "Go to your room!"

SAGITTARIUS-Leo Woman: There is a method in the madness of you Archer Lioness ladies, which a lot of us other gals should study. Somehow you always have a trail of men following you. And they're not just any men, they're smart, they're rich, they're handsome. They also must be masochists, because you play so hard to get that you damn near torture the poor things!

When you finally agree to even date one of them, it's as if you're doing him a favor. The more you treat them like irritating flies, the more they swarm around you. Having your vast reservoir of Jupiter joviality, you enjoy milking every second of their torment. But, at the same time, that Fixed Leo planning in the back of your mind is screening each and every one for marriage suitability. What exactly can make you drop the fly swatter for a man is pure intelligence.

A man who is handsome, rich, and not just smart but creatively brilliant, will transform you into a romantic mush mouth. If he happens to be a Cardinal-Cardinal, LIBRA-Libra, his pulsing Venus can make a true sensual woman out of you-something you probably never thought possible. He'll bring out the very best in you. And when you've got a good thing, you hold on to it, so to speak... .

DECAN PAIRS WITH SAGITTARIUS-LEO

SAGITTARIUS-Leo &

ARIES-Aries (3/21-3/30) 9
ARIES-Leo (3/31-4/9) 8
ARIES-Sagittarius (4/10-4/20) 7
TAURUS-Taurus (4/21-4/30) 2
TAURUS-Virgo (5/1-5/10) 4
TAURUS-Capricorn (5/11-5/20) 4
GEMINI-Gemini (5/21-5/31) 5
GEMINI-Libra (6/1-6/10) 6
GEMINI-Aquarius (6/11-6/20) 2
CANCER-Cancer (6/21-7/1) 5
CANCER-Scorpio (7/2-7/12) 4
CANCER-Pisces (7/13-7/22) 6
LEO-Leo (7/23-8/1) 8
LEO-Sagittarius (8/2-8/12) 8
LEO-Aries (8/13-8/22) 8
VIRGO-Virgo (8/23-9/3) 2
VIRGO-Capricorn (9/4-9/13) 4
VIRGO-Taurus (9/14-9/22) 2
LIBRA-Libra (9/23-10/3) 9
LIBRA-Aquarius (10/4-10/13) 7
LIBRA-Gemini (10/14-10/22) 6
SCORPIO-Scorpio (10/23-11/2) 2
SCORPIO-Pisces (11/3-11/12) 7
SCORPIO-Cancer (11/13-11/22) 4
SAGITTARIUS-Sagittarius (11/23-12/2) 7
SAGITTARIUS-Aries (12/3-12/11) 7
SAGITTARIUS-Leo (12/12-12/21) 8
CAPRICORN-Capricorn (12/22-12/31) 8
CAPRICORN-Taurus (1/1-1/10) 6
CAPRICORN-Virgo (1/11-1/19) 5
AQUARIUS-Aquarius (1/20-1/29) 6
AQUARIUS-Gemini (1/30-2/8) 6
AQUARIUS-Libra (2/9-2/18) 9
PISCES-Pisces (2/19-2/29) 4
PISCES-Cancer (3/1-3/10) 3
PISCES-Scorpio (3/11-3/20) 2

LOVE SCALE SCORES

0 = Forget it! • 1 = Don't be a masochist... • 2 = Why bother? • 3 = Fun for one date. • 4 = It won't last! • 5 = You could do better! • 6 = Romance will fade...
7 = Great buddies! • 8 = Pure passion • 9 = True love. • 10 = Eternal bliss!

STARS OF SAGITTARIUS-LEO

December 13:	Dick Van Dyke
December 14:	Lee Remick
	Patty Duke
	Dee Wallace Stone
December 15:	Tim Conway
	Don Johnson
December 16:	Liv Ullmann
December 18:	Steven Spielberg
	Brad Pitt
	Keith Richards
	Kiefer Sutherland
	Betty Grable
December 19:	Robert Urich
	Jennifer Beals
	Edith Piaf
	Cicely Tyson
December 20:	Irene Dunne
December 21:	Jane Fonda
	Phil Donahue
	Frank Zappa

CHAPTER 12

CAPRICORN

DECEMBER 22 - JANUARY 19

First Decan	Second Decan	Third Decan
CAPRICORN-Capricorn	CAPRICORN-Taurus	CAPRICORN-Virgo
12/22 - 12/31	1/1 - 1/10	1/11 - 1/19

When asked what was wanted for a birthday present,
one CAPRICORN responded, "Someone to take care of me!"

Sign:	Earth - Attainers
Symbol:	The Goat
Planet:	Saturn
Body Talk:	Bones, Knees
Style:	Cardinal

MEET THE CLIMBER...

"I'M MASTERFUL."

This is no pleasant task for me, but someone's got to do the dirty work in explaining to all you clinging, climbing "Kids" why anyone on earth would want to say rude things about you. You certainly don't nit-pick at others like the purist Virgins, nor do you boss the rest of the world around like the generals of Aries. Leos, with all their exhibitionist traits are absolute aliens to you. You can probably understand why people would gossip about the flaky Geminis, yet you still can't grasp why you Capricorns end up being the butt of most of the astrological jokes.

It's because you're so dang serious! Saturn, the disciplinarian and major power planet, hovers over you constantly, like a stern voice nagging you all the time. You are probably plagued with these inner whisperings that you haven't finished all your homework, or paid all your dues. Do you worry that you haven't achieved enough status? Or how about the biggie-that you're falling behind in your perpetual climb toward the summit of the mountain? You may suffer from a chronic fear that you're losing your grip, literally and figuratively. And we haven't even begun to talk about your negative side yet! Just kidding.

As Cardinal Earth signs, you Goats must achieve the highest levels of success or you will feel your life is worthless. Money, career excellence, recognition, physical security, and emotional intimacy are all matters of supreme importance. Because most of you secretly consider yourselves to be the underdogs of the world, you will work tenaciously to get to the top in all those areas.

And the fact is that, whether you give yourself credit or not, you almost always prevail. There you'll be, scrambling up to the very top of the mountain, little, skinny, serious old CAP, with all the rest of us hustlers down below wondering how you, of all the signs, managed to master the difficult route. It's because you've learned your lessons along the way, and that slave-driver Saturn is finally rewarding you with victory.

Now, if this picture seems unrealistic to any of you Goats out there, please don't "kid" yourself. You may cover up your eternal desperation to succeed with a clever, subtle sense of humor. You may profess to be above counting the pennies in your piggy bank on a daily basis, or deny that you live in dread of sudden catastrophe. Unless you have emerged as a new personality after years of psychotherapy, no matter what your decan, I'm sorry to report that the planets have dinged you with an inferiority complex of the worst order. But before you launch yourself into Saturnian doom, do remember that you're the one looking down the mountain at everybody else. You'll outlive and outdo all the others. You may not be chuckling now, but you always get the last laugh.

FIRST DECAN OF CAPRICORN

"I'M MASTERFUL. I'M VERY MASTERFUL."

CAPRICORN-Capricorn	CARDINAL-Cardinal	SATURN-Saturn

All right, so I was a tad rough on all you CAPRICORNS, so what? You guys are always giving yourselves a hard time, anyway, especially you perfectionist 1st Decan Goat boys and girls. But for the moment, you can relax, because I'm going to load you up with compliments galore, and you've earned it. Being at the beginning of this Sun sign means that you get a double dose of lesson-learning Saturn. You are so worldly wise that no matter how high you get on your success ladder, your head will never be in the clouds. And even though close friends may poke fun at some of your funks, you have the most unique ability to enlist the assistance of others on your trek up the hill. Yours is a kind of quiet yet acknowledged influence over most everyone you know. That's why, in your conservative, understated manner, you end up as the chief executive officer in every field you enter.

CARDINAL-Cardinal style when it is in an EARTH-Earth decan, such as yours, suggests big and dramatic movements of earth. CAPRICORN-Capricorns have astrologically built-in power, potentially as devastating as a downright earthquake, and as positively strong as the earthen blocks used to build the pyramids. Add to that, the dramatic Saturn turns of events that always seem to come your way, and you have got to see that you are one of the heavyweight decans, masters and mistresses of the great challenges.

Many of you place so much stress on how much money you have in the bank, or why you haven't been elected president when you're already vice president at age twenty-five, that it may take you years to meet up with your personal power. Well, let me be the first to introduce you to yourself. Aside from your neurotic phobias, you are indeed perfect!

YOUR DARK SIDE

All decans of Earth signs are materialists, so you're not completely alone in your obsession with cash flow. Unless you CAP-Caps contain your panic at the prospect of poverty, however, all that fabulous mastery of yours will be useless. I'd have to say that whether you grew up during the Great Depression, or have studied that era, or maybe just heard some firsthand stories from others" you really believe that the market could crash at any minute. Even if you're rich as Croesus, you never feel as though you have enough to last through a period of hardship.

So, you live as if waiting for another financial disaster. Plus, though you're not blabbermouths like your Sagittarian neighbors, you'll talk about your money woes as if everyone around you could care. We don't. It gets on our nerves. It's in bad taste.

A person doesn't have to be a genius to figure out the source of this mortal fear. With Christmas and Chanukah right around your birthday, you probably have been getting shortchanged since you were a baby Goat. Grandma and Grandpa gave brother and sister two gifts of money, one for birthdays and one for Christmas. But you just got one measly old check, and were told that it counted toward your birthday and the holiday, When it's time to celebrate your having come into the world, all your buddies are off on vacation, so once again you're stuck without any presents. You've been acting so obnoxiously underprivileged ever since, no wonder Santa leaves you lumps of coal in your stocking every year!

YOUR LIGHT SIDE

The best news of all, unless you have some complicating factors in your birth chart, is that this is the "take responsibility" decan. As hard on yourself as you are, and aside from that cash-register mentality, you don't depend on anyone or anything else for your success.

You accept responsibility as the master or mistress of your own destiny. You create substance both in your outer world and in the inner fibers of your being. And, you move in only one direction, upward all onward, no matter how steep the climb. What seems to keep you going, even though to all appearances you don't stand a prayer, is faith, one of the heavenly virtues.

BOTTOM LINE FOR YOUR POWER

I'll bet you money that if you stopped worrying so much about losing all of yours, you'd rid yourself of recurring nightmares and find yourself having a lot more fun. This is a special decan, born during the last ten days of the year. You CAP-Caps represent the faith of mankind that the new year will bring prosperity, peace, and joy on earth. You have brilliant and shining Starpower of the highest order. With that touch of divinity in your perseverance, it simply is a snap for you to be: an *Achiever*.

BODY TALK

Whew, I'm glad the heavy lecture is over. I almost moved myself to tears! Now for the fun part. CAPRICORN rules the knees and all the bones, so you 1st Decan CAPS shouldn't have any trouble in those two areas. Your kneecaps and the backs of your knees are your erogenous zones, bar none. A slight touch or a breath of air from a member of the opposite sex on your knee-joint regions will send a shiver of excitement all throughout your well-built skeletal system. Talk about being well connected!

Once again, most of you don't know how lucky you are. You know the old belief that a Goat can munch on tin cans and not be fazed in the least. Well, not that I've ever actually witnessed such a dietary practice by real Goats, but the idea holds true for you CAPRICORN-Capricorns. You can eat trash like nobody's business and still remain a skinny mini. I hate you all! And so does your opposing sign Cancer, who merely looks at food and gains weight. If for various reasons you do put on a few pounds, never fear. You can stick to deprivation diets longer than any other decan. And you probably just don't need to exercise very much, not after all those mountains you've been climbing.

You have generally wonderful health, though you secretly adore going to doctors just to hear how perfect you are. The typical description of you Goaty Goats is that you look more mature than your age when you're young, and once you hit maturity you never show your age. Are you smiling yet? You should be!

YOUR BEST-BET CAREERS

I can't resist suggesting the most obvious of opportunities for you to use your decan potential to its utmost with mountain climbing. I'm pulling your knee CAP-Caps; you guys wouldn't be caught dead with anything so physically risky. And besides, there's no guarantee of bucks in being in such a noncompetitive sport. You may enjoy a good hike in the hills every now and then, but you're too realistic to climb real mountains for a living. You need to get yourself on a heap of paperwork, or scale the corporate ladder. You usually stick to the more conservative options among the top fields—doctor, lawyer, tax specialist. You have two prerequisites for career happiness. First, you must make money at whatever you do. And second, you have to feel you're good at what you do. Usually, because you work so hard at excellence, the second issue won't be a problem.

With your worldliness, you have an inborn understanding of what the consumers of the world want to buy. As a consumer advocate, or reporter, you can put that skill to use. Or, in land development and commercial real estate, you'll have yourself a real monopoly.

Your shyness, or should I say, your quietness, limits the extent to which you can handle a heavy load of public appearances. However, your mind-set is excellent for training and teaching in whichever field you've chosen to master. Your own handle on discipline makes you a brilliant candidate for behavioral psychology, which is also why men and women of this decan make superlative parents. Thank God for that. You're going to need someone to carry on your dynasty, don't you think?

YOUR BEST-BET LOVE COMBOS

CAPRICORN-Capricorn Man: You male Billy-Goat Gruffs are no doubt armed and ready to be chewed up and spat out in little pieces. Ha, fooled you, didn't I? I'm not going to do anything of the kind. You men are honorable, selective, polite, respectful toward women, and genuinely loving. Of course, that doesn't excuse your emotional retardation, but nobody's perfect.

Yes, you do tend to put your practical thinking way ahead of your emotional longings. You'll pick a gal just because she's a good cook and homemaker, and because she doesn't have expensive tastes that are going to milk you dry. Your eyes don't get misty around her, and she doesn't make your heart, or any other part of your anatomy, go thump-thump-thump. But, I've got to give you credit for mastery of the love affair. What you don't feel naturally, you learn to live without, while you learn to be a wonderful provider and decent lovemaker. Don't even try to hide the truth that the men of this decan are the foremost consumers of sex manuals.

And listen, you're going to need them if you hook up with Ms. Double SCORPIO, your Sextile dream come true. She wants to feel the earth move when she's with a man. She's jealous, and will kick you down the mountain if you cheat on her. But you usually don't cheat. The mere thought of divorce makes you quake with fear-way too socially unacceptable. That's why a Scorpion woman is such a good choice for you. She and you are species that mate for life, or else!

CAPRICORN-Capricorn Woman: While the males of this decan pretty much have their acts together, you girl Goat-Goats disappoint me. After all, I'm Ms. Ultra Independence, and you ladies seem to have been at home rolling your hair during the whole Women's Lib era. What the hell happened? You managed to get out there and fight for equal pay and equal voting rights, but you never got over the "fragile female" routine you pull when in the company of men.

Woman to woman, I have to advise you, these boys can sense it when a girl is desperate. What do you need a man for anyway? You're tenacious, successful on the job, financially self-supporting. Plus, most of you 1st Decan CAPRICORN women never have to watch your weight. Well, don't tell me you need a guy to be supportive emotionally, do you?

Of course you do! There's nothing wrong with wanting intimacy, though you might improve the clingy, clutchy way you go about finding it. Take a couple "cool" pills from your friend Aquarius. Then, when you've chilled out a little, get introduced to a sensitive Bull. Right. Mr. TAURUS-Taurus. Together you will be millionAries, and your babies will be beautiful. Don't laugh, pride in your children's good looks will be yet one more feather in your CAP-Cap. And I bet you'll take all you can get.

DECAN PAIRS WITH CAPRICORN-CAPRICORN

CAPRICORN-Capricorn &		
	ARIES-Aries (3/21-3/30)	8
	ARIES-Leo (3/31-4/9)	7
	ARIES-Sagittarius (4/10-4/20)	3
	TAURUS-Taurus (4/21-4/30)	9
	TAURUS-Virgo (5/1-5/10)	8
	TAURUS-Capricorn (5/11-5/20)	5
	GEMINI-Gemini (5/21-5/31)	5
	GEMINI-Libra (6/1-6/10)	3
	GEMINI-Aquarius (6/11-6/20)	5
	CANCER-Cancer (6/21-7/1)	1
	CANCER-Scorpio (7/2-7/12)	5

LOVE SCALE SCORES

0 = Forget it! • 1 = Don't be a masochist... • 2 = Why bother? • 3 = Fun for one date. • 4 = It won't last! • 5 = You could do better! • 6 = Romance will fade... 7 = Great buddies! • 8 = Pure passion • 9 = True love. • 10 = Eternal bliss!

STARS OF CAPRICORN-CAPRICORN

December 22:	Ralph Fiennes	December 29:	Ted Danson
December 23:	Susan Lucci		Mary Tyler Moore
December 24:	Howard Hughes	December 30:	Tracy Ullman
	Ava Gardner		Tiger Woods
	Ricky Martin	December 31:	Val Kilmer
DEcember 25:	Annie Lennox		
	Barbara Mandrell		
December 26:	Gregg Allman		
	Sissy Spacek		
December 27:	Marlene Dietrich		
December 28:	Denzel Washington		

SECOND DECAN OF CAPRICORN

"I'M MASTERFUL AND I'M MATERIALISTIC."

CAPRICORN-Taurus	CARDINAL-Fixed	SATURN-Venus

For all the gloominess associated with CAPRICORN, you Goat-Bull combos have almost gotten off scot-free. Almost. The Venus glow that softens Saturn's intensity does help you to avoid being your own worst slave driver.

You have strong compassion toward others, which makes you realize you're not the only one who is struggling to get ahead. Without question, you 2nd Decans are the most optimistic and social of all the three Goat groups. And well you should be; you've come into the world on the brink of the new calendar year. When you celebrate your birthday each year, you can celebrate fresh starts, clean slates, and all the achievements that you have-attained already.

Let's not give old Saturn a completely bad rap altogether. With its disciplinary energy, you are able to tackle tasks that seem totally out of your reach. Your Cardinal CAPRICORN drive makes ambitious demands upon you, whereas your Fixed Taurian common sense gives you planning know-how. You guys are masters at making itineraries. Isn't your favorite question, "What's on the agenda?" Isn't it true that you have a file index to all your belongings? And, when you lend books to friends, don't you make them fill out a library card? Though you're not as dollar conscious as the money-minded 1st Decan, you Goat Bulls seem to think that the more tin cans you own the better. Well, you'd prefer them to be gold cans, wouldn't you? I'll bet, among your extensive conservative wardrobe you haven't got one article of clothing that is made from synthetic threads. You love to collect items of value, such as artwork, antiques, coins, and stamps. When you were young, I'd imagine you were the boy with the baseball cards that no one else could find, or the girl with the special edition one-of-a-kind Barbie doll.

Saturn and Venus play nasty tricks together on well-meaning CAPRICORN-Taurus males and females in the area of your love life. As far as you're concerned, a breakup is a brutal war. It's not so much losing a lover that makes you freak—it's the question of how you're going to split up the stuff. "What, not the Lalique crystal!"

YOUR DARK SIDE

I've got two bones to pick with you Goat Bulls, and because you're basically so together, I'm going to let you have it. You exploit your genius for manipulating other people by being an out and out social climber.' You name drop something awful. You love rubbing elbows with the elite. You'll exchange political favors that aren't necessarily ethical. At the worst extreme, you aren't above giving a swift goat kick in the shins to a friend who no longer fits in with the status that you've acquired.

Because of your sensitive Venus influence, you don't commit these manipulative acts without an awareness of what you're doing. You probably have heart-to-heart confessions with shrinks or ministers as you try to make amends. Should a peer dare to accuse you of having used him or her to gain further status, however, you'll bleat with denial. Fear of others discovering that you've hustled your way to the top can lead to stubborn snits, strange paranoids, and periods of total introversion-usually rare in this decan. However, the fact that most of you industrious CAP-Taurian types never forget your humble origins can also be a blessing, as we're about to see.

YOUR LIGHT SIDE

A strong strain of religious thought and feeling runs through this 2nd Decan of CAPRICORN. In your deepest spiritual core, you are immensely grateful to whom or whatever fates or Supreme Being you worship for making you as tenacious as you are. Because you are so motivated to attain material and social status, and because you usually do, you never take your acquisitions for granted. You appreciate the positive strides you've been able to make and the beautiful objects you value. As the saying goes, astrologically at least, you "don't look gift horses in the mouth."

Also, in a completely other vein, as CAPRICORN masters of Taurian materialism, you can make anything. Yep, you're as artsy and craftsy as they come. You probably have one favorite hobby that has nothing to do with making money, it's just something that gives you pleasure. As connoisseurs of colors, materials, and textures, many of you have a nice collection of scraps, old junky items that you transform into useful, beautiful objects. Having an enjoyable pastime not only provides you with entertainment, it's also a healthy outlet for working off Saturnian blues. And, by the way, if you're ever bored, you could always design a Jacqueline Stallone headband with a corporate look.

BOTTOM LINE FOR YOUR POWER

This manipulation and use of others has just got to stop. And you CAPRICORN-Taurians are definitely capable of getting rid of unproductive habits. Once you've learned to sidestep your obnoxious traits, you'll be free to be you, an attainer of the highest order. Technically skilled, and emotionally fulfilled, you can amass all that is your rightful due. You won't waste it or lose it. You appreciate every step up the ladder to the stars, and you pace yourself, conserving fuel and refreshment as you go. Whether you launch a climb for personal glory, or invest your energies into causes that benefit others, you rank superior as: a *Conservationist*.

BODY TALK

The idea of the baby born of a Goat and a Bull is somewhat humorous, don't you think? Very humorous, I should say! I've got to get you Kids laughing because the news in this section is a tad grim; that is, if you're vain or fret about your health. The sad story for you scrappers is that you are born klutzy. Maybe you're top heavy, or maybe you're overly flat-chested. With Cancer in straight-on opposition to you 2nd Decans, the top half of your body is often out of proportion. As a result, with all that climbing you do, you tend to trip and break your brittle bones. And you turn against your doctors, when your stubborn Taurian aspects prevent you from following their advice.

Your compensation prize, for what it's worth, is an interesting or sexy chinny-chin-chin. Whether it's cleft, or Cupid like, it gives your face a look of determination and lovely grace. You men should just go wild and grow yourself a "goatee"—a conservative one, of course! And you ladies won't ever have to worry about having more than one chin!

YOUR BEST-BET CAREERS

If you haven't taken a whirl in politics on one level or another, you've missed the major power punch you Goat Bulls can deliver. From community organizational work, to chairing special task force committees, to holding office in national government, your gift with a gavel is not to be believed. Your natural inclination to associate yourself with the powers that be provides a marvelous entrée to the rich and famous. Even if you're not one of them yet, you'll gobble up their scraps and find yourself well on your way.

Itineraries, agendas, map making, and graphs are chores you can practically do in your sleep. Combine them with any job in corporate planning or trading. With your love of acquisitions, the company stock will shoot up in value.

Being of the more risk-taking breed of CAPS, you 2nd Decans can integrate your compassion for other people's problems into the sometimes delicate areas of crisis counseling. Who knows, you might save the life of a famous celebrity and find yourself in the social circles of your dreams! Because you despise breakups so much, you could make a killing as a divorce lawyer. When I think how much of my equity all my attorneys got from my three divorces, I often wonder if I should try that field.

The Taurian passion for music makes you Goat Bulls avid compilers of extensive musical collections. Take that to the marketplace and open up a record store, or a music studio; you could start an opera company, or manage the careers of other musicians. You'd even do well selling your own artistic wares-provided you can bring yourself to part with some of your beloved belongings.

As the great conservationists, this 2nd Decan can make a remarkable contribution to the environmental causes of the day. You'll convince everyone to stop killing off all the polyesters—who needs their pelts anyway? At the bottom line, you have an almost spiritual respect for the earth. Whether you own lots of it, or dig in it professionally in farming, landscaping, or gardening, you'll sculpt yourself mounds of pay dirt, Here's mud in your eye!

YOUR BEST-BET LOVE COMBOS

CAPRICORN-Taurus Man: When you boys are good, you're great. And when you're bad, you're pathetic nerds. Having been born during the dawn of the new calendar year, you may have grown up with the aura of being special. And since you've got everyone wrapped around your finger, no one ever convinced you that you weren't. So, with this glow of understated confidence, women can't help but be attracted to you. And you can't help but expect them to be!

Let's just say you're used to getting what you want. You'll usually appreciate who you get when you want her. You pamper your Missy with fabulous, valuable gifts. You entertain her with frisky, playful lovemaking. You impress her with your ambitious goals, and take her hobnobbing with your upwardly mobile friends. You'll romance her with Venus-inspired sensitive words. You're her knight in shining armor—at least for the courtship period. Once the marriage contracts have been signed and the honeymoon is over, the honeymoon is over! She'll realize that she's become just another fixture in your life, one more item of value in your collection, a belonging, a possession. Unless she lacks total self-esteem, you're going to get one of your favorite Ming vases smashed over your head.

Then, when she goes to file a suit, you revert to the wronged victim. How could she do this to you? So what if you had a casual fling with your secretary? It meant nothing to you, right? When she dumps you out onto the street while she's holding onto the house, the kids, and the cars, you're ready to jump off the nearest cliff. If you would like to avoid such a sordid scenario, which of course, I have exaggerated for effect, please, hitch up with a 1st Decan PISCES girl. She couldn't care less about all your stuff. All she wants to do is understand your feelings. Isn't that sweet?

CAPRICORN-Taurus Woman: Being the superb mistresses of itineraries that you 2nd Decan women are, you could actually have made out your guest list for your wedding long before you were even a teenager. You Goat Cowgirls are so prepared that, in addition to a handsome hope chest and dowry, you've even got a list of qualifications for the man you'll marry. Haven't you sketched out your future dream house on the hill? Did you put your own down payment on your engagement ring years before you even met Mr. Right?

Far from being a hopeless romantic, you don't just get a crush on a cutie and expect him to do all the work. No, you're an industrious kind of gal and you have your methods all mapped out. You buy his interest, or maybe in some cases, Daddy buys his interest! How can any red-blooded healthy boy say no to all those special favors you're offering just for him to take you to the dance? If he makes the fatal mistake of giving you a good-night kiss, it's going to be like *Fatal Attraction*. Once you decide you want a man, there is no escape for him. He'll end up marrying you just to get you off his back.

Look, there's nothing wrong with knowing what you want and going after it. However, be prepared for "Heartbreak Hotel" unless you realize that you can't buy love. And you won't have to spend a penny, or cast your precious pearls before swine, if you date the deliciously sensual SCORPIO-Pisces, a man who'll love you for you. There's a possible karmic connection here that may surprise even you well-prepared CAP-Taurian ladies. You definitely won't have to sell him on jumping into the sack with you, although you might have to hire a third party to rescue you both from post-orgasmic faints. So put that down on your agenda!

DECAN PAIRS WITH CAPRICORN-TAURUS

LOVE SCALE SCORES

0 = Forget it! • 1 = Don't be a masochist... • 2 = Why bother? • 3 = Fun for one date. • 4 = It won't last! • 5 = You could do better! • 6 = Romance will fade... 7 = Great buddies! • 8 = Pure passion • 9 = True love. • 10 = Eternal bliss!

STARS OF CAPRICORN-TAURUS

January 1:   J. Edgar Hoover
             Frank Langella
January 2:   Cuba Gooding, Jr.
             Christy Turlington
             Tia Carrere
             David Lynch
January 3:   Mel Gibson
             Dabney Coleman
             Victoria Principal
January 4:   Dyan Cannon
January 5:   Diane Keaton
             Robert Duvall
             Pamela Sue Martin
January 6:   Loretta Young
January 7:   Kenny Loggins
             Katie Couric
             Nicolas Cage
January 8:   Elvis Presley
             David Bowie
             Shirley Bassey
January 9:   Richard M. Nixon
             Joan Baez
             Crystal Gayle
January 10: Jim Croce
             Rod Stewart
             Pat Benatar

THIRD DECAN OF CAPRICORN

"I'M MASTERFUL AND I'M VERY INTELLECTUAL."

CAPRICORN-Virgo	CARDINAL-Mutable	SATURN-Mercury

If it weren't for your proximity to cool and idealistic Aquarius, this 3rd Decan would end up feeling like pure dogs instead of just mountain climbing underdogs. As it is, you can't avoid being astrological mutts–unusual mixtures of the Sun's shifting power as it leaves CAPRICORN. But don't put on a sad face, it's not such a bad thing. Your main ruling planet, Saturn, lightens up its pressure on you, which means you don't have to work so hard at everything like all the other CAPS. Mercury comes in to help out, giving you added mental strengths, which, when channeled carefully, can make you natural whiz kids. And the surprise relief comes from neighboring ruler Uranus.

Where the 1st and 2nd Decan Goats stick to the more beaten paths, you Goat Virgins aren't afraid to try some unconventional routes. Being a mutt does have its advantages, let me tell you.

It takes a very perceptive person, shrink, or astrologer to figure you out. Most men and women born during the 3rd Decan of CAPRICORN have long ago developed a useful facade of one kind or another to cover up a native timidity. You might joke constantly in your spicy, cynical, critical manner. You might even have earned the reputation for being tough and opinionated. If those people only knew how often you juggle your emotions around like hot potatoes, they'd truly question their ability in character judgment.

Karmically speaking, you CAPRICORN-Virgos have already learned lessons about professional achievement, financial and social rewards. None of these areas give you a moment's worry. No, your lessons are higher up on the spiritual scale. You worry about weighty, deep, and profound matters, like "Oh, my God, what if I drop dead without warning? I haven't purchased my plot yet!"

YOUR DARK SIDE

Yes, it's true. Your masterful intellects are undeniably brilliant along so many lines, yet the fear of death becomes a morbid, unrealistic obsession that you share with next to no one. Do you have nightmares about earth tremors? How about seafood poisoning? How many wills have you actually written out? More than one, I'll bet. Maybe this sounds from out in left field, but many of your fellow decan members have confessed to scary visits to the doom room, where all hope seems out of sight.

Even though you know, rationally, that these morbid thoughts are unproductive, they may pile up on you with such frequency that you feel as if you have no control over them. Aha, the magic word—control. CAPRICORN-Virgos want lots of it, and earn lots of it. Sure, yours is more of an underplayed, behind-the-scenes kind of control, but basically you manage to steer events and people in the direction you want them to go. As a CARDINAL pushy Goat, you still have Mutable Virgo's flexibility to get you out of a jam when you've pushed too far. Added to that, you have great self-control as well. Your anger, your pride, and your ego are all constantly held in check, So what's the one thing that no living person can control? Death.

YOUR LIGHT SIDE

Fear of mortality and the need to control that which you cannot may cause you needless neurosis, but one of the consequences isn't such a rotten trait. To compensate for your interior tremors, you work double time to make sure that everyone else feels all right. If it's laughter that a friend needs, you'll turn feelings of gloom into mirth. If a pal wants to cry on a shoulder, you've got one ready and waiting. Ultimately, you thrive on serving others, asking little glory in return.

Being a 3rd Decan, you are unusual for starters, and because of the drop of Aquarius in you, you may have unconventional attitudes. But when expressed as a traditional CAP, these ideas are completely acceptable to everyone around you. Even your critical Virgo side doesn't ever sound offensive when you offer your opinion.

BOTTOM LINE FOR YOUR POWER

You have an easy job to do, so give those dumb, glum phobias a good Goat kick out of your thoughts. That way you can finally relax and enjoy the panoramic view over all your other success. All your intelligence and well-honed skills, together with your gift for putting others at ease, can allow you to work miracles. Who knows? Maybe one day you'll discover the cure for death. Within you is the hope of: a *Transformer*.

BODY TALK

Hear ye, hear ye: Good news for all 3rd Decan Capricorns! You're not going to die. Not anytime soon, at least. And not because of your body's ailments. The worst it ever gets will be self-induced ulcers brought on by unrealistic fears. I wouldn't call you bona-fide hypochondriacs. You can handle sniffles and sneezes like breezes. On the other hand, let's not forget this decan's preoccupation with the big, scary life-threatening diseases. Let me reassure you, again, that the forces of the planets have been extremely kind to you guys.

Nimble, fresh, youthful, silky skinned, flexible, rejuvenating are all adjectives to describe the Goat Virgin's physique. Don't act so surprised, you know it's so. You guys are so well-groomed, a wrinkle in your skin is as uncommon as an unsightly spot on your clothes. All right, if you insist on having a specific problem you can worry yourself hairless, because hair growth is slow in the 3rd Decan of CAPRICORN. But you'll never have to pay money for electrolysis!

And yes, there is a specific prized aspect to your body. It's your bounce. Your share of knee-bending influence from CAPRICORN gives you extra spring support, something you'll use to full effect either on your feet or on your back. Nobody who knows you intimately is going to complain about that, including yourself. Am I right? You better believe it, baby!

YOUR BEST-BET CAREERS

If there's one Sun sign who can turn negative thoughts into dollars, it's you old earth-conscious CAPS. And with all that death and dying, you 3rd Decans are always moaning about, you could end up turning your neurosis into megabucks. How about selling life insurance? Legal estate planning, casket design, cemetery construction may all sound morbid, but being prepared for the hereafter is something you've probably spent time doing.

Or perhaps you'd like something more high-minded, having those Mercury inspired smarts that you do. You might use your literary skills as a biographer of others who have already bit the dust, immortalizing them and yourself in the process. Goat Virgins are often fanatics about proper grammar and language usage, so don't overlook editing the written work of others, teaching linguistics, or being available at all times to correct other people's verbal boo-boos. Thank God you do it with humor!

Humor is not something to knock, especially if you combine it with your affinity for the macabre. Write or produce those zany, freaky, outlandish horror movies. Your touch is the Midas one. On any level of show business, the 3rd Decan of CAPRICORN can introduce novel ideas and gain mainstream approval. Because of your CARDINAL-Mutable style pattern, as an actor, cinematographer, script reader, or director, you get the best results without causing waves.

One facet of this last group of Goats is that you aren't so concerned about what everyone else thinks of you. Take, for example, my friend, the bold Mayflower Madam, Sydney Biddle Barrows (1/14). She simply started her own classy version of what we commonly call the oldest profession in the world. So what if she eventually got shut down? She's not suffering financially, not with all the book and film rights of her life story that she's sold.

Well, Ms. Barrows' specific path may not be yours, though whatever you've chosen to do will or should be unique. As a transformer, you need to feel that your work is making a difference in the perceptions of others. Money is never a goal unto itself for you CAP-Virgos. So why is it that you always have so much of it? Well, astrologically this is an "inheritance" decan! That means legacies are due you, and legacies you'll leave behind. (Now stop! You aren't going to die for a long time!) If you haven't received yours yet, don't be surprised when long-lost Uncle Festor wills you his pig farm. You'll finally know what I mean about you guys being able to bring in the bacon!

YOUR BEST-BET LOVE COMBOS

CAPRICORN-Virgo Man: You know how I'm always ragging on most men for their lack of intimacy in relationships? Can you believe that you suffer from the reverse problem? Hard to imagine, but such is often the case among the emotionally complex males of this decan. You'll shoot the breeze with your buddies, or discuss your brainy opinions with colleagues, all with confidence. Yet, in the throes of a *tête-á-tête* with a loved one, you'll spill your guts. Yuck!

Oh, you make a fabulous first impression. Women look at you with your youthful, well-dressed self-assuredness and start to see dollar signs and wedding rings immediately. Then you take her home, and coyly seduce her onto your bouncy mattress. No problems yet. Then, when she gets her things together and starts to leave, your strong facade dissolves. You'll beg her to stay, you'll confess that you're afraid of sleeping alone in the dark. You'll recount all your childhood nightmares and let her know how easily you were hurt before. Unless she's got a martyr complex and wants to be dumped on, she'll be on her way, pronto.

Listen, you could always marry a rock; it won't leave you in the middle of the night. Or, you could learn to share your insecurities with friends and family, and not put that kind of pressure on your lover. Whether or not the preceding description fits you exactly, you'll always balance beautifully with a 1st Decan SCORPIO woman. She's Ms. Detective and won't mind hearing about all your inner turmoil. She'll kiss it and make it all better. Aaahhh...

CAPRICORN-Virgo Woman: I hate to drive a point into the ground, but this old "fear of death" issue hits hard on the sensitive women of this decan. So, what does that have to do with love? It means that you'll make some inappropriate choices for yourself. Just because a guy looks so rugged and strong doesn't mean that he's immortal. Yet, that's what you're looking for, isn't it? A man who'll fight off those things that go bump in the night—er, the inhuman ones.

So you date tough guys, so what? Hey, I think a man on a motorcycle with chains is kind of appealing, too. Unfortunately, unless he happens to have had a Harvard degree, you and he won't have a darn thing to talk about. And even though you couldn't really care less what your parents think, you'll send them to early graves with your parade of muscle-bound bruisers.

Ladies, please stop confusing physical power with character power. If you want strength, and sensitivity don't pass by Mr. TAURUS. His Venus will romance the dickens right out of you. With his staying power and your natural bounce, even your neighbors will think there's an earthquake going on!

DECAN PAIRS WITH CAPRICORN-VIRGO

LOVE SCALE SCORES

0 = Forget it! • 1 = Don't be a masochist... • 2 = Why bother? • 3 = Fun for one date. • 4 = It won't last! • 5 = You could do better! • 6 = Romance will fade... 7 = Great buddies! • 8 = Pure passion • 9 = True love. • 10 = Eternal bliss!

STARS OF CAPRICORN-VIRGO

January 11: Naomi Judd
January 12: Howard Stern
Kirstie Alley
January 14: Faye Dunaway
Andy Roonie
January 15: Martin Luther King, Jr.
Joan of Arc

January 17: Muhammad Ali
Jim Carrey
Benjamin Franklin
January 18: Cary Grant
January 19: Dolly Parton

CHAPTER 13

AQUARIUS

JANUARY 20 - FEBRUARY 18

First Decan	Second Decan	Third Decan
AQUARIUS-Aquarius	AQUARIUS-Gemini	AQUARIUS-Libra
1/20 - 1/29	1/30 - 2/8	2/9 - 2/18

An AQUARIAN declined an invitation to have lunch with a friend,
saying, "Sorry, I'm too busy saving the world!"

Sign:	Air - Thinkers
Symbol:	The Waterbearer
Planet:	Uranus
Body Talk:	Legs, Muscles
Style:	Fixed

MEET THE IDEALIST...

Once the Sun passes through the dark, earthy reaches of Capricorn, it arrives in the altogether different realm of AQUARIUS. Here, in this cool, high, clear, Air sign, we find an unusual motley crew, made famous by what is widely known as our current Age of Aquarius. Your era, when it dawned in the free-speaking, freedom-loving 1960's, brought about powerful changes in attitudes; not unlike the very goals you Aquarians have in your daily lives. The greatest benefit thus far throughout the New Age, at least where Jacqueline Stallone is concerned, has been in the rediscovery of astrology. Boy, was that a turnaround! Up until then, if I'd have asked someone what their "sign" was, I would have been answered with an "Uh, you mean my street sign?"

Now this doesn't mean that all you AQUARIANS follow the stars. The only things that all AQUARIANS follow are their own unconventional opinions. And just because you ladies and gents sponsored an age that began with hippies, love beads, be-ins, and streakings, doesn't mean that you're all radical left-wing liberals. Good old middle-of-the road AQUARIAN Ronald Reagan's black hair dye would go white if he even heard that suggestion! Whatever your political persuasions, however, you've been given special gifts for rallying the masses. As symbolized by the human Waterbearer, you bring a refreshing, positive message of community, of hope, and of progress. As the Fixed sign of the Airy creatures, you don't just talk about ideas like some flaky Geminis we know, or think about everything in the manner that certain Librans contemplate their navels. You'll do something with your ideas, especially when they can serve mankind. How altruistic you are!

If swallowing this image of yourself is a bit like drinking too much sweet nectar, halt your gag reflex and listen to how your ruler Uranus alters the picture. It's crazy, it's rebellious. It's off-the-wall. Without its power, we might end up calling you all Mr. and Mrs. Mother Teresa. Your planetary master brings intensive insights, wild risks, surprise changes for better or for worse, and also is said to rule electricity. It's no coincidence that Thomas Edison, inventor of the light bulb, was born in AQUARIUS, under the jolting influence of Uranus. So, don't be surprised when you suddenly light up like live wire with a cockamamy idea or invention. It could be the answer to the prayers of civilization. Ever hear of "the seven-year itch"? Sure, you have. Well, it derives from astrology's studies that Uranus spends seven years in each sign and does crazy, wacky, unpredictable things wherever it is. We can say much the same thing about all you electric AQUARIANS—you always feel like you've got an itch.

FIRST DECAN OF AQUARIUS

1/20 - 1/29

"I'M UNCONVENTIONAL. I'M VERY UNCONVENTIONAL."

AQUARIUS-Aquarius	FIXED-Fixed	URANUS-Uranus

You men and women born at the height of the Sun's power in these first ten days of AQUARIUS define the essence of everything I've just been describing. You are pure refreshment from beginning to end. I'll bet all you 1st Decan Waterbearers actually do offer everyone you know a fresh glass of H_2O to take off the edge. Or maybe you just suggest to them that they go and clear their heads with some deep breaths of clean air.

Let me sing your praises before I take you to task, even though most of you seem immune to criticism-it just rolls off your back like so much water. Remember you are a FIXED-Fixed specimen, consistent in your own ways, as unusual as those ways can be. So we can accurately expect you always to champion independence, progressive thinking, and originality, in yourself and for others. In broad terms you are generous to the needy, considerate of the unfortunate, friendly, and wonderfully pleasant. Also, as a mental AIR-Air. decan, you are thoughtful and studious. You must be very well-rounded, right?

Yes, that's the big picture. But, when we take a closer look at you helpful Bearers of new ideas, we find something that seems to be missing: emotion. "How can you say that?" "That's not true!" "I'm going to close this book right now." I can just imagine all your objections. I can practically quote the letters you'd like to write, about how you were brought to tears by the hunger in the third world, how you were moved to organize an abused children's clearinghouse.

Well, that's all fine and dandy; don't stop your good work, either. But what about the time that you split up from your ex and didn't shed a tear? And what about that period when you were juggling two love interests at the same time and didn't feel a shred of guilt? Maybe you have done some work on getting in touch with your feelings, which I'd only encourage you to continue. Do be aware that this decan has the reputation for being terrific in team efforts, and a big bomb in the one-on-ones. You guessed it—you're top candidates for Bachelor decan!

YOUR DARK SIDE

Your aloof, detached demeanor when dealing with deep emotions is a Pandora's box that I'm not about to open. There's also a positive side to your cool that I can't completely condemn. When other people are falling victim to overpowering waves of sadness, you'll come up with a plan to solve their problems, rather than being drowned in their woes. Now, it's those plans of yours that I'd like to discuss with you.

Has it ever been pointed out to you that they're unrealistic? Has anyone ever called you just a little naive? Has your idealism ever made you the laughingstock of your peers? You say that you don't care about what other people think. You also say that every now and then one of your harebrained ideas does pay off. You argue that it's better to follow your beliefs than stand around with your thumb up your, um, your nose. Absolutely.

Unfortunately, those double Uranus vibes in you aren't at all practical. Regardless of what other people think, you've got to be experiencing some moments of disappointment. Maybe you didn't anticipate that your friends had attended too many charity balls lately and so passed on yours. You had a great idea to convert the barn into a theater space, but you didn't count on having to do the hammering and nailing yourself. And where you had anticipated a few days of rehearsal, the rest of the cast took months to learn their lines. Forgive me for reminding such students of society as you are, but as you know, "Rome wasn't built in a day."

YOUR LIGHT SIDE

Sometimes, your naive, innocent remarks can induce sincere affection in others. Your loving sense of humor pokes fun at the world without hurting people on an individual basis. And don't go changing your generous intentions. You may think you have more water in your jugs than you actually do, but the positive help you give when you pour out your supply for others does make a difference.

The most wonderful AQUARIUS-Aquarius gentleman on the planet was Mr. George Burns (1/20). If he had merely followed the rules of practicality, he would have never become a legend in his own time. He improved and healed the world with laughter—an age-old cure for everything that ails you, or ails anyone for that matter! He remained ageless for decades.

What all you 1st Decan AQUARIANS have in common with the cigar-smoking George is a youthful, never-ending supply of sheer vitality. Despite your idealism, you never become bored or jaded. When you come up against a wall of criticism, you'll stick to your efforts no matter what. I can nitpick at your minor shortcomings, but basically you are evolved spiritually and ethically. And what's even nicer is that you don't demand approval or flattery, which makes me want to give it to you all the more! Anyone else fallen for that ploy with you lately? Oh well, it works!

BOTTOM LINE FOR YOUR POWER

To truly be a more well-rounded individual, please take some time out to explore your private feelings. Also, do understand that not all your save-the-world campaigns are going to be accepted or supported by everyone. Be prepared to carry the load alone in certain instances. In the meantime, congratulate yourself on the refreshing manner in which you bring hope and concern to those who really need it. You have a talent to get a gang in motion, to make them wake up and live. You are the tops as: a *Revitalizer*.

BODY TALK

As the zodiac clock ticks along and distributes body parts to each Sun sign, moving from head to toe, it starts to run out at the end. Being the next to last sign, AQUARIANS have to take what's left from between the Capricorn's domain over the knees, and the Fish's control over the feet. You 1st Decan Waterbearers are going to have to be satisfied with having lovely shins and calves. Call it potluck, or call it true fortune because there's more here than meets the eyes. I know you ladies would much rather have been given big boobs, and you men would give your right arm to have the male Scorpion's big you-know-what. Poor things, maybe both of yours will grow!

All joshing aside, don't overlook the sexy appeal that just a little bit of leg showing can have. Both sexes should immediately invest in a pair of peddle-pushers, and wait for mouths to drop. It's not only your tendons and lower leg muscles that have been so gracefully sculpted. From head to toe, both men and women of the 1st Decan of AQUARIUS have a flexible, strong, lean musculature. Don't act so cool, you know you've got body beautiful if ever there was one. If you didn't think so, you wouldn't enjoy walking around in the nude so much. All right, so you're not showing off, you're just Airing out!

Health-wise, your opposition to Leo can lead to heart trouble. Fortunately, your revitalizing powers are so strong, you'll recuperate in no time. Remember, you've got forever-young George Burns as a decan relative! Do watch out that you aren't so busy doing social work that you neglect having regular cholesterol checks. And be careful where you disrobe. As popular as you are, your unconventional choices for showing your birthday suit may go over like lead balloons. You don't want to make everybody jealous, do you?

YOUR BEST-BET CAREERS

I don't have to dig too far to come up with some unconventional professions that can occupy you peppy folks for lifetimes. Starting with any branch of social work, from employment at a home for juvenile delinquents, to launching homeless shelters, to convalescent homes for the elderly, you're all in your element.

If playing Nurse Nightingale isn't your cup of tea, turn to the more entertaining side of group organization, and land yourself a corporate personnel director title. Or open up a nudist colony and go to town as resident camp counselor. Party planning is your middle name, isn't it? Being a regular idea guy or gal, you can't miss the bank in advertising or magazine publishing, especially when your products and topics are New Age related. You come up with the concepts and leave the detail, to the Earth signs to carry out. No offense!

In general, this decan scores low with the bucks. But wait, Uranus may surprise you with a payload you never expected. Karma rewards the generous in mysterious ways, you know. Buy lottery tickets, yours may have the winning number. Just don't donate the whole jackpot to your various causes. As I'm about to discuss, you'll need some cash to support your active love life.

YOUR BEST-BET LOVE COMBOS

AQUARIUS-Aquarius Man: You think you know yourself, fight? You mental airborne lads, imagine yourselves to be caring, thoughtful, loving mates, don't you? As the popular sayings go: "I'm so sure!" "Like no way, dude!" In your dreams you are the lover of the century, in real life you're just a "wham-bam-thank-you ma'am" man. Then how come so many women keep coming back to you for more? Because they're masochistic, I guess.

What is so ironic is that you 1st Decan AQUARIAN boys see yourself as the antiestablishment forces, pointing at marriage as an outdated practice. Yet you're behaving like good old male chauvinists, the type who've been around since the beginning of time. The type that women have been failing for since the beginning of time. Oh, you're charming as all get out, spouting your ideal-istic beliefs like poetry over gourmet feasts. You're not half-bad in the sack either, unless a woman starts to cry in the middle of your orgasm.

But, hey, I'm idealistic, too. I have faith that if you fellas are willing to risk your lives saving the poor and downhearted street people, then you can be brave enough to let yourself fall in love. You'll note that I've scored you with high potential in many combinations. Start with a LIBRA-Libra, her Venus will convince you to take the plunge. Be forewarned, love is a scary mystery. It will bring up all kinds of gooey feelings that might even make you cry when you're having an orgasm!

AQUARIUS-Aquarius Woman: Ladies, ladies, please, what have you got that all us other fiery, watery, or earthy types are lacking? What love potion have you concocted that makes so many men encircle you like a flock of vultures? Don't act so naive, just, open the curtain and look out the window. Could it possibly be that it's because you couldn't care less? Maybe you do care, though I'd have to say that the majority of females whom I've studied in this decan would much rather demonstrate mouth-to-mouth resuscitation in a CPR class, than French kiss a guy who didn't turn her on. And, as we all know, an unavailable ice princess is every virile man's private dream. They all want to conquer you and melt your little heart, and all you do is yawn.

Unless you're truly committed to old maid status, with a few casual romps in the hay for entertainment thrown in, do me a favor. Take a love consciousness-raising class and meet a Fire sign, preferably an ARIES. He'll boss you into submission. And if you do put out, emotionally as well as physically, he'll be so grateful he'll run one of your beloved humanitarian campaigns. Suddenly the word ring won't seem like a four-letter word at all. There are some other women out there who wouldn't mind trying some of those extra men that you've been keeping on a string. Thanks!

DECAN PAIRS WITH AQUARIUS-AQUARIUS

LOVE SCALE SCORES

0 = Forget it! • 1 = Don't be a masochist... • 2 = Why bother? • 3 = Fun for one date. • 4 = It won't last! • 5 = You could do better! • 6 = Romance will fade... 7 = Great buddies! • 8 = Pure passion • 9 = True love. • 10 = Eternal bliss!

STARS OF AUARIUS-AQUARIUS

January 20: Lorenzo Lamas
January 21: Geena Davis
January 23: Humphrey Bogart
January 24: Neil Diamond
              Maria Tallchief
January 26: Eartha Kitt
              Paul Newman

January 27: Bridget Fonda
January 28: Alan Alda
              MIkhail Baryshnikov
January 29: Oprah Winfrey
              W.C. Fields

SECOND DECAN OF AQUARIUS

1/30 - 2/8

"I'M UNCONVENTIONAL AND I'M CONTROVERSIAL."

AQUARIUS-Gemini	FIXED-Mutable	URANUS-Mercury

Look up in the sky. It's a bird, it's a plane, it's, it's ... it's the soaring 2nd Decan of AQUARIUS, the Waterbearing Twins! What a surprise! You swift, electric shocks of humanity come in two varieties: talkers and big talkers. It's no accident that the "Great Communicator" Ronald Reagan (2/6) ranks among the members of the AQUARIUS-Gemini Decan. Some of you may gain attention through strong silence, or others through daring, physical stunts. Once the spotlight is on you, though, no matter how different your style from another of your kind, you'll milk it for all it's worth. When you relate an experience, it will never lose in the telling, that's for sure. When you have a point to make, you'll have an audience and you'll make an impact.

So what if you change your opinions frequently? That's just the way that planetary ruler Uranus has of reminding you to keep everybody guessing all the time. To complicate the composite that you are, there are also those extra changeable Gemini sides of you that love stirring up controversy. One remarkable trait that all this windy, wordy energy brings is your ability to talk absolutely off the top of your heads while you appear to be experts in areas that are completely foreign to you. That's mental Mercury for you!

As the 2nd Decan of AQUARIUS, you still embody the progressive, humanitarian spirit of both the 1st and 3rd Decans. However, you're not as likely to get caught up with organized activities to do your good deeds. Being a mix of Fixed and Mutable styles, maintaining rigid schedules over a period of time is a major drag for you. The key word for both male and female Waterbearing Twins is—timing. To score with your power edge of surprise, you always want to strike when the time is right. Sometimes, your instincts will trick you, and you'll fall flat on your twin set of water jugs. No problem, you'll just talk your way out of a scandal. When the timing is right, you can deliver a major power punch.

As you'll discover, the list of stars in this decan is practically endless. It's about electric magnetism and about staying in the ring long enough for the fat lady to sing, which means forever. Many of the stars would be pumping gas now if it weren't for their decan's trick of trying new approaches, and stunning the public with unconventional means. I could go on and on about the adorable Farrah Fawcett (2/2) whose chart shows her to be much more complex than you'd imagine. She took quite an unexpected turn with her career and succeeded in proving herself to be a very accomplished serious actress.

The ongoing goal for all you AQUARIAN-Geminis will be getting to know yourself and getting in touch with those timing instincts. That's easier said than done....

YOUR DARK SIDE

How can you get to know yourself when you're always changing? Seems almost too obvious, doesn't it? Besides, you think you know yourself, and you do—for today. But, weren't you very different a week ago? And who knows what interests and goals will concern you next month?

Perhaps you've observed someone else in the middle of a serious identity crisis, the kind where they leave their spouse, children, home, and job to run out to search for themselves. Come on, learn how you might actually be operating, all the time. The Jupiter/Mercury combined influence has a curse that goes along with it. Although you'll be receiving more flashes of mental insights than you can count, you might be so busy taking them in or telling others about them that you won't have that all-important time to digest them. Your words will be empty rhetoric and you'll be accused of being superficial. That would be a sad state of affairs for one as bold and well-meaning as you, don't you agree?

The even more obvious solution seems so difficult for most of you. If you truly wanted to know yourself, and take advantage of your instinct for good timing, achieve your humanitarian goals, together with love, security, and recognition, you'd take the time to seek advice. Ouch, Mercury the Messenger doesn't like to be on the receiving end of advice, does he? Or do you?

YOUR LIGHT SIDE

As essential as timing is for your success, you have astrologically implanted sensors for upcoming trends. We don't call you cool and with-it and hip, for nothing! To enhance that sensitivity, you've got a bag of Uranus surprises to get you instantaneous attention. The icing on the cake is your tasty gift for Mercurial gab.

Put these positives together, and you can magnetize the masses, pep them up, and sway them to action. Not everybody is going to agree with your ideology, though they may find themselves going along with your various plans just because they like you.

The attitudes of you AQUARIAN-Geminis are controversial because they've never been tried before. Having been blessed with the art of persuasion, you can actually convince perfect strangers to try your unconventional means. Wait till they get the Uranus surprise of their lives when they find out that your ideas work!

BOTTOM LINE FOR YOUR POWER

Unless you can swallow your individualistic pride and take sound counsel from those whom you respect, you might suffer the sad end of being a flip-flop on someone's foot. By trusting the right outsiders, you'll be clothing the naked, and improving the wicked in genius ways. The cosmos has put you here to change society for the better. Your Starpower will shine forever when you lead us forward into the future as: a *Reformer*.

BODY TALK

My personal belief is that good health and good looks reflect an individual's state of mind. Because your mind is always changing, so are your appearance and physical well-being. This decan has been given nice legs from AQUARIUS, and graceful, lean arms from Gemini. Doesn't seem very remarkable to me, and it certainly must not be to you, because both sexes are famous for trying to alter their physical picture. From a health standpoint this is good news. Having your weak spots in the areas of lung problems and nervous disorders, your knack for self-reform comes in handy. When you get regular checkups, Doc is going to reward you with a lollipop for practicing preventive medicine on yourself. Don't worry about your ticker, though. Since a lot of you have already become vegetarians, your cholesterol is admirably low.

Don't even get me started about some of the ridiculous hairdos that you Waterbearing Twins create. Honestly, how many colors and chemicals are you going to try on your naturally lovely locks before you're satisfied? Perhaps you enjoy a little shock appeal? Just don't get so carried away that it looks like you've stuck your finger in an electric socket.

Your fashion statements can be so bold, you make me look like a conservative dresser. Besides, it's fun to guess what outrageous outfit you'll try next. Remember, when it comes to style in this decan's case, a little goes a long way. With your sex appeal, the same can be true. In the bedroom you love to exercise. Unless, of course, you're Ronald Reagan. Or, unless Nancy is holding an itty-bitty gun to your head!

YOUR BEST-BET CAREERS

You better believe that your gold mine lies in your talents of verbal persuasion. You are limited in how long you'll stay with any one pursuit, but hopefully, at least for a stint, you'll devote yourself to political reform, Write a controversial clean air bill, or anti-pollution law, and see how fast it gets on the books. Ronnie Reagan is in good company with New Dealer Franklin Roosevelt. Both presidents faced strong criticism from many sides, but somehow they proved to be in tune with the times.

There's nothing like jumping from one extreme to the other, but since you 2nd Decan AQUARIANS are always doing it yourself, I might as well go to my second-choice recommendation for you. You make great hairdressers. Not only do you come up with attractive new looks for your clients, but you also entertain them with wild tales as you snip away. Don't pooh-pooh this vocation. I know more than one AQUARIAN-Gem salon owner who makes me look like I'm financially underprivileged.

As skillful as you are at stirring up controversy, don't miss an opportunity to work in the news media, particularly TV broadcasting. News anchoring and political commentary are both up your alleys.

The artistic path is bumpy for the 2nd Decan AQUARIANS. The long haul can last two seconds the way you all jump from one thing to the next. Unless, of course, you want to try graffiti or primitive tribal dancing.

Money in this decan runs in cycles—surprising highs and near devastating lows. I'd suggest that you each date bankers.

Back to the more generous members of the AQUA-Gems, I must say, that as hard as maintaining relationships can be for most of you, you make fabulous parents. That's why our next section can become a real soap opera. Leaving hubby or wifey isn't your problem, but what about the kids? Not an easy issue for you ethical types, is it? Well, you can always join or lead a support group for single parents, can't you?

YOUR BEST-BET LOVE COMBOS

AQUARIUS-Gemini Man: Guys, do I have some dish on you! Is it true that you're into sex orgies? What do you mean you've always wanted to have a ménage a trois? You like to talk dirty? Lies, right? Filthy, rotten lies. You couldn't behave in so base a fashion! After all, you have impeccable ethics. Sure you do, and they include getting as much nooky as possible without having to pay a price. How are you going to be able to spread your gospel of progress to the nations of the world if you have some emotional broad attached to your side? But then again, how can you go to work in the morning if nobody's been putting out for you lately?

I hope the saints will forgive me for being crude. I just want to get my point across, in the event that any one of you has been guilty of the typical AQUARIAN-Gemini mate sin: It's called "lying by omission." You somehow forgot to tell her you were already living with another woman. It just slipped your mind to mention that you've been a confirmed bachelor since day one. You told her that you were taking her to meet some charming friends of yours. but you neglected to say that you were hoping everybody would end up in bed together. You just wanted to try it, right?

Well, maybe you want to try some cold showers. Or, if you insist on experimenting with new alternatives. how about dating your neighbor decan, Miss AQUARIUS-Libra. Maybe with her common background, she'll be more tolerant of you than I am. Or stay single, and experiment on an inflatable doll. You're good with hot air!

AQUARIUS-Gemini Woman: Don't get nervous, ladies, I'm not going to give you the same shakedown I gave to the men of this decan. On the contrary, you ladies behave like ladies (well, for the most part). But your libidos run on the same highs and lows as everything else you do. Sometimes you think the man who's courting you is "Mr. Perfect", sometimes you'd like to send him to dog obedience school. Sometimes you find yourself fantasizing about the futuristic joy of your wedding day. Other times you envision the kitchen and the bedroom as your personal hell.

Like everything in your existence, the magic will happen when the timing is right. You may need to hold out for years, pursuing your professional dreams, getting your idealistic message across to the masses, just getting to know yourself. If you're open to love. it can happen to you. It has to take you over like an electric charge, enough voltage to keep the current flowing through all your other cycles. Sounds like I'm being a little idealistic, doesn't it? Not if you get electrocuted by a Venus-kissed LIBRA-Libra. It's mad, it's crazy, it's sock-it-to-you chemistry that is going to save your world. Just don't tell him about your colorful past. What he doesn't know won't hurt him—right, girls?

DECAN PAIRS WITH AQUARIUS-GEMINI

LOVE SCALE SCORES

0 = Forget it! • 1 = Don't be a masochist... • 2 = Why bother? • 3 = Fun for one date. • 4 = It won't last! • 5 = You could do better! • 6 = Romance will fade... 7 = Great buddies! • 8 = Pure passion • 9 = True love. • 10 = Eternal bliss!

STARS OF LIBRA-LIBRA

January 30:	Franklin Delano Roosevelt
	Vanessa Redgrave
	Phil Collins
January 31:	Norman Mailer
	Tallulah Bankhead
February 1:	Clark Gable
	Margaux Hemingway
	Lisa Marie Presley
	Pauly Shore
February 2:	Farrah Fawcett
	Christie Brinkley
	Garth Brooks
February 3:	Blythe Danner
	Morgan Fairchild
	James A. Michener
February 4:	Alice Cooper
February 5:	Jennifer Jason Leigh
	Barbara Hershey
February 6:	Tom Brokaw
	Ronald Reagan
	Axl Rose
	Natalie Cole
	Zsa Zsa Gabor
February 8:	James Dean
	Lana Turner
	Ted Koppel
	Nick Nolte
	Mary Steenburgen
	Gary Coleman

THIRD DECAN OF AQUARIUS

2/9- 2/18

"I'M UNCONVENTIONAL BUT I'M DISCRIMINATING!"

AQUARIUS-Libra	FIXED-Cardinal	URANUS-Venus

By now I must sound like a broken record every time we hit a 3rd Decan of any sign and I have to explain that the Sun's movement makes that decan weird. Well, repetitive though I may be, let's not overlook that AQUARIANS are unconventional for starters.

Add to your Uranus-inspired element of surprise, a romantic and high-minded Libran Venus, plus a dash of neighboring Piscean Neptune, and you folks don't stand a prayer at being "normal." Ah, who wants to be normal anyway, right?

I like the Waterbearing Scale Balancers. You're the quiet AQUARIANS. Sure, you've got your own set of irregular opinions, and you'll be happy to argue them with good, clean Fixed logic if so asked. Your Cardinal style components can make you forceful when necessary, though never objectionable. Don't forget, you've got such weirdos born within your decan as Honest Abe Lincoln and inventive Thomas Edison. They're proof of how cool being not normal can be.

Thank God for your Venus. Ever heard me say that before? It's true. You, as opposed to the 1st and 2nd Decans, are very much in touch with your feelings. While the rest of the Waterbearers may find themselves serving refreshments to the world all alone, yours is absolutely a marriage decan. You need love and companionship, and you can offer it in return. Otherwise, your precious, refreshing water supply would just peter out.

YOUR DARK SIDE

We'll hear more about your other delightful traits in a moment. What surprises me is that, given all those positives, you attract some major losers into your life. You're no pushover, so I know you know they're users. With that discriminating Libran side, you're not so easily fooled as to think they're anything more. In your AQUARIAN socialistic way you'll continue to be generous to them, while you climb up on those Libra scales and debate about what you should do about getting rid of the riffraff.

Interestingly, according to all the premises of astrology, each decan attracts qualities that it lacks in itself. Since you lack negative aspects, you must be drawing them in unconsciously. So, the damage that gets done is just as unconscious. It may take years before you realize that the fun-loving loud pals with whom you've been jet-setting are manipulators and cons. And you thought that you were being unconventional.

To whatever degree you might experience such influences, do keep tabs on your unconscious. You may get too close to Piscean self-deception for comfort. You don't want their problems on top of yours, do you?

YOUR LIGHT SIDE

Probably, the reason that you are blind to flaws in some of your peers is that you are astrologically groomed for seeing only the best in others. Though it may take its toll on your energies from time to time, this attitude can also have great benefits for most of you.

In other respects your judgment is notably clear, precise, and ethical. When it comes to issues, cultural likes and dislikes, basic choices of career and mate, you won't waste precious time balancing your scales. Your motives are as pure as the refreshing, unique "aqua vita," tonic of life, that you serve. You live high on the spiritual ladder, and it takes an army of opposition to pull you down. The New Age is your age, a time to explore modern solutions to ancient problems.

BOTTOM LINE FOR YOUR POWER

Don't be such a saint that you avoid negative confrontations and in so doing lose your lofty stature. When you remain true to your individualistic beliefs, you'll have a magical, easy way of improving everyone around you. With so many positives, yours is a lucky decan. Your job, though it may sound humble, can have a far-reaching power, if you set an example to the world as: a *Teacher*.

BODY TALK

Any decan with Venus rulership almost always loves to be touched, and you Uranus/Venusites are no exception to the rule. With planetary emphasis on all your muscles, your calves, hips, and buttocks, we can be sure that going for regular massage treatments is an AQUARIAN-Libran practice. Each one of you probably has your very own specific, erogenous zone. Being an Air sign, we can only guess what you enjoy having done to it!

Okay, so you're just a teeny bit kinky. I refuse to spank you for your offbeat sensuality-you might like it too much. I only wish you'd approach your health with the same amount of interest. Sticking to diets, exercise programs, and conventional medical advice is just a big bore to you Waterbearing Scale Balancers. Why is it that you always require a second opinion? Or a third and fourth opinion? Oh, well, being inventive, you'll usually develop homeopathic cures that will work just as well.

Watch all your "oral" vices, please. Just because you're into holistic healing doesn't mean you can visualize yourself sober when you're walking a shaky line. Substitute my favorite, sweet carrot juice, for heavy wines, and you'll become an addict to the healthful, refreshing tonic. Just don't overdo it; your hands will turn orange and people will think you really are from another planet!

YOUR BEST-BET CAREERS

Everything you do must serve two purposes, to teach and to be true to your differences, or in other words, to be creative. Therefore, anything but a conventional desk job is open game for you AQUA-Libs. If we begin with the very act of teaching, we can find you lecturing and demonstrating in the related fields of sociology and psychology. Try out your spiritual beliefs in a New Age seminar. Then again, there's always your fascination with outer space. A course in astronomy, or electromagnetic conversions could utilize your Ph.D. to the max. Or take a step further than science, and instruct in the various fine and cultural arts.

Your creativity may produce useful inventions that will earn you major dollars and major kudos. In medical technology, home appliances, and musical devices, don't be afraid to tinker to your heart's content.

This is an animal-loving decan, if there ever was one. While the 1st and 2nd Decans of AQUARIUS are worrying about feeding the people of the world, this 3rd Decan will go hungry to give an old dog a bone. You guys and gals can set up S.P.C.A. branch offices, or start a fund to protect endangered species. Save the Whales, already!

If you have your mind set on being a movie star, go for it! Are you surprised? Your lack of ego and ability to take rejection in stride will keep you hanging in for the long run. Or take all those quiet, strong opinions of yours and pour them into novel writing. Maybe yours will fall into the science fiction category. You can use all our out-of-body experiences as background material. Just remember to thank me for the suggestion when your book hits the bestseller list.

More than the other two decans of AQUARIUS, you FIXED-Cardinal types do need a certain amount of financial security. Being the lucky ones, you usually have it almost as if by osmosis. Any dollar bills growing on your trees lately?

YOUR BEST-BET LOVE COMBOS

AQUARIUS-Libra Man: With your throbbing Venus, heating up Uranus, which as we've seen can sometimes be cold as ice, you gentlemen may be chagrined to find that you literally melt for certain women. You're a total pushover for a pretty face, and Lord have mercy on you if she's got a killer bod. You could become an unwilling love slave.

What happens all too often for many of you Waterbearing Scale-Balancing guys is that these bimbettes aren't so dumb as to not take advantage of your weakened state. She'll get to know all your vulnerable areas. She'll start flashing that special smile that you can't refuse, bat those lashes, and sashay those hips. She'll very subtly begin to mold you into her idea of the perfect mate. So, one morning when you wake up and smell the coffee, and realize that you've been ground down into a conventional, boring, subservient wimp, you'll go haywire.

What you must avoid like the plague is a woman who wants you to be anything other than what you are. All your unique, if slightly weird traits, must be appreciated. The minute a gal starts saying things like, "You should really get a normal job," dump her. But please do not, I repeat, do not, remain single for long; it would be a crime against your romantic nature. Dash right out and find a playful, proud SAGITTARIUS-Leo. She's so independent, she won't want to bother trying to change you. And you'll charm the riding pants right off her. There's a drop of opposition in this combo, but you like it hard, don't you?

AQUARIUS-Libra Woman: You nutty girls don't give a darn what the dude looks like, how much money he makes, whether he can spell his own name, or how big his ... um ... his car is, do you? Nah, your only criteria when shopping in the male department is that he be an artist. Let's see, how many types have you already dated? The bearded French painter? Remember him, with splotches of paint on his fingernails? You must have had at least one rock musician. Bass players, I've heard, really know how to pluck a gal's heartstrings. Oh, and there were those years with that Irish poet. What a temper he had!

Well, if you're choosing what and whom you want, why aren't you refreshing, thoughtful belles in states of bliss? Why? Because, these wild and weird guys literally dwarf all of your creativity. You'll place your pet projects on a back burner so you can help him mount his show, or publicize his event. Plus, someone has to go out and earn a living, and you've been elected. Suddenly all your Venus passions have been tamed, and you've turned into a domestic engineer. Poor thing, no wonder you're always bursting into tears for no reason.

This isn't an easy situation to solve, so I'm going to have to break one of my own rules and urge you to stay on your own turf. Meet and marry a man of your own decan. Since you're both so good at balancing, you'll complement the hell out of each other. You can compromise and take turns being creative. With your mutual love of little furry creatures, I can guarantee there will be a lot of petting going on!

DECAN PAIRS WITH AQUARIUS-LIBRA

LOVE SCALE SCORES

0 = Forget it! • 1 = Don't be a masochist... • 2 = Why bother? • 3 = Fun for one date. • 4 = It won't last! • 5 = You could do better! • 6 = Romance will fade... 7 = Great buddies! • 8 = Pure passion • 9 = True love. • 10 = Eternal bliss!

STARS OF AQUARIUS-LIBRA

February 9:	Joe Pesci	February 15:	Jane Seymour
	Mia Farrow	February 16:	Ice-T
February 10:	Roberta Flack	February 18:	John Travolta
	Laura Dern		Yoko Ono
February 11:	Burt Reynolds		Matt Dillon
	Jennifer Annisont		
February 14:	Gregory Hines		
	Meg Tilly		

CHAPTER 14

PISCES
FEBRUARY 19 - MARCH 20

First Decan	Second Decan	Third Decan
PISCES-Pisces	PISCES-Cancer	PISCES-Scorpio
2/19 - 2/29	3/1 - 3/10	3/11 - 3/20

Practically drowning in Kleenex and tears, a PISCES complained,
"Why don't I ever learn from past mistakes?"

Sign:	Water - Feelers
Symbol:	The Fish
Planet:	Neptune
Body Talk:	Feet
Style:	Mutable

MEET THE DREAMER...

Finally the Sun comes to its last country, the weird, wonderful, frightening, and oceanic world of the mysterious and mystifying PISCES. Every possible human trait that astrology has forgotten to dole put to the other signs gets dumped on all the poor Fishes. Or should I say, "Gee, are you guys lucky, you have so many options!" You swimmers come in the widest assortment and types of all. More mental geniuses populate your seas, along with more of the greatest seers and visionaries, artists, musicians, lovers, religious martyrs, alcoholics, bums, and con artists than any of the other signs-put together.

Neptune rules your waters, and where Neptune goes, anything goes! The king of the ocean can offer a PISCEAN self-discovery or self-deception. The choice is yours. Your symbol, the Two Fish shapes pulling in opposite directions while tied together by a string, basically says it all. No matter what your decan, your heightened sensitivities to everybody and everything, can sometimes stress you and stretch you to extremes. You'll try to avoid snapping in two by escaping into your Neptunian, fluid, dreamy dreams.

Since you're a Mutable Water sign, there is no predicting your modus operandi for contending with troubled rivers. Each one of you is different from the next, and within the course of your life you can alter your basic approach drastically. You may start out as a guppie and grow into a shark, or vacillate between barracuda and flounder modes.

Whenever I meet a PISCES, I find myself lowering my loud voice, guarding my Sagittarian tongue, careful not to bruise the thin skin of the gentle soul to whom I'm speaking. Even if he or she has just pickpocketed me! It's riot because I fear the wrath of the Fish, but because I'd be the last person on earth to diminish the dreamer. The rest of us need you to go into realms we're afraid to explore. You complete the karmic cycle of astrology, and though being you may not always be so easy, all of us depend on you for our very lives. Every person from each of the other decans should have a PISCES in their life, on one level or another. Even opposing, critical Virgo can learn from you. You must be powerful!

FIRST DECAN OF PISCES

2/19- 2/29

"I'M DEMOCRATIC. I'M REALLY DEMOCRATIC."

PISCES-Pices	MUTABLE-Mutable	NEPTUNE-Neptune

Double whammy, hocus-pocus, voodoo, trickery? How come people are always accusing you 1st Decan PISCES of using magic to do what seems to come naturally to you? Each decan of the Swimmers is psychic, but yours takes the cake. With double Neptune in force, you don't just tap into other people's emotions, you are able to connect with them on an unconscious level, hear what they're thinking, look into their pasts, and anticipate their next moves. Maybe you don't see yourself as extrasensory perceptive, or maybe you haven't experienced this side of yourself. Or maybe you're so used to it, you just take it for granted. Believe me, when it happens it can blanket you like a storm, and as the saying goes, you'll be "blinded by light." It might turn you into a scared little fish on a hook ... Or a power-hungry piranha. In any case, glide lightly when your magic powers are in force. They have minds of their own.

Other than that, you're pretty normal. With MUTABLE-Mutable style, you may have lofty ambitions, though you'll take a lot of detours before arriving at your final destination. Good for you, you need to take in all the sights, sounds, and feelings of the world, so that you can be reminded you're not alone in it. You are driven to share, both in what you take in and in what you give back. If any other decan is reading this, they probably won't fully understand what I'm saying. But I think you PISCES-Pisces telepathics are getting the gist. You're all so kind, you always indulge anyone when they feel like sharing!

And just to prove my point, take the historical example of PISCES-Pisces George Washington, the very first pillar of democracy. If he hadn't been a dreamer, we'd all still be subjects of jolly old England. Georgie was so keen on sharing that he couldn't tell a lie, nor could he keep his flippers off the many mistresses he kept in addition to Martha.

YOUR DARK SIDE

Speaking of our country's past, why don't you snap out of your reverie for a moment so I can do some Fish butt kicking. When you decide that you can't cope, or that you don't want to cope, you'll go flicking your dolphin fins straight down into the lower depths of your personal past. Your lover might hint that you could be a bit more neat around the apartment, and suddenly you're in a tailspin. You'll relive childhood traumas of being criticized for not being tidy. You'll recall how painful it was when your mother took you off your bottle. Some psychiatrists call this regressing. I call it distressing!

Neptune has a naughty side, and sometimes plays some lowdown tricks on you. You can actually return to scenes in your past and find that they've been distorted. You may go back and see yourself as the kid who was always losing, when in reality you were a super-achiever. This leads to all kinds of confusing emotions that are as hard to unravel as a tangled fishing line. Sometimes it's all so overwhelming that you fabricate your own memory blocks.

If you feel that this type of exit hatch has never been your route, then you've already embraced your light side. Don't be shocked, however, when you start hitting little glitches and you can't remember your brother's name, or what you were thinking two seconds before, or what nine times nine is. By the way, where did you leave the scissors?

YOUR LIGHT SIDE

Hold up a prism, or a beautiful crystal, to the window, and watch what happens. Or turn on a Jacques Cousteau special and fix your eyes on the mystical, glorious patterns of colors that swim before you. Can you see yourself in those reflections and refractions? Can you believe that's how other people see you? See, you don't have to be Shirley MacLaine to be a channel. A PISCES-Pisces will do just fine, thank you very much!

Without words or even your own intentions, your translucent shine can magnetize people, things, animals, experiences-all that comes within your sphere. You see them in their auras, and they, not even aware what you are doing, take part in your spell. You communicate with your sixth sense, speaking with the eyes, healing with your vibrations. Your greatest potential is the ability to share on the spiritual plane. I've heard that it's better than sex. Is it so?

BOTTOM LINE FOR YOUR POWER

Don't laugh at this mystical stuff, it can make your wildest dreams come true on the spot. Believe in your magical powers and trust them to guide you on positive paths. Wait, don't get carried away. Remember that you control your perceptions and keep yourself out of those waters that have already flowed under the bridge. Rare and rich as those beautiful streaks of light that you reflect, you are: a *Visionary*.

BODY TALK

Whoops, I almost hypnotized myself. I guess that's what you Fishy Fish people are always doing to others, because of them there eyes. 1st Decan PISCEAN eyes are notoriously saucer-shaped, and always ready to fill up with tears, for no reason at all. The tough boys of the decan are probably ticked at me. Hold on, I didn't say that you were crybabies, I just said that you had watery eyes, okay? At least you'll never have to spend money on Visine! And, by the way, those long, moist, piercing looks both sexes can give, can knock members of the opposite sex unconscious. So don't knock it, sock it to us.

Speaking of socks, since PISCES rules the feet, the 1st Decan gets to experience a wide range of physical sensations centered in their little tootsies. While the whole body's nerve endings rest in the bottom of your soles, your super-sensitivities may pick up just about anything. In general, health is erratic with this group, so do take every and all precautions to keep in the pink of things. Stay away from friends who aren't feeling well, even though you just love feeling needed. You're so democratic, you'll insist on sharing their cold!

In the meantime, don't underplay the magnificence of your peepers. If you wear glasses, get contact lenses. Don't worry about them distorting your vision, you've got an excess in that area.

YOUR BEST-BET CAREERS

You've probably assumed that I'm going to push you right into the fields of the occult and supernatural, but I'm going to do exactly the opposite. Nothing like confusing the already confused, is there? Unless you are prepared to give up all conventional holdings, don't let yourself enter into a situation where these divine psychic gifts are being used for money. Use them in conjunction with other work that keeps you grounded and structured. Routine can be your best friend, and self-employment a lonely vacuum. We don't want to lose you to the outer limits, after all.

You certainly can't go wrong utilizing those colorful images you are always seeing. Start with a job as an illustrator, graphics designer, or film colorist. Ask Ted Turner for a job; he can tell you that it's the wave of the future. Glass tinting and blowing, fabric weaving, textile design are professions where your talents can't fail you.

The spiritual depths of you PISCES-Pisces people can be tapped when you work with others in connection with organized religions, including roles as priests, rabbis, ministers, nuns, or church administrators. Then, when something makes you weep, you can share the feeling with the entire congregation.

Traditional astrology says that any career in the vicinity of the ocean is a must for you. We're talking oceanography, sailing, commercial fishing, dolphin training, entertainment director on cruise ships. Use your vivid imagination to add to that list.

Wherever you drop your line, don't even think for a minute that you're going to fade into the woodwork. In fact, with that beautiful aura glow that all you PISCES 1st Decans have, careers in beauty and modeling will have you shining in the spotlight. I hope your ESP won't pick up on all the naughty thoughts that those who look at you will be having. As we're about to see, the Neptune-Neptune born can become the fresh fish of the day, on just about anybody's diet.

YOUR BEST-BET LOVE COMBOS

PISCES-Pisces Man: Oh, you handsome, delicious, loving devils, you. What is that cologne you're wearing? Could it be Love Potion Number Nine? Heck, you, probably haven't got a clue about how you attract schools of bait-nibbling little girl fishies. Well, neither do I! When I think about it rationally, there's no way that I could fall for Mr. Dream Machine. But I have before, and, who knows, I could do it again, all against my better wishes. Please, leave us Fire sign women alone-we can't handle you.

What's so hard about handling a male PISCES-Pisces, you ask? Have you ever tried to hold a fish in your hands? It's such an ordeal. They need water, they need oxygen, too; they need greenery to look at, they need a gentle touch. Obviously, some women out there don't mind taking care of needy men. You probably know them all on a first-name basis, or even more intimately.

There are two ways the finer of the species can feel after having been seduced by that special scent of yours, and then rudely awakened by the hard work that is required to keep you fulfilled. She'll either go insane or become addicted to those creative love sessions that you offer as a reward. If you want her to be in the second category, then go for a 2nd Decan CANCER. Nurturing a man's ego is her specialty. And she's a damned good cook to boot! With her strong sense of privacy, she'll never sell out your secret lovemaking tips. By the way, what is that thing you do with your toes? Hmmm…

PISCES-Pisces Woman: If your love life isn't making you cry or writhe with suffering, then you probably think you're doing something wrong. Why is it that, with all your visionary clarity, you insist on seeing love as equal to misery? Don't tell me you thrive on it. You don't have to tell me, I already know. Neptune has tricked you into believing that if a man doesn't make you feel like you're being pulled apart at the seams, you couldn't really love him.

As a result, you lovely, feminine joys immerse yourself into long, tortuous affairs, over and over again. The meaner or more inconsistent he is, the more devoted you become. Maybe you should wear a sign on your behind that reads Kick Me, I'm Already Down. Or maybe, you should think about dreaming up a better scenario where romance includes getting along with your man.

In that picture, include the possibility of what could happen if you matched up with Mr. CAPRICORN-Taurus. He likes to suffer every now and then, too. However, he appreciates your creative ideas in the bedroom even more! Where did you dream up that position that you girls are so famous for? You know which one I mean!

DECAN PAIRS WITH PISCES-PISCES

LOVE SCALE SCORES

0 = Forget it! • 1 = Don't be a masochist... • 2 = Why bother? • 3 = Fun for one date. • 4 = It won't last! • 5 = You could do better! • 6 = Romance will fade... 7 = Great buddies! • 8 = Pure passion • 9 = True love. • 10 = Eternal bliss!

STARS OF PISCES-PISCES

February 19:	Smokey Robinson	February 25:	Pierre Auguste Renoir
February 20:	Cindy Crawford	February 27:	Elizabeth Taylor
February 21:	David Geffen	February 29:	Antonio Sebato, Jr.
February 22:	Drew Barrymore		
	George Washington		

SECOND DECAN OF PISCES

3/1- 3/10

"I'M DEMOCRATIC AND I'M POSSESSIVE."

PISCES-Cancer	MUTABLE-Cardinal	NEPTUNE-Moon

Let's see, you like to share, but you're extremely private. You believe in spreading the wealth, but you're pretty retentive about some of your pet possessions. You are the epitome of the Two Fish swimming in different directions. You must be very confused, or very versatile.

Actually, as the PISCEAN decans go, you're emotionally the most balanced of all. How can that possibly be true? Well, the string that holds the PISCES-Cancer together is the best sense of humor to ever hit any decan. Yours can span from the goofiest, to the spaciest, to the darkest zones. They don't call hanging out with you the *Twilight Zone* for nothing.

As children of the Moon, as well as Neptune, you understand innately the beginning of all the creative processes. You're always budding with blooms of glorious, artistic creations. You might break into tears in the middle of a sitcom, or start laughing like a hyena during a Shakespearean tragedy. These outbursts may seem inappropriate to people in your company, but they're usually the birth of one of your own visionary projects. If you follow these feelings in your guts, you'll soon be hatching caviar eggs. There's money, power, fame, and glamour in this decan. Too bad about some of the pitfalls that accompany all these riches. But, thank God for your extra Crab shell.

You, above all, can handle the ruts that crop up in your road, or the dams that block your waterways. You'll just pretend that you don't see the barriers. As long as you don't use destructive means, which isn't always the case, your lack of realism is exactly what allows you to achieve the impossible. They don't get much more outrageous than you!

YOUR DARK SIDE

Where do you think the expression "drinks like a fish" comes from? From proof that PISCES, and especially the consuming Cancer-kissed 2nd Decan of PISCES, are the biggest boozers of the zodiac, that's where. What's your poison? Gin? Vodka? Beer, wine, rye, tequila, whiskey, rum, moonshine, schnapps? Stop me when you can't stand it anymore. Let's get dangerous. How about marijauna, cocaine, speed, tranquilizers? I hope to God you're all shouting "no" right now. If any Fish-Crab combo out there feels he or she has an alcohol or drug, or, yes, even a food dependency problem, of any sort, know that you're not alone. And know that you're ruining your life!

The Moon casts dark shadows over you at times, emotional bummers that make you want to run and hide. Then old Neptune whispers in your ear, "Ya wanna get high, man?" Sure you do, you love getting high. What a great escape from the political chaos of the day, right? Wrong. You know as well as I what happens when you use artificial means to get off. I could paint a really lurid picture for you, though certainly not one as vivid as your imagination could conjure. It's a horror show!

I'm certainly not telling the 2nd Decan of PISCES something that any person with an IQ of three doesn't know already. What you might not know, however, regardless of whether you're a teetotaler, or whether you have all these vices under control, is that you don't need anything extra to get you high. You already are, naturally.

When everybody else has to work so hard to expand their consciousness, all you have to do is kick back and dream. What a cheap date you could be!

YOUR LIGHT SIDE

If I could only convince you how many people would pay zillions of dollars to have what you have, you might begin to appreciate it a little more. You are the geniuses of the zodiac. We're talking my number-one hero, Michelangelo, who is a member of your decan, okay? Here's where you, too, can find your natural highs.

When you look at beautiful scenery, or hear dramatic music, or are moved by something you've read, you feel every part of it and come alive. You start to hatch your own fish egg ideas, as nutty as you please, just to prolong the feeling. Imagine how good you feel when you take in these sensations. The high just keeps on going when you share them with others.

You PISCES-Cancers don't merely enjoy art, you don't simply find that you're pretty good at creating things or stories or what-have-you. You breed art. It would be impossible for you not to be creative. In the same way that it would be impossible for a Sag like me not to philosophize for several hundred pages.

Your PISCEAN sensitivities can give you the embryo of an idea, and then your Cancerian side nurtures and develops it over time. It is a lot like giving birth when you create something. No wonder you're always thirsty or hungry—you're feeding what's inside of you. This may sound completely foreign to those of you who aren't yet in touch with this potential. Be open to it.

The MUTABLE-Cardinal Style pattern says that destiny finds you, and when it does it happens fast. Today you're a bus driver, tomorrow the world-famous "Yellow Submarine" cartoon animator. Anything can happen if you'll let yourself dream that it might.

BOTTOM LINE FOR YOUR POWER

If any of those escapist Neptune tendencies are limiting your being the very best that you can be, go visit your neighbor Aquarius. This world and lifesaver probably has a great seminar for you to join so that you can rid yourself of anything that stands in your way. With so many positive stars shining above you, it would be a shame for you not to use your creative genius, and get to experience the real high times ahead, as: an *Artist*.

BODY TALK

While the PISCES side of your decan has given you dainty, soft feet, the Cancer influence brings tiny, minuscule waists. I hope that any excess drinking you do is of water. You wouldn't want to trash such a naturally delicious shape, now would you? Probably other people think that your breast and hip measurements are wider than they are. Let's not tell them the truth, shall we? It's just your waist's way of tricking the eyes.

Astrologically, you haven't been given anything to worry about healthwise, except for the abuses that we've already discussed. Besides, you've reformed since I gave you the lecture, right? As long as you're moderate in all those areas, you'll live longer than the tenacious goats of Capricorn. The only pause for concern a Fish Crab blend may have will be with dry-skin patches or skin rashes. Scales and shell combined do make for some genetic oddities, I suppose. Lavish your body with aloe vera day and night. Your possessive side will soak it right up.

The body survey says that PISCES-Cancer men and women have more tattoos per capita than the rest of the decans of the zodiac. Anchors and the word Mom tend to be the most popular choices to engrave on your various body parts. Or, because you're so artistic, maybe you've designed your very own original motif. Don't scorn the idea. Think about how much mileage you could get from inviting a member of the opposite sex over to see your etchings—the ones on the wall and the one you-know-where.

YOUR BEST-BET CAREERS

I don't know where to begin and it doesn't even matter, because an, choice for you has to come under the heading of art. From painting, to sculpting, to photography, to architecture, you score on the top of the charts with the visuals. Thank God for the Crab in you. When the money starts pouring in, you'll invest in a good strongbox, and there it will stay.

As a poet, playwright, screenwriter, or novelist you'll create worlds never before experienced by humanity. Start a literary magazine, or run a theater, and you'll be drowning in cash receipts.

Though you may be natively shy, get yourself on a stage or in front of the camera as an actor. The minute you enter the dream world of the play, or film, you'll be giving the audience a contact high. Don't overlook your PISCES-Cancer feet and miss out on a chance to dance your way to fame and fortune. And where there's music, it's a shoo-in that a member of your decan had a hand in its composition or performance.

Cooking, gardening, and baby making are about as creative as anyone gets, all of which you folks do with genius. If you insist that you aren't artistic, you can always get a job as a professional mourner. You're so talented at shedding those tears. Also, I've heard it's a great way to pick up chicks or dudes. You're a dead ringer for that job, so to speak … .

YOUR BEST-BET LOVE COMBOS

PISCES-Cancer Man: How sweet you gentlemen are with your shy, sensitive lures. You male Fish Crabs can romance a woman like nobody's business. You'll spout poetry, wipe away a tender tear at the movies, draw a sketch of her at the park. You'll comfort her about all those awful men who treated her with their mean old double standards. Isn't your favorite line the one about how you support Women's Lib? Fat chance.

I've heard some of the other lines you con artists create, and they're probably the reason I say that this decan has such a good sense of humor. You've got to be kidding yourself if you think that you really mean the very things that you'll later contradict. I love the one about how the two of you should just take your clothes off and talk about your feelings. Later, when you're in the throes of passion, she'll realize that you didn't care a bit about talking. You just wanted to take advantage of her. You brute. No, not true? Maybe you did want to just talk and also to take advantage of her. That's the confused you, right there.

In marriage it gets worse. The pattern reverses. You know, you'll tell your wife that it's nooky night and when the perfect moment arrives, you'll decide you just want to share your feelings about the day. Then, when she kicks you out of bed, if you're the bad brand of PISCES-Cancer jerk, you'll march over to the comer bar and drown your sorrows. You guys may be artistic geniuses but you can also be screwed-up messes. Unless you evolve higher than the worn stage, stay single. If you've decided to quit the push-me-pull-you pattern, I'd be more than happy to introduce you to your fellow PISCEAN of the 3rd Decan. She'll keep you so busy in bed you won't have time to swim in different directions.

PISCES-Cancer Woman: You goofy gals, nut cases all, you are committing the cardinal sin of romance, the one every teenage girl learns to avoid. It's not in how you charm the boys, that's your strong point. You giggle, toss your tresses, bat your eyelashes, wiggle your fins. They eat it up. You entertain your fella with the most spaced-out talk this side of Neptune or the Moon. No problem there; he'll be fascinated. And when you take him home to your Fish Crab hole to show him your tattoo, he'll get higher than a kite thinking what a unique catch he's gotten.

Then, the next day, you call up all your girlfriends and tell them about your dream man. Pretty soon, he won't have time for you because all your cronies have booked him. You just couldn't resist sharing, could you? Or maybe you could. The emotional storm that hits you each time Romeo runs off is enough to destroy you. How could the dolt do it to you? How could your best girlfriend pull such a lowdown stunt? How could you keep repeating the same old mistake?

It's all so simple. Trust your Cancer possessiveness and don't advertise your man. What your girlfriends don't know won't hurt them. If you must share with them, tell them that you're dating a Scorpion Fish who has a weensy stinger. The "weensy stinger" part will be a lie, but if he is a 2nd Decan SCOR-PIO, you might soon be sending your cohorts wedding invitations. This man will be there for you when you need him. Since he's such a good detective, and you're an utter mystery, the two of you can play cops and robbers together. Wait till you get a blast of his gun!

DECAN PAIRS WITH PISCES-CANCER

PISCES-Cancer   &   ARIES-Aries (3/21-3/30) 3
ARIES-Leo (3/31-4/9) 4
ARIES-Sagittarius (4/1-4/20) 6
TAURUS-Taurus (4/21-4/30) 8
TAURUS-Virgo (5/1-5/10) 7
TAURUS-Capricorn (5/11-5/20) 8
GEMINI-Gemini (5/21-5/31) 2
GEMINI-Libra (6/1-6/10) 5
GEMINI-Aquarius (6/11-6/20) 4
CANCER-Cancer (6/21-7/1) 8
CANCER-Scorpio (7/2-7/12) 7
CANCER-Pisces (7/13-7/22) 8
LEO-Leo (7/23-8/1) 3
LEO-Sagittarius (8/2-8/12) 4
LEO-Aries (8/13-8/22) 3
VIRGO-Virgo (8/23-9/3) 4
VIRGO-Capricorn (9/4-9/13) 7
VIRGO-Taurus (9/14-9/22) 6
LIBRA-Libra (9/24-10/3) 5
LIBRA-Aquarius (10/4-10/13) 5
LIBRA-Gemini (10/14-10/22) 3
SCORPIO-Scorpio (10/23-11/2) 8
SCORPIO-Pisces (11/3-11/12) 9
SCORPIO-Cancer (11/13-11/22) 8
SAGITTARIUS-Sagittarius (11/23-12/2) 5
SAGITTARIUS-Aries (12/3-12/11) 2
SAGITTARIUS-Leo (12/12-12/21) 3
CAPRICORN-Capricorn (12/22-12/31) 5
CAPRICORN-Taurus (1/1-1/10) 6
CAPRICORN-Virgo (1/11-1/19) 5
AQUARIUS-Aquarius (1/20-1/29) 6
AQUARIUS-Gemini (1/30-2/8) 4
AQUARIUS-Libra (2/9-2/18) 2
PISCES-Pisces (2/19-2/29) 5
PISCES-Cancer (3/1-3/10) 7
PISCES-Scorpio (3/11-3/20) 9

LOVE SCALE SCORES

0 = Forget it! • 1 = Don't be a masochist... • 2 = Why bother? • 3 = Fun for one date. • 4 = It won't last! • 5 = You could do better! • 6 = Romance will fade... 7 = Great buddies! • 8 = Pure passion • 9 = True love. • 10 = Eternal bliss!

STARS OF PISCES-CANCER

March 1:	Harry Belafonte
	Ron Howard
	Timothy Daly
March 2:	Desi Arnaz
	Eddie Money
	Jon Bon Jovi
	Karen Carpenter
March 3:	Alexander Graham Bell
	Jean Harlow
	David Faustino
March 4:	Chastity Bono
March 5:	Rex Harrison
	Andy Gibb
March 6:	Michelangelo
	Tom Arnold
	Rob Reiner
March 7:	Tammy Faye Bakker
March 8:	Lynn Redgrave
March 9:	Raul Julia
	Jeffrey Osborne
March 10:	Chuck Norris
	Sharon Stone

THIRD DECAN OF PISCES

"I'M DEMOCRATIC. I'M ALSO SEARCHING."

PISCES-Scorpio	MUTABLE-Fixed	NEPTUNE-Mars

Here we are at the very last decan stop of the very last sign of the zodiac. Kind of makes me feel sentimental. How about you fish Scorpions, you too? I'll bet that you are, because nostalgia, sentimentality, moroseness, guilt, sadness, longing, and all intense emotions run high in your decan. As babies of runaway, escapist Neptune and direct, driving Mars, there's no way on the planet that you MUTABLE-Fixed types could ever grow up to be lightweights. This is the stage of the game where you emerge as the genius of the geniuses, or the damned astral dunce who has to start the whole cycle over again.

You'll succeed big, or fail badly. The powers and talents that have been given to the 3rd Decan of PISCES are characterized by an emotionally charged intelligence that doesn't even score on the IQ scale. It's that high!

Spooky things can happen to each and every one of you in your relationships, with friends, family, and lovers alike. If you're living right, you should feel as though you've connected with your past lives a hundred times or more.

The word karma comes around so many times in your life that if you don't believe in it now, you will when I get done with you. Don't search so desperately for the mysteries of the universe outside yourself that you take your own revelations for granted. And make sure that you're a good PISCES and that you share them with all of us. And don't think that you've escaped the escapist tendencies of the 1st and 2nd Decans. Your addictions can be just as dangerous as theirs, especially because yours involve other people.

Being the completion of the zodiac wheel, the point at which the whole circle starts over again with fiery Aries, you do brush up against the Rams and pick up even more of Mars' driving force. As fearless as this makes you, many of you still are frightened by your inner powers. Don't be. Having all the cosmic waves that you Fish Scorpions have been given only happens once in several lifetimes. Unless you fall prey to the petty problems of your decan, you have the very highest potential of all. How's that for Sagittarian hyperbole?

YOUR DARK SIDE

I'll play you a few notes of your dreaded obsession. It starts with an S and ends with an X. Got any clues? I'll bet you do. Where do you think you PISCES-Scorpios go when the going gets rough? To b-e-d, that's where, with just about anyone who is willing. And what a wonderful, dreamy escape a multiple orgasm can be, right?

All right, maybe not all you Fish Scorpions sink so low. Maybe you consider yourself to be as prudish as an opposing Virgo. Don't you find that when you do become intimate with someone, you aren't really in the moment? Aren't you just trying to occupy the hours in which you'd otherwise be searching for mystical answers to questions that are giving you headaches? Sex is kind of like a big aspirin for you, isn't it?

It shouldn't be my job as an astrologer to tell you what disgusting things can happen to you physically and psychologically when you use sex as a drug. If you do fall victim to this urge on occasion, remember that you've got friendly Neptune to cool your Mars drive when your blood gets boiling. Thank your lucky stars for that.

YOUR LIGHT SIDE

Intercourse is so commonly associated with the 3rd Decan of PISCES because it's a quick trick for doing your higher mission, that of becoming one with others. There are more spiritual ways of having intercourse, which should also be familiar to you folks. If you have connected with your lighter side, you probably have already experienced your own astrological gift of being able to achieve mental and emotional oneness with others. How about with objects? Have you ever done it with plants? You can merge your soul with thought, actions, feelings, and with the entire universe. We stargazers like to call the Fish Scorpions the special God children, Of course, all creatures are God children, but your decan recognizes this above all.

And just because you're so evolved doesn't mean that you've done away with all worldly requirements. If so, all that Scorpion shrewdness would be a big waste. Your MUTABLE-Fixed style allows you to infuse your material goals with cosmic blasts of energy. Not only do we find the highest intelligence quotients in this decan, we also uncover individuals who aren't so secretive as to not share their discoveries with all the land.

BOTTOM LINE FOR YOUR POWER

With your genius you ought to know exactly how to stop escaping into fleshly excess and how to rise above any obstacles in your course. You can be a super galactic achiever on every plain. You are the rarest and richest of the zodiac, because you've got the power to link us to the powers of the universe. It's a basic job, but without you we would all be lost. You are: a *Unifier*.

BODY TALK

Since the planets haven't skimped on your personality, they decided to go lean and mean on you physically. With PISCES commanding your feet and Scorpio dominating the sexual organs, this could translate as small you-know-whats. I'm sorry, ladies and gentlemen. Don't be upset. There's always prosthetic surgery or shoe padding if being short and narrow really bums you out. Besides, as the song says, "it's not the meat, it's the motion"!

Being small in other areas isn't such a crying shame, either. How about those cute, tiny buns of yours? Calvin Klein should hire the lot of you to model his size-one jeans. If for some reason your chart has balanced you out, say with some big Sag Jupiter dimensions, you may not be singing the same blues as the rest of the decan. You're going to have to watch your weight, however, where the other Fish Scorpions stay petite.

Medically, you are vulnerable. Thank heavens for your own scientific inquisitiveness. You'll be giving yourself semiannual physicals, just to make sure you're shipshape. When lurking germs try to bite you, you just bite right back. Feisty little devils, aren't you?

YOUR BEST-BET CAREERS

You are without question a self-employment decan. You blow fellow workers out of the water with your genius IQ. We'd hate to see some big Aries try to compete with you on the job. So, if you plan on toiling at home, make sure you build a laboratory to putter in. Science is where you prevail. Physics, microbiology, nuclear medicine, are all experimental areas where you can make a killing.

Or get a partner with a big gun and open up your own detective agency. You've got the most clever knack for finding escaped criminals. Especially with your background in escapism! You could always take those searching impulses into the sea. Scuba diving is a natural for you, and while you're down there, pick me up a couple pearls, okay? How about a strand?

Since you're such a specialist in sexual reproduction, open up a sperm bank. Before long, you'll be able to buy the World Bank. Being able to unify yourself with other people's problems, you can find employment in any area of therapy or religious counseling. You know how to keep a secret when you should, and helping others attain their dreams is a natural for you.

Speaking of dreams, ever thought about writing a book on visual imagery? How about launching an international sleep study? One of your fellow PISCES-Scorpios, Edgar Cayce (3/18), had no formal education even though he was a devout student of the *Bible*. As a young man, he discovered that by placing a book under a pillow at night he could absorb its entire subject matter by morning. Saves you money on college tuition, doesn't it?

At this final stage of the zodiac ladder, you're so close to the Stars that it really doesn't matter what you do. Open up any professional directory, close your eyes, flip the pages until the feeling strikes you, and *voilà*, your destiny awaits you. I wouldn't recommend any other decan to dabble in such a mystical business, except for this one. Whoops, in case your finger landed on Housekeeping, skip to your next choice. Even though I've complimented other decans for skills in that area, it's not for you. See what a wonderful influence you are on me? That's the nicest insult I've ever given anyone.

YOUR BEST-BET LOVE COMBOS

PISCES-Scorpio Man: We're done with the insults. I've already chastised you dear Fish Scorpion men sufficiently for that habit you used to have for excessive skin diving. That's all in the past. From here on out you're going to be the best that you can be, which is pretty darned amazing, I should say.

You men have tender, loving hearts. You're just dreamy. You'll offer a woman friendship, devotion, support, and appreciation. It doesn't get any better in the hay than you. Simply be forewarned that not all the girl fishies in the sea know how to appreciate you. A lot of them are, so used to being mistreated that they'll think there's something wrong with you. Has any woman told you that she loves you like a brother lately? Brother, is right.

As you can see, you've got a long list of positive connections to make in the zodiac. Please, make sure that you pick someone as smart as Miss CAP-Cap. You deserve someone who'll love you back, and for all the right reasons. Whomever you pick, she should have a feeling of déjà vu about her. Otherwise, Neptune will have you sneaking out the back door at night. And you said that you'd quit that stuff!

PISCES-Scorpio Woman: Beautiful, lovely sea maidens, why do you always look so sad? The sex wasn't really that good, was it? You're so delicate and kind and feminine, why do men get so scared of you and leave you in the lurch? Would you believe it's because you are so smart, you make them feel inadequate?

Or, perhaps because you are so sweet and gentle, men get frightened that they'll crush you. They usually do, the louses. So what do you do to the guy who broke up with you because he couldn't live up to your expectations? You go out and sleep with his best friend. And so on and so on. How many football teams have you scored lately?

You should go chat with your Aquarian girlfriends and learn how to develop a thicker skin. Even if you aren't suffering from the above syndrome, do go meet your match in opposing VIRGO-Capricorn. You'll achieve bliss becoming one with him. By the way, his book collection is the best. The two of you can read the one about permanent love, and then pass it on to your children. You'll never want to escape this karmic connection, ever.

DECAN PAIRS WITH PISCES-SCORPIO

LOVE SCALE SCORES

0 = Forget it! • 1 = Don't be a masochist... • 2 = Why bother? • 3 = Fun for one date. • 4 = It won't last! • 5 = You could do better! • 6 = Romance will fade... 7 = Great buddies! • 8 = Pure passion • 9 = True love. • 10 = Eternal bliss!

STARS OF PISCES-CANCER

March 12:	Liza Minnelli	March 18:	Queen Latifah
March 14:	Albert Einstein		Bonnie Blair
	Billy Crystal		Charlie Pride
March 15:	Andrew Jackson	March 20:	Carl Reiner
March 16:	Jerry Lewis		William Hurt
March 17:	Rudolf Nureyev		Jessica Lange
	Nat King Cole		
	Kurt Russell		

CHAPTER 15

SPOTLIGHTS

MEET THE STARS...

ARIES

BETTE DAVIS, an ARIES-Leo, born on April 5, is one of my heroines. She was a leader, like all Aries, and she carved out a path for women in Hollywood in a way nobody else could. She had all the defiance of her decan, and all the *Starpower*!

TAURUS

I've been talking to TAURUS-Taurus **SHIRLEY MACLAINE** (born April 24)
for years about astrology.

GEMINI

GEORGE BUSH (born June 12), a GEMINI-Aquarius is the born politician with style and spirit.

CANCER

CANCER-Scorpio **MILTON BERLE,** born on July 12, is a great role model for the next generation.

LEO

ROBERT MITCHUM, a LEO-Sagittarius, born on August 6, knew what he was all about!

VIRGO

SOPHIA LOREN, a VIRGO-Taurus, born on September 20, has this decan's eternal beauty and strong constitution—it doesn't get any better!

LIBRA

JULIO IGLESIAS was born on September 23, which makes him a LIBRA-Libra and puts lots of Venus in his chart. For this man, a great career is nothing without a terrific love life.

SCORPIO

WHOOPI GOLDBERG, born on November 13, is a SCORPIO-Cancer. Her wit breaks me up, I even copy her hairstyle!

SAGITTARIUS

PHIL DONAHUE, a real SAGITTARIUS-Leo born on December 21, has a Sag's love of controversy and a Leo's pride. He's also got a very private side that few people see.

CAPRICORN

For **KIRSTIE ALLEY,** a true CAPRICORN-Virgo (born January 12), her talent will only get better and her mystique is for real. It takes a very perceptive individual to figure this beauty out!

AQUARIUS

BURT REYNOLDS, an AQUARIUS-Libra (born February 11) proves it takes more than sex appeal to stay in there!

PISCES

The charming PISCES-Cancer **LYNN REDGRAVE** (born March 8) is so elegant—so English! She is a No-Hollywood-Bullshit chick!